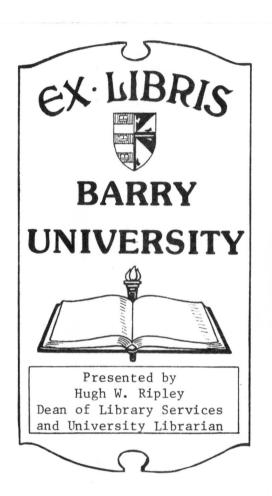

D1156981

DATE DUE

Raiders
&
Blockaders

The American Civil War Afloat

WILLIAM N. STILL, JR.
JOHN M. TAYLOR
NORMAN C. DELANEY

Brassey's
Washington · London

Editorial Offices:	Order Department:
22883 Quicksilver Drive	P.O. Box 960
Dulles, VA 20166	Herndon, VA 20172

Brassey's books are available at special discounts for bulk purchases for sales promotions,
premiums, fund-raising, or educational use.

Library of Congress Cataloging-in-Publication Data

Still, William N.
Raiders and blockaders : the American Civil War afloat / by
William N. Still, Jr., John M. Taylor, and Norman C. Delaney.
p.   cm.
Includes index.
ISBN 1-57488-164-7
1. United States—History—Civil War, 1861–1865—Naval operations.
2. United States. Navy—History—Civil War, 1861–1865. I. Taylor,
John M., 1930– . II. Delaney, Norman C. III. Title.
E591.X83 1998
973.7′5—dc21   98-16579
CIP

First Edition
10 9 8 7 6 5 4 3 2 1
Printed in the United States of America

CONTENTS

....

Foreword   vii

1

"When Can You Start?" The Strange
Occupation of James Bulloch
NORMAN C. DELANEY   1

2

The Historical Importance of the USS *Monitor*
WILLIAM N. STILL, JR.   13

3

Defiance: Raphael Semmes of the *Alabama*
JOHN M. TAYLOR   23

4

Technology Afloat
WILLIAM N. STILL, JR.   35

5

The Yankee Blue Jacket
WILLIAM N. STILL, JR.   52

....

iii

CONTENTS

6

The Confederate Tar
WILLIAM N. STILL, JR.   80

7

The Overblown *Trent* Affair
JOHN M. TAYLOR   100

8

"Porter . . . Is the Best Man"
WILLIAM N. STILL, JR.   111

9

At Semmes's Hand
NORMAN C. DELANEY   123

10

A Naval Sieve: The Union Blockade in the Civil War
WILLIAM N. STILL, JR.   131

11

Admiral Goldsborough's Feisty Career
WILLIAM N. STILL, JR.   141

12

Corpus Christi: The Vicksburg of Texas
NORMAN C. DELANEY   151

....

CONTENTS

13

Showdown off Cherbourg
JOHN M. TAYLOR   166

14

The Raider and the Rascal: P. D. Haywood's
Cruise of the Alabama
NORMAN C. DELANEY   183

15

Reluctant Raider
JOHN M. TAYLOR   194

16

Confederate Behemoth: The CSS *Louisiana*
WILLIAM N. STILL, JR.   205

17

Potomac Flotilla: A Gunboat Captain's Diary
JOHN M. TAYLOR   214

18

Franklin Buchanan and the Mobile Squadron
WILLIAM N. STILL, JR.   224

19

John Taylor Wood: Confederate Commando
JOHN M. TAYLOR   242

Index   255

FOREWORD

....

The role of the opposing Civil War navies has inexplicably been a neglected area of interest in American history. And the engagements on the rivers of what was then considered "The West" have received even less attention. Author and historian Shelby Foote, the julep-voiced star commentator on Ken Burns's PBS miniseries "The Civil War," once lamented to me in a *Naval History* interview the "shortage of naval material," excepting the battle between the ironclads *Monitor* and *Virginia*, "and maybe Farragut's busting into Mobile Bay," he said, because they are perceived as the war's only "colorful and dramatic" naval battles. His explanation for the dearth of study on the war in the West is that "much more material exists about the Eastern theater of the war, especially photographs and newspapers." He's right. But that is beginning to change.

The beauty of *Raiders and Blockaders* is that the essays it features are as well conceived and written as they are well researched. William Still is probably the most respected Civil War naval historian alive. And Norman Delaney and John M. Taylor have established themselves as authorities in the field, as well.

Here, in one volume, we're treated to the stories of great Civil War naval personalities: Raphael Semmes, captain of the notorious Confederate commerce raider *Alabama;* the Union Navy's man in the West early in the war, Mississippi Squadron commander David Dixon Porter; Matthew Fontaine Maury, the father of oceanography who resigned his U.S. commission to join

....

the Confederate States Navy; the controversial old man, Louis M. Goldsborough, whom many criticized for not cooperating with the Union Army; and the U.S. Naval Academy professor-turned-Confederate commando, John Taylor Wood. Dr. Still also concisely covers the enlisted ranks on both sides, much as the venerated historian Bell I. Wiley did with his classic works on the lives of Billy Yank and Johnny Reb, the common soldiers of the Civil War.

This book covers the major theaters of the war at sea; the political ramifications of the Confederacy's relationship across the Atlantic with Great Britain; the epic battle between the USS *Kearsarge* and the CSS *Alabama* off the coast of France in 1864; and the lesser-known "siege" of Corpus Christi, Texas. It features a critical analysis of the performance of the Union blockade—still a matter of debate among historians—details the technology of iron and steam that made ships of wood and sail obsolete, and exposes a "diarist," one whose writings have been used as source material in the past, as an impostor.

So why has the naval history of the Civil War been neglected? Perhaps the real reason is that shipboard duty at the time has been portrayed as plodding and tedious. And sailors of that era had a reputation—deserved or not—of exhibiting low moral fiber, especially while they were in port.

Another reason could be that naval engagements were unlike the great land battles—Antietam, Shiloh, Gettysburg, Chattanooga—with their storied charges, flanking movements, high-ground conquests, and desperate defenses, involving tens of thousands of men. Even the best-known Civil War sea battles took hours to unfold, their antagonists slowly maneuvering into position, often resulting in the weaker parties making good an escape. The naval "battlefields," such as they are, present a problem as well, because visitors are unable to tread the "ground" where the sailors fought.

Perhaps, too, historians have steered away from the subject because many of the Union naval operations concerned the blockade of Southern ports, which most of the time, whether successful or not, was unexciting service and not nearly as glamorous as pitched battle. And the Southern blockade-runners, while seen as more romantic than their Union counterparts, often were depicted as shady characters, less interested in supporting the Southern cause than in advancing their own personal interests. And besides, most were seen not necessarily as deft professionals.

But Civil War naval operations were important, and this volume collects some their best stories. "Stories" is a key word here. When I was asked to write this short essay, I felt a tinge of "old-home week," because many of these capsule treatments first appeared in a Civil War history magazine that I once helped to edit. As a matter of fact, I'm proud to say that I think I may have worked on a few of these myself. I remember once a rather well-known academic historian, who liked to expound on how many hundreds of other academics could penetrate his obtuse work, took one look at the magazine, pointed his condescending nose skyward, and said, "Oh. That's popular"—practically choking on the "p-word" as though he were uttering some sort of obscenity. "Why, yes. At least 125,000 people read it every month," he was told. Still he scoffed, convinced that no serious study of history could—or should—be understood and enjoyed as entertainment by the general populace.

I'm sure the circulation of that magazine is even larger now, since Civil War history got a major boost from Ted Turner's epic motion picture *Gettysburg*, and different generations are being exposed to the human-interest stories that have gripped the American psyche for more than 130 years.

All this is not to say that academic study is unimportant. Popular authors will tell you it's just as important for them to get the facts correct. But give me the author who can get the history right and still tell an entertaining story. That is what Pulitzer Prizes are all about. "What the academics have done to history, equating facts with truth," says Shelby Foote, "is a murderous thing. The truth is how the facts came into being, what effect the facts had, not the facts themselves." "Truth" is the way Mr. Foote chooses to define popular history and the manner in which he writes. He has made history digestible to large audiences, as have the authors of the pieces contained in *Raiders and Blockaders*.

So, popular it is. More and more people are becoming interested in the stories of this conflict. And ever more good writers are tackling the saga of the war at sea. That is the point. It *is* popular. Thank Heaven for it.

Fred L. Schultz
Editor-in-Chief
Naval History magazine
Annapolis, Maryland
March 1998

1

"When Can You Start?" The Strange Occupation of James Bulloch

NORMAN C. DELANEY

Through May 8 and 9, 1861, two Southerners conferred on a matter that would be vital to the future of the new Confederacy, the building of a navy. The two were the Confederacy's newly appointed Secretary of the Navy Stephen R. Mallory and an experienced naval officer, James D. Bulloch. Bulloch had volunteered for Confederate naval service, but now Mallory surprised him with an extraordinary assignment. He was ordered to Europe to procure ships, some of which would become commerce destroyers, prowling the seas and preying on Northern merchantmen. The thirty-eight-year-old volunteer realized the responsibility being placed upon his shoulders. The survival of the new nation might well depend upon his success.

James Dunwoody Bulloch, native of Roswell, Georgia, is one of the least known and most important naval figures of the Confederacy. And had things worked out differently, historians would today be writing of "Bulloch of the *Alabama*" or "Bulloch of the *Florida*" instead of dashing Rebel sailors Raphael Semmes or Eugene Maffitt. But without the tireless work of Bulloch there would very likely have been no *Alabama* or *Florida* for Semmes or Maffitt to make their reputations on.

He was born in 1823 to a distinguished Southern family, one that later married into a distinguished Northern clan and produced a president of the

United States, Theodore Roosevelt. In 1839 Bulloch was warranted a midshipman in the United States Navy, and then rose to the grade of lieutenant after fourteen years as a midshipman, passed midshipman, and master. During the Mexican War he served in California operations aboard the U.S. store ship *Erie* and the schooner *Shark*. Then in 1852 he was assigned to the U.S. mail steamer *Georgia* to gain experience with the new steam engine technology. But by then Bulloch was disillusioned with regular naval service, and dreading the prospect of waiting years for promotion to commander, he decided to leave it. However, his letter of resignation, written in June 1854 after a cruise aboard the steamer *Black Warrior,* cited only "reasons of a purely private nature."[1]

Along with other naval lieutenants who resigned from U.S. service, Bulloch remained in commercial mail service as a civilian. And by 1861 he had become "completely identified with the shipping interests of New York," holding neither property nor financial interests in the South. But when war erupted, his decision to support the South came easily. He later wrote: "My heart and head were with the South. My sympathies and conviction were both on that side, although my personal interests were wholly, and my personal friendships were chiefly, in the North." Then on April 13, 1861, while in Louisiana, Bulloch wrote Confederate cabinet member Judah P. Benjamin offering his services.

However, before Bulloch could serve the Confederacy, he felt bound to return the mail steamer *Bienville,* which he then commanded, to her owners in New York. His refusal to sell or surrender the *Bienville* to Louisiana authorities was supported by President Jefferson Davis himself, and the ship was finally allowed to depart from New Orleans. It reached New York on April 22. (Ironically, the *Bienville* was already chartered by the U.S. Government to transport Federal troops to Washington. Later she was used as a blockader off Bulloch's native Georgia.)

Avoiding detainment in the North, Bulloch traveled to the Montgomery, Alabama, office of Secretary Mallory for a meeting. There the secretary came directly to the point: "I want you to go to Europe. When can you start?"

Bulloch was appointed civilian naval agent to secure steamers and naval stores and equipment. And Mallory assured him of wide discretionary power and adequate funds. His methods would follow those of another agent,

Commander James D. Bulloch, the Confederacy's indispensable purchasing agent in Europe. *(From* The Confederate Navy *by J. Thomas Scharf)*

Major Caleb Huse, C.S.A., who had already been sent to England to purchase arms and ammunition for the Confederate army. Mallory would also later send three commissioned officers with instructions to purchase or build ships in Europe. They were James H. North, George T. Sinclair, and Matthew Fontaine Maury, who, although operating independently of Bulloch, would all rely upon him to disburse naval funds.

Mallory, knowing the urgency of acquiring a navy, had chosen the ideal person for this difficult assignment. In Bulloch he had more than a competent officer familiar with the latest naval technology. He had also found a man possessing initiative and resourcefulness. And Bulloch was an even-tempered individual who would avoid treading on sensitive toes. But Mallory's man wanted most of all to command a ship, and hoped that the successful performance of his task in England would earn him a commission and a command.

Arriving at Liverpool in June, Bulloch began making his contacts. He set up an office with Fraser, Trenholm & Company, a Liverpool branch of a Charleston banking firm. And soon he had arranged for the building of two wooden cruisers by two separate contractors—Fawcett, Preston, & Company, and Laird Brothers. But in neither contract negotiation did Bulloch represent himself to the builders as an agent of the Confederate Government. Nor did he say anything to them about the purpose of the vessels; he just felt certain that the truth was known. However, he did take a special interest in the Laird vessel, the "290." This vessel, larger and better armed than the other, would be the ideal commerce destroyer, and Bulloch hoped and believed he would eventually command her.

Secrecy was of great importance to the success of Bulloch's undertaking since he and other Southerners in England were under surveillance by agents of the United States Government. The able American ambassador, Charles Francis Adams, was determined to uncover all activities that could aid the South. Thus, Bulloch carefully studied the Queen's Neutrality Proclamation and the Foreign Enlistment Act for loopholes. The latter presented the greatest problem, for it prohibited the equipping in England of the ships of belligerent nations. Bulloch hoped, naturally, that that nation would soon abandon her neutrality and become an active partner against the United States. However, in the meantime, great care had to be taken lest Confederate actions embarrass a potential ally.

As difficult as the Foreign Enlistment Act made things for Bulloch in England, the situation in France was even worse. In June of 1861 Emperor Napoleon III forbade French subjects to cooperate *"in any manner whatever"* in equipping or arming the warships or privateers of any belligerent nation.

While construction continued on his cruisers, Bulloch and Major Huse obtained a large quantity of military hardware, including the armaments Bulloch would need for his two ships. However, since his first ship, the *Oreto,* would not be ready for service until late 1861, Bulloch decided to use the time to bring those supplies to the Confederacy. He secretly procured a swift steamer, the *Fingal,* a ship that would nominally be the property of an English company and might, if circumstances warranted, be so considered officially. And though concerned that he might be exceeding his authority,[2] Bulloch took command of the ship.

After several days at sea the agent and his *Fingal* made an emergency stop at the Azores to take on water. This stop was fortunate, for there Bulloch found Terceira Island, an ideal location for outfitting his cruisers once they departed England. Elated with his discovery, he pressed on for home with little trouble and a lot of good luck. The *Fingal's* run into Savannah, Georgia, was even facilitated by a Southern pilot brought aboard the ship at Bermuda.

With the *Fingal* and her goods safely at anchor, Bulloch had good reason to be pleased with himself. His cargo included 14,000 Enfield rifles, one million ball cartridges, two million percussion caps, and large quantities of revolvers, sabers, rifled cannon, gunpowder, and medical supplies. And it was an added windfall for the South because no commission had to be paid to a middleman.

Conferring again with Bulloch, this time in Richmond, Mallory responded enthusiastically to his report. He was now prepared to grant his agent a commission and command of the first cruiser completed in England. Lieutenant North, originally sent to Britain to build ironclads, was to command the next completed ship.

Bulloch was pleased at the prospect of command but surprised when informed of his promotion to commander. His fifteen years of official U.S. service, with less than one year in the grade of lieutenant, were insignificant compared to the seniority of officers like North, who had been a U.S. naval lieutenant since 1841 and had thirty-three years of service. Stating his willingness to accept a lieutenancy, Bulloch warned Mallory that "criticism and a feeling of discontent in many quarters" would "vent itself on me as its cause." But the secretary saw no reason to deny Bulloch the appointment and insisted he accept.

Once again aboard the *Fingal,* Bulloch waited impatiently while she was prepared for the return voyage. His conversation with Mallory had "excited ambitious hopes," and he resented each day of inactivity. But the Federal blockade of Savannah was formidable, and the commander finally had to admit the impossibility of getting the *Fingal* to sea. And he was plagued by notions that North had taken command of the *Oreto* during his prolonged absence. Finally, Mallory approved Bulloch's request to return to England on another vessel. And he appointed an assistant navy paymaster at Savannah, Clarence R. Yonge, as Bulloch's clerk—a worker who impressed Bulloch as being a "quiet, modest, young man."

On February 5 Bulloch and Yonge left Wilmington, North Carolina, by blockade runner and arrived at Liverpool on March 10. There, the commander was astonished to find the *Oreto,* although fully provisioned, lying idly at anchor. Lieutenant North, despite his complaints to Mallory about inactivity, had failed to take advantage of his opportunity to assume command and depart. Perhaps relieved at the lieutenant's lack of initiative, Bulloch was just the same disappointed in North for permitting the ship to remain vulnerable to seizure. And although he now formally offered him command of the *Oreto,* North declined. He stated he preferred to remain in Scotland to produce an invincible ironclad ram which he intended to command.

Although he congratulated Bulloch on his success and promotion, North was unable to contain his true feelings. In an angry letter to Mallory, he exploded: "Rank to a military man is everything and that rank has been taken from me." Aware of North's feelings toward him, Bulloch could not afford to dissipate his energies by feuding with his fellow officer. He wrote North: "You and myself are of an age to be above the display of childish jealousies and offishness, and I propose that we continue to meet as at our first acquaintance and not to avoid each other's glance as was the case this morning."

North was not alone in regarding Bulloch's promotion as outrageous. Commenting about "the row in naval circles," Lieutenant John M. Stribling, C.S.N., noted that "the excitement about it has not yet subsided." Finally, Bulloch complained to Mallory that "a certain clique of naval officers" were determined to prevent him from ever getting a command. Mallory promptly settled the matter by informing North that Bulloch outranked him and that he himself was not interested in petty issues of rank and seniority.

Bulloch needed all the support he could get in what was a seemingly impossible task. The jealousy of fellow officers was the least of his difficulties. He felt the strain of the incessant pressure applied by United States agents and their spies, men who were attempting to frustrate his work. British authorities had also been alerted regarding the purpose of the *Oreto* and only needed hard evidence of her intended mission before seizing her.

The new commander's first task, then, was to get the *Oreto* to sea. His legal authorities in England had convinced him of his right to have ships built as long as their purpose, ownership, and destination were kept secret. Bulloch pondered the possibility of getting arms aboard the vessel, but unannounced inspections by British Foreign Office agents made this impossible. So when the *Oreto,* now the *Manassas,* sailed on March 22, 1862, she was ostensibly an English merchant ship with a British captain and crew. But a master in the Confederate navy was actually in charge of her. He was John Low, with orders from Bulloch to bring the ship to Nassau and deliver her to a Confederate commander. Guns and munitions would arrive later aboard SS *Bahama.*

At Nassau the ship was eventually turned over to Lieutenant James N. Maffitt, C.S.N., an experienced blockade-runner. The ship then became the CSS *Florida,* and after many delays, was taken to sea. But Maffitt's ship was still not in condition for cruising, and he was compelled to run her into Mobile Harbor for additional work and equipment. She eventually got to sea early in 1863, a full year after her completion. It was then that her successful cruise as a commerce destroyer began.

Later, after cruising the West Indies and the coast of Brazil, she would arrive at Brest, France, on August 23, 1863, in need of a thorough overhaul. However, the ship's presence in France would come at an awkward time for Bulloch; he was engaged in sensitive operations there. And the commander later said he believed that the *Florida's* arrival was an important factor in his failure to obtain all but one of the ironclads he was building in France.

Back in Britain work on the "290" (soon to be the *Enrica,* and later named the *Alabama)* was completed, and she was finally launched on May 15, 1862. To Bulloch she was no ordinary ship. He had developed a fondness for her as "a piece of handiwork which had come to completion under my own eye." Then, on June 11, Bulloch received orders from Mallory assigning the "290" to someone other than himself. Commander Raphael Semmes, who had commanded the CSS *Sumter,* the first of the South's commerce destroyers, was without a ship. The *Sumter* had been bottled up at Gibraltar by a Federal blockade and had been found unfit for further service. Bulloch's "piece of handiwork" was his to command.

Interestingly, Semmes had earlier declined Bulloch's generous offer of command of the "290" in deference to Bulloch's own desire to command her. Then he left Europe for the Confederacy. However, North, now a commander, still expressed interest in a ship, so Bulloch offered him the command as a courtesy. But only days later, learning that Semmes had received orders for the "290" and was returning to England from Nassau, Bulloch rescinded his appointment of North.

Actually, what mattered more to Mallory than who commanded the "290," was what would keep Bulloch busy in England. Mallory was convinced that Bulloch, North, and George T. Sinclair, each commanding an ironclad ram, could together gain "imperishable renown" by breaking the blockade and recovering New Orleans. With this in mind, he considered Bulloch's work indispensable and instructed him to immediately contract for the building of two ironclads, in addition to providing funds for North's vessel, under construction at Glasgow, Scotland. One million dollars was credited to Bulloch's account in England, and another million was promised. So the commander lost no time in negotiating for two ironclad rams to be built by Laird Brothers.

Now, even as he was forced to swallow his own great disappointment at losing the "290," Bulloch also had angry and disappointed Commander North to deal with. But he still believed that he would command one of the ironclads and was determined not to lose his next opportunity. He pointedly reminded Mallory of this desire to command a ship, and wrote:

> I aspire to purely professional distinction, and I feel that to toil here, as it were, in exile and then to turn over the result of my labors for the use of others is willingly to consign myself to oblivion. To retain the commission of commander and yet never to command a ship seems to me a mockery.

Then suddenly his own quarrels were eclipsed; he learned from sources close to the British Government (perhaps in the government itself) that authorities were preparing to seize the "290" in forty-eight hours. Bulloch acted without delay and on July 29 staged a "trial run." And the ruse worked; the "290" escaped to a destination known only to Bulloch and her captain, a British merchant officer specially chosen for his judgment and discretion.

On August 13 Bulloch, Semmes, and other Confederate officers left Liverpool aboard the chartered steamer *Bahama*. Bulloch felt that he should accompany Semmes to the rendezvous "to smooth away as much as possible his embarrassments and difficulties in assuming the command of a new ship with a strange and untried crew." At Terceira, the Confederate agent's previously discovered hiding place, they found the "290," and after three days of loading coal, stores, and guns, she was ready; the Confederate ensign was raised and the ship was formally commissioned CSS *Alabama*.

The sailors who volunteered to serve aboard the *Alabama*, enticed by generous wages, good treatment, and prize money, were then enlisted for the cruise. And as she prepared to sail, Bulloch left her to return to England aboard the *Bahama*. Among the Confederates to whom he bade farewell were his young half-brother, Irvine S. Bulloch, serving as midshipman, and Clarence Yonge, now Semmes' paymaster. Although he had not prevented Yonge from sailing, Bulloch had changed his opinion about him and had warned Semmes that he was "an unsteady and unreliable young man, whose judgment and discretion were not to be trusted."

Bulloch maintained his special interest in the *Alabama*, "without one pang of envy toward her gallant commander." And he planned for a coaling tender to meet the cruiser at pre-arranged stations for fueling and the exchange of intelligence. However, Semmes had to give up this practice because of the increased risk of discovery. Subsequently, since reports from Semmes were infrequent, Bulloch had to rely largely on newspaper accounts to follow the career of his favorite vessel. But to his immense satisfaction the number of overhauled and burned merchantmen steadily rose, and Northern accounts became more shrill in denouncing the "pirate" Semmes.

After the escape of the *Alabama*, United States agents in England became alarmed, lest other vessels being prepared for the South escape to sea. British officials were embarrassed too at the way they had been caught napping, and they resolved it would not happen again. Thus, the *Alexandra*, a gift to the South from Fraser, Trenholm & Company, was prevented from ever leaving port despite a court decision in her favor.

In addition to the problems of tightened British surveillance, Bulloch's work was hampered by the defection of his former secretary. In January 1863, while the *Alabama* was in port at Jamaica, Yonge was dismissed by Semmes for drunkenness and theft. The young man, privy to secret information about Confederate operations in England, then became an informer for the United States. Angry and bitter, Bulloch blamed himself for having allowed Yonge to remain in Confederate service in spite of his doubts about him.

Bulloch was also worried about the future of the two ironclad rams being built by the Lairds. In October 1863 Captain Samuel Barron, C.S.N., became ranking Confederate naval officer in Europe, and it was his responsibility to deliver these vessels to the Confederacy. Soon other officers, all hoping to command or serve aboard cruisers or ironclads, converged on the convenient waiting ground, France. Bulloch was concerned lest these officers prove embarrassing to the French Government. Also, their presence produced a dramatic increase in leaks of sensitive information. In fact, the loose tongues of some of these men may well have contributed to Bulloch's ultimate failure to launch additional cruisers and ironclads.

As completion of the Laird rams neared, Bulloch realized the difficulty of getting them to sea. He tried arranging for a French company to serve as contractor, but this scheme failed. Then on September 3, 1863, no doubt influenced by Southern military defeats, the British Foreign Office ordered the rams seized. This left Bulloch no choice but to sell the vessels to the British navy. And North, too, was forced to sell his Glasgow ironclad, a project which had turned into a monstrous white elephant.

Believing that Napoleon III had become more sympathetic to the South, Bulloch now moved his operations to France. There he contracted for six vessels, four corvettes similar to the *Alabama,* and two ironclads. But this French experience thoroughly soured Bulloch on dealing with foreign governments. He had become disillusioned with the lies and duplicity of even so-called friends of the South, and he wrote bitterly to Mallory: "I have not yet found in Europe a single person who did not expect to receive remuneration for any service he might render to the Confederate States."

Then *Alabama* was sunk by the USS *Kearsarge* off Cherbourg, France, on June 19, 1864. Her loss was a psychological blow to the South, and Mallory demanded immediate replacements for her. But there was no longer any possibility that they would come from France, because Napoleon had suddenly lost his interest in the South. Once again Bulloch had to save what he could by selling the French cruisers and ironclads.

However, through a complicated arrangement with the Danish Government, Bulloch managed to get one of the French ironclads under his control. This vessel became the CSS *Stonewall,* assigned to Commander

CSS *Florida*, Bulloch's first acquisition in Britain. *(U.S. Naval Historical Center)*

Thomas J. Page. But the *Stonewall,* the South's last hope to break the Northern blockade, would never make it. Later, to Bulloch's disgust, her timid commander would procrastinate for weeks before finally steaming for America. The war would end before he arrived, and Page would take the *Stonewall* into Cuba's Havana Harbor to sell her to pay off his crew.

Successes for Bulloch became infrequent as the fate of the Confederacy was gradually sealed. But, remarkably, he was still able to obtain several blockade runners late in the war. And, to replace the *Alabama* and the *Florida* (rammed and captured by the USS *Wachusett* in Bahia Harbor, Brazil, in October 1864), Bulloch secretly purchased a splendid merchant ship, the *Sea King.* Renamed the *Shenandoah,* with Lieutenant James I. Waddell in command, she cruised the Pacific and Arctic oceans and raised havoc among the vessels of the American whaling fleet. Unaware until July 1865 that the war had ended, Waddell sailed the *Shenandoah* to England, arriving there in November.

With this dismal end to the war, Bulloch canceled all contracts, paid his creditors, and turned all remaining funds over to Fraser, Trenholm &

Company. Then he was pushed to confront his personal problems. His controversial work for the Confederacy had jeopardized his future in the United States. And excluded from President Johnson's general amnesty, he was forced to remain in England with his family. But there, as a British citizen, he had no trouble earning a livelihood with his knowledge of the mercantile cotton trade, and in subsequent years he became a Tory and a partisan critic of Prime Minister Gladstone.

Bulloch occupied his later years writing recollections of his war activities. And, published in 1883, they provided a fascinating, low key account of his important work as a "secret agent." The book, a testament to Bulloch's unsung role in history, expressed no vindictiveness toward wartime enemies or associates who had disappointed him (Yonge excepted). Instead it showed James D. Bulloch to be a remarkable individual whose accomplishments deserved greater recognition. The cruisers he built captured the imagination of the South and made their captains—Semmes, Maffitt, and Waddell—legendary figures. That he played a less glamorous role than these men made him no less a hero in the service of the Lost Cause. And when he died in Britain in 1901 that is how he probably hoped he would be remembered.

Notes

Copyright © 1982 Historical Times Inc.
This chapter first appeared in the March 1982 issue of *Civil War Times Illustrated*.

1. Undoubtedly, Bulloch was still shaken by the death of his wife, Elizabeth, earlier that year, after only two years of marriage. An intensely private person who revealed little of his romantic or personal life, he never elaborated on his resignation motives, or any connection they may have had with Elizabeth's death.
2. Later, at Bermuda, Bulloch was relieved to find dispatches from Mallory giving permission for the blockade-running enterprise.

2

·················

The Historical Importance
of the USS *Monitor*

WILLIAM N. STILL, JR.

In 1851, John Ruskin wrote: "Take it all in all a Ship of the Line is the most honorable thing that man, as a gregarious animal, has ever produced." In that same year, however, Sir Henry Bessemer gave his first demonstration that molten iron could be converted to steel. Ten years later, a ship would be laid down, constructed partially of iron, that would symbolize the end of Ruskin's "most honorable thing."[1] That ship was the ironclad warship, USS *Monitor.*

A recent authority has written: "Of all the warlike technology of the zenith of the Industrial Revolution and of the Age of Progress, none has loomed more impressively, generated more public controversy, or captured the general imagination of powers with naval pretensions than the ironclad warship."[2] Today, only one ironclad, the HMS *Warrior,* is still afloat, presently being restored in England. Although it is one of the first of the armored warships, it is by no means the most famous. That distinction probably belongs to the *Monitor,* presently lying some sixteen miles off Cape Hatteras, North Carolina, at a depth of approximately 230 feet.

Virtually from the time it was under construction during the first year of the Civil War, its fame was assured. Its unique raft-like structure support-ing a turret generated thousands of words in the newspapers. The contro-

An artist's rendition of the famous clash between the *Monitor* and the *Merrimack*. (*U.S. Naval Historical Center*)

versy surrounding the *Monitor's* inventor-builder, the Swedish-American, John Ericsson, contributed to its fame. Then came its celebrated battle with the CSS *Virginia* (formerly the USS *Merrimack*), perhaps the only naval combat which achieved its place in history mainly because it was indecisive. As Bernard Brodie wrote:

> The engagement in Hampton Roads on March 9, 1862 would never have gained so much renown had either the *Merrimac[k]* or the *Monitor* sunk the other. It was the uselessness of their long and furious cannonade, contrasted with the signal victories of the *Merrimac[k]* over unarmored ships on the previous day, that made the affair a landmark on the story of the warship.[3]

Writing of this battle, Oliver Wendell Holmes asked: "Is it not the age of fable, and of heroes, and demi-gods over again?"[4] The combat captured the imagination of the American public then and later. Various naval officers, members of Congress, as well as newspapers and periodicals, including the influential *Army and Navy Journal*, discoursed on the epochal importance of the encounter.[5]

The *Monitor* action in Hampton Roads produced such an intense enthusiasm in the North that a "monitor craze" swept the Union. Three weeks after the battle, ten improved Ericsson monitors were contracted—the Passaic class—which would see more service than any other class of monitors. Until the end of the war the navy would concentrate on monitor construction.[6]

The monitor craze crossed the Atlantic. Shortly after the battle, Charles Francis Adams, U.S. minister to Great Britain, wrote to his son that the *Monitor* had become the "main talk of the town."[7] The London *Times* wrote: "Whereas we had available for immediate purpose 149 first-class warships, we now have two, both armored vessels. . . . There is not now a ship in the English Navy, apart from these two, that it would not be madness to trust to an engagement with the little *Monitor*." In a similar tone, Ephraim Douglas Adams wrote: "More than any other battle of the Civil War the duel between the *Merrimac* and the *Monitor* struck the imagination of the British people."[8] The Hampton Roads engagement was not only a sensation in England but also throughout Europe.[9] John Bigelow, U.S. consul general and minister in Paris, wrote in his memoir:

> That event had done more to re-establish [the U.S.] as a national power in Europe and inspire respect for our military resources than anything that has occurred since the rebellion. The Nations who were rejoicing in our weakness . . . two months ago . . . have suddenly discovered that the race is not always to the strong, and that it was the mercy of Providence rather than their own wisdom or sense of justice which prevented their being plunged into a war which in the natural course of things might have resulted in sinking half their navy before they would have heard of its arrival in our country.[10]

Although Bigelow exaggerated the *Monitor*'s power as well as the effect the battle had on European governments, he nevertheless was correct on the ironclad's impact on public opinion.

The Hampton Roads engagement did, however, impress the French government. A French frigate observed the combat from the southern entrance to Hampton Roads. Its commanding officer wrote a long, detailed account of it, concluding that "I can right now foresee how useless it will be for ordinary ships to try to fight against these floating fortresses armed with rifled guns of nine and eleven inches in diameter." Referring to the *Monitor* as a "work of genius," his report influenced Napoleon III to hasten the modernization of his fleet.[11]

Historians would continue to perpetuate the fame and importance of the *Monitor* after the war. A majority of historians writing in the latter decades of the nineteenth century agreed with James Ford Rhodes in that "the *Monitor-Merrimac[k]* struggle was undoubtedly a great turning point in naval warfare." Bruce Catton wrote in 1956, "March [1862 was] memorable for the most momentous drawn battle in history—a battle that nobody won but that made the navies of the world obsolete." Winston Churchill also commented that "the combat of the *Merrimac[k]* and the *Monitor* made the greatest change in seafighting since cannon fired by gunpowder had been mounted on ships about four hundred years before." And finally, William C. Davis described the *Monitor* as a "model for the warship of the future."[12]

James P. Baxter demonstrated some thirty years ago in his brilliant study on the ironclad, however, that the influence and importance of the *Monitor* both on the naval construction policies of the European governments as well as on the development of the modern capital ship have been greatly exaggerated. At the time of the Hampton Roads contest, more than one hundred ironclads were under construction in various countries. Baxter went on to say:

> Though the influence of the battles of Hampton Roads on the policy of European governments has been greatly exaggerated, few naval actions in history have made so profound an impression on the popular imagination. The combats of March 8 and 9 symbolized the passing of the old fleets and the coming of the new. Symbols they were, and not the cause, for they did not initiate the great revolution in naval architecture, they crowned it. They taught the man in the street what the naval constructors already knew: that shell guns had sounded the doom of the wooden navies of the world. On the chief problem confronting the naval constructors of Europe—the best design for seagoing ironclads—these battles threw little light. Nevertheless fate had provided for the first fight of ironclads so incomparable a setting that the *Merrimack* and *Monitor* have monopolized public attention in the United States, to the exclusion of the scores of ironclads then already built or building in Europe.[13]

In an article published in 1981, Larry E. Tise, then director of the North Carolina Division of Archives and History, emphasized the historic and symbolic value of the *Monitor* to the American people.[14] Dr. Tise is correct. To the majority, however, the value of the *Monitor* is related to the

Battle of Hampton Roads—a military or naval value. The vessel has another symbolic value, perhaps equally important: its place as an example of American technology and industry.

The Civil War was fought at a time when the United States was beginning to accelerate toward industrial importance. The nation was already one of the industrial leaders in the world in 1860, with manufacturing employing almost one-seventh of the labor force.[15] Before the war American contributions in technology were gaining recognition. The U.S. exhibits at the Crystal Palace Exposition in London in the mid-1850s impressed Europeans.[16] New inventions illustrated American ingenuity. Cyrus McCormick's reaper and especially the sewing machines of Elias Howe and Isaac Singer were sold abroad. By the war's outbreak Singer's European outlets were selling more sewing machines than some 3,000 salesmen were able to market in the United States.[17]

Recent writings in the economic history of the United States in the mid-nineteenth century have suggested that the Civil War actually retarded the nation's growth.[18] This may well be true, but the war clearly stimulated developments in technology. "It was the first struggle," John W. Oliver wrote, "in which science and machinery played a dominant part, and it was the first time that technological innovations and improvements were applied on a large scale in a major war."[19] Bernard and Fawn Brodie wrote: "The American Civil War was a colossal proving ground for improved weapons of all kinds. For the first time the achievements of the industrial and scientific revolution were used on a large scale in war."[20] Ericsson himself wrote that "the time has come, Mr. President [Lincoln], when our cause will have to be sustained not by numbers, but by superior weapons. By a proper application of mechanical devices alone will you be able with absolute certainty to destroy the enemies of the Union."[21] The most famous of the "mechanical devices" was designed by Ericsson, the ironclad *Monitor*.

> "A . . . feature of the *Monitor* story, perhaps the most important one for her place in the international history of technology," wrote Theodore Ropp, "is that she was one of the most successful ship prototypes in history. *Monitor*, like the later *Dreadnought*, became a generic term, in the *Monitor's* case for light-draft, coast defense ironclads and for vaguely similar light-draft ships which were used in both world wars and Vietnam."[22]

Monitor-type warships were used by various navies. The last American naval vessel designated a monitor, the *Cheyenne*, was decommissioned and scrapped in 1925.[23] The Passaic-class monitor, *Camanche*, remained afloat as a coal barge in San Francisco at least until World War II.

Baxter in his study on ironclads stressed the revolutionary importance of these early armored vessels. The ironclads were the transitional warships from wood to iron. However, armor was only one of the technological innovations in the nineteenth century that revolutionized the navies of the world. During the century occurred the shift from sail to steam. The screw propeller, rifled and breech-loading ordnance, shells, and the revolving turret were other innovations.[24]

The *Monitor* incorporated many of these technological improvements. It carried two 11-inch Dahlgren smoothbore cannon that could fire shells, it was driven by screw propellers of Ericsson's design, and it was steam-powered by two single-cylindered steam engines also designed by Ericsson. Of the naval technological developments of the century, the introduction of the steam-powered warship was, in its tactical, strategic, and ultimate political consequences, by far the most important. Although historians have emphasized the engagement between the *Monitor* and the *Virginia* as the first combat between two ironclads, they rarely point out that this was also one of the earliest engagements between two warships maneuvering entirely under steam propulsion.[25]

In addition to steam machinery and propellers, there were more than 250 patentable inventions by Ericsson on the *Monitor*. Isaac Newton, the ship's first engineer, estimated "that she contained at least forty patentable contrivances" in the turret.[26] And the turret itself was the most important of these technological innovations.

Although the *Monitor* was not the first ironclad in action, it was the first turreted armored vessel to engage an enemy. The success of Ericsson's vessel gave a great impetus to the adoption of the armored turret. The concept of a turret was not new, however. Ericsson himself recognized this when he wrote: "A house, or turret, turning on a pivot for protecting apparatus intended to throw warlike projectiles, is an ancient device. . . . Thinking back, I cannot fix any period of my life at which I did not know of its existence."[27]

Along with Ericsson's gun tower, several turrets were either under construction or had been proposed. Theodore R. Timby of New York later

The *Monitor*'s crew on deck. *(Library of Congress)*

would claim that the idea was his; James B. Eads, a western river builder, designed a turret that was installed on the Milwaukee-class monitor; and Captain Cowper P. Coles of the Royal Navy developed a cupola that the British government adopted even before they learned what had happened at Hampton Roads.[28] Nonetheless, the *Monitor*'s success provided the turret concept with credibility, and it was a major factor in the emphasis on turreted warships both in the United States and abroad. Until the end of the war the U.S. Navy would concentrate on monitor construction. Of the forty iron-clads laid down by the Union during the war, thirty-five were of the monitor type.[29] As Davis said, the "turret alone would have made Ericsson immortal; it was the most successful innovation in nautical warfare of the century."[30] Although Davis's statement is probably exaggerated as to the turret's significance, there can be no question about its importance.[31] The centerline turret would be a major characteristic of the modern capital ship.

It is almost certainly questionable that the *Monitor* was the forerunner of the modern warship, as has frequently been said. Both Baxter in his work on the ironclad and Stanley Sandler's on the modern capital ship convincingly disallow that theory. It was not the raft-like monitor but the large, high-freeboard, centerline, multiple-turret armored ship that was the forerunner of the modern capital ship. Modern ship design was primarily a result of developments in Europe. Yet, with its turret, forced-air ventilation in living spaces, and other unique features, the *Monitor* was, within the context of the mid-nineteenth century, a most advanced warship and unquestionably had a great impact on design in the United States for many years.

Today, the *Monitor* is undoubtedly the best known warship in American history, recognized by most children. Even compared to famous vessels still afloat, such as the *Constitution, Constellation, Missouri,* and *Olympia*, it stands alone. The *Monitor* is both a historic artifact and a symbolic monument of enormous importance to the American people. As such, it is worthy of the public and private resources necessary for its full documentation.

Notes

1. Quoted in Elting E. Morison, *From Know-How to Nowhere: The Development of American Technology* (New York, 1974), 147–48.
2. Stanley Sandler, *The Emergence of the Modern Capital Ship, 1860–1870* (Newark, DE, 1979), 15–16.
3. Bernard Brodie, *Sea Power in the Machine Age* (Princeton, 1941), 171.
4. Quoted in Rear Admiral Albert Gleaves, *Life and Letters of Rear Admiral Stephen B. Luce* (New York, 1925), 3.
5. George T. Davis, *A Navy Second to None: The Development of Modern American Naval Policy* (New York, 1940), 9, 9n.
6. William N. Still, Jr., "Technology Afloat," *Civil War Times Illustrated* 14 (November 1975): 42.
7. Worthington C. Ford, ed., *A Cycle of Adams Letters, 1861–1865,* 2 vols. (Boston, 1920), 1:123.
8. Ephraim D. Adams, *Great Britain and the American Civil War,* 2 vols. (New York, 1925), 1:276.

9. Lynn M. Case and Warren F. Spencer, *The United States and France: Civil War Diplomacy* (Philadelphia, 1970), 266.

10. Ibid., 267.

11. Ibid., 265–67.

12. Bruce Catton, *This Hallowed Ground* (New York, 1960), 160–61; Sir Winston Churchill, *History of the English-Speaking Peoples,* 4 vols. (New York, 1956), 4:202; William C. Davis, *Duel between the First Ironclads* (Garden City, 1975), 165; Gleaves, *Stephen B. Luce,* 289.

13. James P. Baxter, *The Introduction of the Ironclad Warship* (Cambridge, MA, 1933), 285; Kenneth Bourne, *Britain and the Balance of Power in North America, 1815–1908* (Berkeley, 1967), 239–40. See also Regis A. Courtemanche, *No Need for Glory: The British Navy in American Waters, 1860–1864* (Annapolis, 1977), 157; Sandler, *Emergence of the Modern Capital Ship,* 65. For an example of an exaggerated effect, see Stephen B. Luce, "The Story of the Monitor," *Naval Actions and History, 1799–1899,* published in the Papers of the Military Historical Society of Massachusetts (Boston, 1902), 12:127–54.

14. Larry E. Tise, "Off Carolina Searching for the *Monitor*," *Civil War Times Illustrated* 20 (July 1981):38–41, 44–45. This was a special issue devoted to the *Monitor,* the only issue of that magazine devoted to a particular ship.

15. Sidney Rather, James H. Soltow, and Richard Sylla, *The Evolution of the American Economy* (New York, 1979), 241.

16. Charles Singer et al., eds., *A History of Technology,* 7 vols. (Oxford, 1985), 5:818.

17. Ibid., 819.

18. Susan P. Lee and Peter Passell, *A New Economic View of American History* (New York, 1979), 227–29. Thomas Cochran was the first historian to challenge the idea that the Civil War stimulated economic growth. See Thomas Cochran, "Did the Civil War Retard Industrialization?" *Mississippi Valley Historical Review* 48 (1961): 197–210.

19. John W. Oliver, *History of American Technology* (New York, 1956), 276. See also Singer, *History of Technology* 5:809.

20. Bernard Brodie and Fawn Brodie, *From Crossbow to H-Bomb* (New York, 1962), 133–34.

21. William C. Church, *The Life of John Ericsson,* 2 vols. (New York, 1890), 2:34.

22. Theodore Ropp, "The *Monitor's* Changing Appeal," in *The* Monitor*: Its Meaning and Future* (Washington, 1978), 72–73.

23. *New York Times,* 4 October 1925.

24. Still, "Technology Afloat," 5.

25. Brodie, *Sea Power in the Machine Age,* 177.

26. Church, *Life of John Ericsson,* 1:261.

27. Ibid., 2:114.
28. Baxter, *Introduction of the Ironclad Warship,* 324; Still, "Technology Afloat," 42; Phillip K. Lundeberg, "The *Monitor:* Fragile Survivor," *The* Monitor: *Its Meaning and Future,* 67.
29. Still, "Technology Afloat," 43.
30. Davis, *Duel between the First Ironclads,* 18.
31. As mentioned earlier, most authorities place more emphasis on steam propulsion.

3

Defiance: Raphael Semmes of the *Alabama*

JOHN M. TAYLOR

The story of the Confederacy at sea is to a large extent the story of Raphael Semmes, the most successful 19th-century practitioner of the naval strategy of commerce raiding. Commanding first the *Sumter* and then the famous *Alabama*, he led the near-destruction of the Federal merchant marine and was the only naval officer on either side to fight two battles at sea. He helped to defend Richmond in the final year of the war and was the only officer in Confederate service to hold flag rank in both the navy and the army.

Born in Charles County, Maryland, on September 27, 1809, Semmes was orphaned at the age of 13. Reared by two uncles, he enjoyed a middle-class upbringing in the Georgetown section of Washington, D.C., and the eastern shore of Maryland. He had little formal schooling, but became a voracious reader, especially of history.

Semmes's relatives secured a midshipman's appointment for their adopted son, and the 16-year-old Raphael entered the U.S. Navy in 1826. He spent most of the next five years at sea, cruising the Caribbean and the Mediterranean. He studied wind currents and navigation and developed an appreciation for nature—plants, marine life, and wildlife—that would never leave him. In April 1832 he was promoted to "passed midshipman" but, like many of his contemporaries, he faced a difficult period of unpaid shore duty. Unable to count on the navy for a livelihood, Semmes read law with his brother, Samuel, in Cumberland, Maryland. Over the years, this second profession would stand him in good stead. On May 2, 1837, Semmes married Anne Elizabeth Spencer, a member of a prominent Protestant family in Cincinnati.

For the next five years Semmes alternated between a sporadic law practice and postings to naval stations along the Florida coast and the Gulf of Mexico. While stationed at Pensacola in 1841 he purchased a plot of land in Baldwin County, Alabama, on the west bank of the river that separates Alabama from the Florida panhandle. The move was an important one for Semmes, for, in moving to the house that he called Prospect Hill, he was putting down roots in the Deep South. From then on, Semmes regarded himself as a citizen of Alabama, and came to credit the Southern planter class with qualities that he himself admired: elegance, hospitality, and disdain for mere money-grubbing.

As time went on Semmes wearied of the navy, with its uncertain compensation, snail-like promotions, and preoccupation with seniority. The war with Mexico held out the possibility of distinction, but a disaster at sea in the first year of the war threatened a premature end to Semmes's navy career. While commanding the brig *Somers* on blockade duty off Veracruz on December 8, 1846, Semmes lost his ship and thirty-nine men in a gale. In any 19th-century navy the loss of a ship could mean the end of her skipper's career, and no one realized this better than Semmes. He met the challenge head on, requesting a court of inquiry. There he painted the storm as an act of God for which the *Somers* had been as prepared as any ship could be, and the surviving officers supported his testimony. Semmes was exonerated.

Three months later, the Alabamian commanded one of the naval guns moved ashore to assist General Winfield Scott in the siege of Veracruz. Shortly thereafter he was chosen to bear a message from Washington to General Scott concerning a U.S. Navy officer who had been taken prisoner by the Mexicans. Semmes left the Home Squadron and spent the remainder of the war with the army, most of the time as a volunteer aide to General William Worth. At the close of the war Worth wrote to Scott, "To Lieutenant Semmes of the Navy, volunteer aide-de-camp, the most cordial thanks . . . are tendered for his uniform gallantry and assistance."[1]

Notwithstanding this record, the navy put Semmes on extended leave in 1849. He took the opportunity to move his family to Mobile, probably so that his children could enroll in the schools there. He attempted to launch a law practice while writing a memoir of the Mexican War, which appeared in 1851 under the cumbersome title *Service Afloat and Ashore During the Mexican War*. The book was well received, in part because of its thoughtful examination of Mexican social institutions.

In 1855 the navy discovered a vacancy in the ranks of commanders, and by the workings of the seniority system that he despised, Semmes was promoted to commander. In February 1856 he again requested sea duty and was briefly given command of a mail steamer. The following November, however, he was assigned to the Lighthouse Service as an inspector of stations. For most of 1857 Semmes combined his fledgling law practice in Mobile with visits to lighthouses along the Gulf of Mexico. He appears to have discharged his responsibilities efficiently, for in September 1858 he was called to Washington to serve as secretary to the Lighthouse Board. For the next two and a half years he occupied a small office in the basement of the Treasury Department, transacting the day-to-day business of the board.

There, Semmes was an interested observer of the collapse of the Union. His sympathies were entirely with his adopted South. An avid reader, he was convinced that the South was a victim of economic op-pression—that policies determined in Washington, had resulted in a transfer of wealth from the South to the North. Tariff legislation, in his view, had protected New England industries at the expense of the South, stifling competition and obliging Southerners to pay artificially high prices for manufactured goods.

Semmes had read extensively in the area of constitutional law, and he was convinced that the Union was a voluntary compact from which any state could withdraw. In his view, much depended on the outcome of the election of 1860. Although Semmes was a Southerner to the core, his presidential preference was for Democrat Stephen A. Douglas, whom he viewed as the one candidate who would allow slave states the same access to the territories as the free states enjoyed. The election of Abraham Lincoln, in his opinion, meant disunion.

On January 11, 1861, Alabama seceded from the Union, following the example of South Carolina, Mississippi, and Florida. For all of Semmes's later zeal for the Confederate cause, he did not immediately resign his Federal commission. He was not a man of means, and the seniority that he had built up in the U.S. Navy was his family's principal economic asset. His wife, Anne, was distraught. Her own family in Ohio were Unionists, and she urged her husband to stay with the Old Navy.

After considerable soul-searching, Semmes resigned his commission in the U.S. Navy on February 15 and headed south. In Montgomery, Alabama, the first capital of the Confederacy, he was commissioned a commander in the Confederate navy and promptly sent back to the North on a sensitive purchasing mission. On instructions from President Jefferson Davis, he traveled through New York and southern New England, ordering munitions for the Confederacy. Contemptuous of the thirst for profit that motivated his business contacts, Semmes doubted that there would be a war.

Back in Montgomery, Semmes applauded the Confederate decision to attack Fort Sumter and thereby to precipitate war. Convinced that the Federal merchant marine would prove to be the Yankees' Achilles' heel, he urged Secretary of the Navy Stephen Mallory to endorse a strategy of commerce raiding. At the same time he persuaded Mallory to give him command of a converted packet ship, promptly named the *Sumter*, which would become the first Confederate cruiser. It took Semmes two months to convert the vessel into a warship. Although blockaded in the Mississippi passes by a Federal flotilla, the 500-ton *Sumter* made a daring escape on June 30, 1861, and the Confederacy had its first cruiser at sea.

At the outset of the war Raphael Semmes was almost 52 years old, and beginning to gray around the temples. He was of average height for his day, about five feet eight inches, and in later life claimed never to have weighed more than 130 pounds. Taut and spare, he carried himself with an erect military bearing. In an era when full beards were the fashion, Semmes instead sported an imperious, pointed mustache that led his crewmen to call him "Old Beeswax."

In strategic terms, the tiny Confederate navy faced three tasks. One was to keep open the important waterways of the South. This objective depended heavily on Confederate fortunes in the ground war, and for this reason, if for no other, was doomed to failure. A second was to break the Federal blockade, so the Confederacy could import military goods and export the cotton that was the South's greatest economic asset. The Con-

Raphael Semmes leans nonchalantly against his aft pivot gun in a photograph taken at Cape Town. *(Library of Congress)*

federacy proved unable to break the blockade, but Mallory's introduction of a handful of ironclad warships caused considerable anguish in Washington.

Mallory's final objective was to take the war to the enemy, through commerce raiders, in such a way as to force the Union to sue for peace. Although the *Sumter* was a primitive steamer, capable of no more than 10 knots, the fact that she could maintain such speed without regard to the wind made her a deadly predator in a time when virtually all merchantmen were sailing ships. In addition, although there were few seagoing vessels in the Confederacy, they could be purchased abroad.

Off Cuba with the *Sumter*, Semmes stopped and burned his first U.S. merchantman, the *Golden Rocket*, on July 3, 1861. The destruction of his first victim was an emotional moment for Semmes. For decades he had served the U.S. flag and defended it; now he was waging war against it. In the six months that followed, Semmes burned seven Northern ships and—unable to send prizes through the Federal blockade to a Southern port—bonded ten others. His operations sharply reduced Federal sea trade in the Caribbean.

Semmes took the *Sumter* across the Atlantic, but critical maintenance problems eventually forced him to call at Gibraltar, where the *Sumter* was blockaded by three Federal warships. Having made the most of his vessel's limited capabilities, Semmes directed that she be laid up. Returning to the Confederacy from Great Britain, he traveled as far as Nassau before receiving orders to return to Britain and take command of a cruiser under construction there, destined to become the famous *Alabama*.

The new Confederate raider was outfitted for sea in great secrecy, and to avoid a contravention of British law, she received her ordnance as well as her new commander and crew in the Azores. The *Alabama* represented the zenith of a hybrid marine form, ships powered by both sail and steam. She measured 220 feet in length and 32 feet in beam, and displaced 1,040 tons. She carried enough coal for eighteen days of cruising and had an innovation found on few ships of her day—a condenser that could provide a gallon of fresh water per day for each man on board, enabling her to remain at sea for extended periods. Her twin-bladed screw could be raised out of the water to avoid drag when the ship was under sail. She would occasionally make as much as 12 knots under sail, to which her engines could add another 2 or 3 knots. Semmes was under orders to avoid engagements with enemy warships, for his was a special mission. The *Alabama*, as Semmes wrote in his memoirs, "was the first steamship in the history of the world—the defective little *Sumter* excepted—that was let loose against the commerce of a great people."[2]

The *Alabama* had been at sea for only ten days when, on September 5, 1862, she sighted the first of 65 victims she would claim over the next twenty-two months, the whaler *Ocmulgee*. Semmes burned her. He spent two months in the Azores, destroying eight vessels in all. Then the *Alabama* made her way westward, destroying ships that carried Northern grain to Europe. Semmes even considered a raid against shipping in New York harbor, but his ship was low on coal, and he reluctantly headed for a rendezvous with his tender in the Caribbean. In New York and New England, shipowners filled the newspapers with tales of the "pirate" Semmes.

On the *Alabama,* as on the *Sumter,* Semmes dealt with his prisoners as humanely as conditions permitted. Captured crews were usually housed on deck, but were afforded some protection from the elements. When the prisoners included women passengers, the *Alabama*'s officers vacated their cabins. Because prisoners were a nuisance, Semmes got rid of them as quickly as possible. Sometimes he landed them at a neutral port, but more often he transferred them to a captured ship whose cargo he had bonded.

Although Semmes had passed up the temptation to show his flag in New York harbor, he hoped to play a role in the land campaign in Texas. There, a Federal force under General Nathaniel P. Banks had captured Galveston in October 1862. Confederate forces had subsequently recaptured Galveston, but the city was blockaded by five Federal warships when the black-hulled *Alabama* arrived there on January 11, 1863.

Semmes considered his options. The city that he had contemplated bombarding was now in friendly hands, and he could hardly take on five enemy warships. While he deliberated, the Federals detached one of their number, the *Hatteras*, to check out the stranger. It was a fatal error. Semmes steamed slowly south, luring his pursuer away from reinforcements. Night had fallen by the time the *Hatteras* reached speaking distance of the *Alabama*. Semmes, in reply to the Yankee's hail, first identified his ship as British. When the wary Federal captain dispatched a boat to verify his story, Semmes identified himself as the CSS *Alabama* and loosed a broadside at point-blank range.

The *Hatteras* was an underpowered side-wheeler that could not trade broadsides with the powerful *Alabama*. The Federal gunboat struck her colors after only 13 minutes, and soon sank in the shallow waters of the Gulf. Semmes rescued the survivors and set course for the Atlantic. He seized and burned two merchantmen in the last week of January, bringing the *Alabama*'s total to 30.

Working the heavily traveled sea lanes off the bulge of Brazil, the *Alabama* captured no fewer than 11 enemy merchantmen during February and March. For all the outrage in the Northern press concerning the *Alabama*'s depredations, pursuit of the raider was disorganized and ineffectual. Semmes was amazed that the Union did so little to protect its merchantmen, noting that the presence of two or three heavier warships in the major sea lanes could have seriously hindered his operations.

From South America, Semmes set sail for the Cape of Good Hope. He made some repairs at Cape Town, but his two months in South African waters were not notably productive. Indeed, the success of the *Alabama*, assisted by the *Florida* and a ragtag collection of Confederate coastal vessels, was making prey scarce. Of the *Alabama*'s eventual total of 64 prizes, 52 were taken during her first 10 months at sea—that is, the period between September 1862 and June 1863.

From South Africa, Semmes took the *Alabama* on a six-month cruise in Asian waters that carried the raider as far as present-day Vietnam. Although the cruise was not productive in terms of prizes, Semmes had the satisfaction of viewing in Singapore no fewer than 22 Northern merchantmen, immobilized by reports and rumors of the *Alabama*. Aboard the raider, however, all was not well. Semmes was troubled by poor morale among his predominantly British crew and by maintenance problems on his once-sleek vessel. He himself was becoming increasingly restive. Off Indonesia he actively sought combat with a Federal vessel, the *Wyoming*, then patrolling the Sunda Strait.

On Christmas Eve 1863 the *Alabama* set her course westward. The raider's boilers were operating poorly, and some of her timbers were split beyond repair. After another stop at Cape Town, Semmes turned northward. He intended to put his ship into drydock, either in Great Britain or France, but he realized that if he did so he would run a strong risk of being blockaded in port as the *Sumter* had been. He told John Kell, "Should we fall in with one of [the enemy's cruisers], not too heavy for us, we will give him battle before we go into dock."[3]

At noon on June 11, the *Alabama* dropped anchor off Cherbourg. Semmes thought that his cruise was over. He wrote to the Confederate naval representative in Paris on June 13 that his health "has suffered so much from a constant and harassing service of three years, almost continuously at sea, that I shall have to ask for relief."[4] On the same day, however, Semmes received word that changed these plans. The USS *Kearsarge*, John A. Winslow commanding, was en route to Cherbourg and would arrive imminently.

The Confederate commander faced a crucial decision. He knew that his ship needed a refit and that some of his fuses were defective. The prudent course would have been to have his ship laid up, as he had with the *Sumter*. But Semmes's fighting blood was up, and he had no great respect for his enemies. He sent a message to be transmitted by the U.S. consul to Captain Winslow: He intended to fight.

On the morning of Sunday, June 19, 1864, the *Alabama* entered the English Channel. Semmes steamed directly for his antagonist, some four

The only known photograph of the *Alabama*, showing her coaling at Singapore in December 1863. *(Tennessee State Library and Archives)*

miles away. He never divulged how he hoped to defeat the sturdy *Kearsarge*, but he doubtless hoped to inflict damage with his pivot guns before coming into the effective range of Winslow's Dahlgrens. Unfortunately for Semmes, his first broadsides inflicted no serious damage. When the range was about 900 yards, Winslow turned to port and opened fire with his own starboard battery. The two antagonists thus fought clockwise on a circular track, eventually at a range of about 500 yards. They made seven complete circles during the course of the action, reminding one Northern sailor of "two flies crawling around on the rim of a saucer."[5]

The firing from the *Alabama* was rapid but wild. Nevertheless, about 20 minutes into the action a 110-pound projectile from Semmes's Blakely glanced off the *Kearsarge*'s counter and lodged in her stern post. The stern post—a large, curved timber that anchored the planks of the upper hull—was a vulnerable point on any vessel, and the impact, according to the *Kearsarge's* surgeon, shook the ship from stem to stern. Had the shell exploded it might have crippled the Federal warship, but it did not, presumably because of a defective fuse.

Almost immediately the battle began to turn. A shot from the *Kearsarge* destroyed the *Alabama's* steering apparatus, and for the remainder of the engagement the Confederate cruiser had to be steered with tackles. Shells from Winslow's Dahlgrens smashed into the *Alabama* at the waterline. Shortly after noon Semmes gave the order to abandon ship. He and Kell then had the great good fortune to be rescued by the yacht of a wealthy Briton who had observed the action, and who took a number of survivors directly to Southampton.

While the Lincoln administration fumed, Semmes was lionized in England. British admirers replaced the sword lost with the *Alabama*, and he was wined and dined by the aristocracy. Nevertheless, Semmes was bitter over the loss of his ship, blaming the one-sided battle on the *Kearsarge's* protective chains and his own defective powder.

Notwithstanding the defeat off Cherbourg, Semmes's record with the *Alabama* was astonishing. During his 22 months at sea he had burned 54 Federal merchantmen and had bonded 10 others. After the war, when British and U.S. negotiators determined that Great Britain owed the United States $15.5 million for damages by ships sold to the Confederacy, the amount charged to the *Alabama*—$6.75 million—was by far the most. In addition to her remarkable toll in merchant shipping, the *Alabama* had sunk an enemy warship, the *Hatteras*, and had brought untold embarrassment to the U.S. Navy. Semmes's record would not be approached by any sea raider until the advent of the submarine.

After a short holiday in Europe, Semmes made his way back to the Confederacy. In Richmond he was promoted to rear admiral and given command of Confederate gunboats on the James River. When Richmond fell, he burned his boats and formed his men into a naval brigade that served under General Joseph E. Johnston in the final weeks of the war. Commissioned a brigadier general in the Confederate Army, he became the only Confederate officer to hold the dual ranks of general and admiral. In December 1865 he became one of the few Confederate officers to be arrested in violation of his terms of parole, as President Andrew Johnson's administration considered bringing him to trial for violations of the rules of war. After Semmes had spent two months in prison, the government reluctantly concluded that it had no case and ordered his release. Semmes returned to Mobile to practice law and to write his memoirs.

Memoirs of Service Afloat During the War Between the States was the first important Confederate memoir to appear after the war, and Semmes took his responsibility seriously. The first seven chapters are an eloquent defense of the right of secession, one that allowed Semmes to make good use of his readings in constitutional law. The narrative that follows is a rollicking account of the voyages of the *Sumter* and the *Alabama*, interspersed from time to time with Semmes's digressions on scientific and sociopolitical topics.

When Semmes turns his attention to nature—the violence of a storm, the picturesque vista of old Cadiz, or the pastoral South African countryside—the reader is reminded of the author's deep interest in the world around him. Viewing the reefs off Tortuga, he likens coral to stonemasons of the deep, and their reefs to miniature cathedrals. He delights in the *Alabama's* stop at the Arcas Islands off Mexico:

> The naturalist would have reveled at the Arcas, in view of the debris of sea-shells, and coral, and . . . in watching the habits of the gannet, man-of-war bird, and a great variety of the sea-gull . . . . As the keel of one of our boats would grate upon the sand, clouds of these birds would fly up, and circle around our heads, screaming in their various and discordant notes at our intrusion.[6]

Much of the book is a political polemic. Semmes portrays the Civil War as a struggle between good and evil in which the South was clearly on the side of the angels. His lurid descriptions of burning ships suggest that he overcame early any aversion he may have had to destroying merchant vessels. After a while the reader becomes conscious of the author's harsh unwillingness to credit his foes with any honorable qualities: A naval officer of Southern birth who remains in Federal service has clearly done so from the basest of motives.

As for slavery, Semmes could not conceive of blacks prospering in a situation where they were left to their own devices. Slavery had been abolished in Jamaica and other British colonies in the 1830s, and Semmes had not been impressed with the result. He considered the antislavery agitation in the North to be hypocritical, designed by all except a few zealots as a way of distracting the country from the economic exploitation of the South.

Because all except one of his victims were merchantmen, Semmes has not always been given full credit for his initiative, pugnacity, and daring. The fact is that he operated in an atmosphere of constant danger and in this environment was bold almost to a fault. His initial breakout from the Mississippi River, in the *Sumter*, required considerable daring. His projected raid into New York harbor with the *Alabama*, although not carried out, was bold in conception. His attempt to disrupt enemy landings off Galveston resulted only in the sinking of the *Hatteras,* but reflected his determination to get the most out of the single vessel available to him. What Semmes would have accomplished if he had commanded more than a single warship can only be conjectured, but his initiative and resourcefulness would have made him a formidable antagonist.

Notwithstanding the fact that he had no home port, he kept two wooden vessels at sea for the better part of three years without an overhaul and without losing either a crewman or a prisoner to disease. As a strategist, he demonstrated that a nation with a weak navy could inflict great damage on any foe with a substantial merchant fleet. He was the first commerce raider to operate in the age of steam, and he may have been the best of all time.

Notes

1. Colyer Meriwether, *Raphael Semmes* (Philadelphia: George W. Jacobs, 1913), 60.
2. Raphael Semmes, *Memoirs of Service Afloat During the War Between the States* (Louisiana State University Press, 1996), vii.
3. John M. Taylor, *Confederate Raider: Raphael Semmes of the* Alabama (Washington, D.C.: Brassey's, 1994), 191.
4. Ibid., 196.
5. John M. Taylor, "The Fiery Trail of the *Alabama*," *Military History Quarterly*, Summer 1991.
6. Semmes, *Memoirs of Service Afloat*, 539.

4

....

Technology Afloat

William N. Still, Jr.

The Civil War is frequently referred to as the first modern conflict. Among the reasons cited for this assertion, technology is given a prominent place. The railroad, electric telegraph, aerial observation (balloons), rifles, repeating small arms, and ironclad warships were all employed during the war. The last item mentioned has been considered the most significant naval development during the period. Yet as James Baxter demonstrated some thirty years ago in his brilliant study, *The Introduction of the Ironclad Warship*, the armored vessel-of-war was introduced and battle tested in various forms long before the Civil War.

The ironclad warship is only one of the technological innovations in the 19th century that revolutionized the navies of the world. During that century began the shift from sail to steam, from wood to iron, from solid shot to shell. The screw propeller, rifled and breech-loading ordnance, the revolving turret, the mine, and the semisubmersible were also introduced. As in the case of the ironclad, these innovations in naval technology had their origin before the Civil War.

The adoption of steam propulsion on warships changed the whole nature of maritime strategy. Undoubtedly, this was the most revolutionary development in naval science since the displacement of the galley by the sailing ship. Ships en route across the ocean could now go in direct lines instead of in sweeping deviations determined by the winds. Battle tactics which had previously been determined by the direction and velocity of the wind now had to be completely revised.

Yet forty years would elapse between the appearance of Robert Fulton's steamboat in 1807 and the widespread adoption of steam propulsion in warships. There were various reasons to explain this delay, including the huge investments in sailing ships by naval powers and the inefficiency of the early steam engines. The first paddle-wheel steamers had little speed, a huge fuel consumption, and very little cruising radius. The paddle wheels were, moreover, obviously and fatally vulnerable to gunfire, and the huge paddle boxes took up so much space along the side that they left little room for the standard broadside battery.

Ultimately, solutions were found for these problems and others, the most notable being the perfection of the screw propeller, which eliminated the exposed paddle wheels and enabled designers to put the engines below the water line. In 1843 the *Princeton,* the first screw warship in the world, was launched. By the beginning of the Civil War most major navies had converted or were converting to steam. This is not to say that steam had completely supplanted sail. While floating batteries, coast defense vessels, and river boats might be powered by steam alone, steam continued for many years to be used as merely auxiliary to sail in seagoing ships.

The introduction of steam coincided roughly with revolutionary developments in naval ordnance. There were four main improvements in ordnance during the period: the introduction of shell guns, improvements in interior ballistics, rifling, and the change to breech-loading.

At the end of the Napoleonic Wars (1814) naval guns were little different in construction and performance from those used in the Spanish Armada campaign (1588). The standard naval gun was still the cast iron, smoothbore, solid-shot muzzle-loader effective up to 300 yards. The shell was a hollowed-out spherical projectile filled with a fused bursting charge. Although fired from 24- and 32-pounder guns, they were considered too small to be effective. In 1824 the Paixhans gun, named after its inventor, French artillery officer Henri-Joseph Paixhans, especially designed to fire large shells, was introduced and immediately demonstrated its power by splintering an old warship. Though the gun rendered the wooden ships so vulnerable as to deprive them of their fighting power, navies did not generally adopt shell guns until the annihilation of the Turkish fleet at Sinope during the Crimean War clearly demonstrated their effectiveness on a large scale.

The science of interior ballistics, which combines chemistry, mathematics, and physics in order to study the various strains and reactions within the gun itself when fired, produced remarkable improvements in ordnance. Experiments during most of the 19th century were directed chiefly to strengthening gun barrels to enable them to fire heavier projectiles with heavier charges without bursting. Gunmakers experimented with wrought iron and steel, but unfortunate explosions caused ordnance experts to concentrate on cast iron until late in the century.

Captain J. T. Rodman of the United States Army designed a smoothbore gun cast with a hollow bore; the interior metal was chilled first so that the exterior metal shrank onto the hardened inner core. The Rodman guns did not appear until the eve of the Civil War, but when they did, it became possible to cast 15-inch and even 20-inch smoothbore shell guns that could be fired safely.

In the early 1850's Commander John A. Dahlgren of the United States Navy developed a 9-inch smoothbore shell gun that was a result of his study of pressures and strains generated in the barrel at firing. With its "soda bottle" shape, Dahlgren's gun was designed to have most of its metal around the breech, concentrating the strength where the interior pressure was heaviest. Dahlgren smoothbore guns were so successful that by the time of the Civil War they were the most popular guns used by the navy.

Apparently American ordnance experts experimented very little with breech-loading ordnance before the Civil War. Breech-loading guns were quite well known in Europe by this time but excited little interest in the United States. However, this was not true of rifled ordnance.

The army began intensive experimentation with rifled cannon late in the 1850's and by the beginning of the Civil War had several hundred rifled pieces of artillery. Most of them were old smoothbores that had been rifled, but a number of them were new pieces designed by Robert P. Parrott, president of the West Point Foundry. The Parrott gun was shaped like a Rodman but with the addition of a heavy wrought iron band shrunk around the breech. The navy used 8- and 10-inch Parrott guns as its standard rifled ordnance during the Civil War.

In a sense the shell gun was responsible for both rifled ordnance and armor. The development of shell guns required armoring the sides of warships, and the development of armor required a heavy ordnance with greater penetrating power.

The Crimean War was a landmark in the development not only of the shell gun, but also of the armored warship. During the conflict the French Government constructed several ironclad batteries which participated in bombardments. After the war the *Gloire,* the first seagoing ironclad, was built. The British followed with the *Warrior,* the first iron-hulled, ironclad, steam-driven battleship.

The introduction of iron armor has obscured another revolutionary innovation appearing about the same time—the iron-hulled ship. As early as 1844 the United States Navy commissioned an iron-hulled warship, the *Michigan.* Nonetheless, naval shipbuilders did not accept the superiority of iron to wood in hull construction until the Civil War years and later.

Even in underseas and mine warfare important developments were made before the Civil War. David Bushnell had invented a practical submarine, the *Turtle,* which operated in New York Sound during the American Revolution. The Russians used contact and electrically discharged mines in the Crimean War with varying success.

Therefore, when the Civil War broke out the revolution in naval technology was well under way. The war became a testing ground for the new developments. As Bernard Brodie wrote, "For the first time the achievements of the industrial and scientific revolution were used on a large scale in war."

Technology played a determining role in the implementation of Union naval strategy—a strategy that was dominated by initiating, maintaining, and strengthening the blockade. The Civil War was not the first conflict in which steamers were used in a close blockade nor was it the first one in which steam propulsion was indispensable to the blockade's effectiveness. As K. Jack Bauer has pointed out in his recent study of the Mexican War, the navy's role in blockading the Gulf coast of Mexico was most difficult as well as significant.

The Union blockade during the Civil War was also difficult to carry out. Sailing warships could not stand in close enough to the low, dangerous Southern coast, and at the same time steamships had no deposits of coal nearer than Hampton Roads or Key West. Consequently, until late 1861 the blockade was really a paper one. The occupation of Ship Island off the coast of Mississippi in September and the seizure of Port Royal, South Carolina, provided logistic support bases, but it was months before the blockade really became effective. In some places success was achieved by capture and army occupation, as at Fort Pulaski off Savannah, Georgia, at Fernandina and St. Augustine, Florida, and along the sounds of North Carolina. At other points it was accomplished by what Admiral Samuel F. DuPont called an inside blockade: stationing a small number of vessels in an inside anchorage instead of a large number beyond the bar. This was done at Hampton Roads, Wassaw, Ossabaw, and St. Simons Sound, Georgia; Jacksonville, Florida; and the Head of the Passes at the entrance to the Mississippi River. At Wilmington, Charleston, and Mobile the combination of hydrography and defenses made an outside blockade necessary.

In theory blockade runners and blockading ships benefited unequally from steam power. Being under way, the former could run past a line of blockading ships and be out of range before the latter could raise anchor and give pursuit. But the most serious effect that steam propulsion had on a blockade's effectiveness was to limit a blockader's range. As Walter Millis has written, a steam warship could range the ocean with a speed and certainty unknown to sail, but was a slave to its coaling ports. Fuel was the most critical logistical need for the blockading squadron. By 1863 the four squadrons required more than 3,000 tons of anthracite coal a week. Admiral Du Pont wrote after receiving word of General Robert E. Lee's advance into Pennsylvania that "if the rebels now raiding in Pennsylvania knew it, they would destroy the Reading Railroad and cut off every squadron from its coal, which would be virtually destroying them. We are now living from hand to mouth for want of it."

Steam propulsion affected not only a blockade but other naval tactics as well. Bernard Brodie wrote in *Sea Power in the Machine Age* that steam propulsion's influence on naval tactics could be stated in one sentence: It very nearly canceled out as a tactical factor the influence of the wind, which had previously been all-important in battle at sea. This was illustrated early in the war at Port Royal when Du Pont proved that warships with steam power and better ordnance were the equal of forts and their land-based guns. Du Pont simply steamed his vessels into the harbor and engaged the forts on their inner and weaker sides until they were abandoned. The same steam power also permitted Admiral David G. Farragut to run past the strong points covering narrow channels at New Orleans, Port Hudson, and Mobile Bay. As Admiral John D. Hayes has recently pointed out in his introduction to the published Du Pont letters, "Given sufficient speed and room to maneuver, ships of either wood or iron could by pass forts to gain control of navigable waters."

This mobility was also reflected in Confederate warships challenging Union blockaders and then successfully returning to their bases. The ironclads *Chicora* and *Palmetto State* attacked Union vessels off Charleston in January 1863. The *Albemarle* attacked Union vessels in Albemarle Sound in 1864 and successfully retired up the Roanoke River to Plymouth. This mobility greatly increased the raiding cruiser's chances of running down merchant vessels and was a major factor in the *Alabama's* and other Confederate cruisers' successes. And, of course, river warfare was made possible because of steam propulsion, since sailing ships could not maneuver unless fortuitous winds blew both up and down stream as needed.

Steam resulted in the tactic of ramming, which was erroneously believed to have played a prominent part in the naval battles of antiquity between rowed galleys. The sinking of the *Cumberland* by the ironclad *Virginia* at Hampton Roads was the first successful ramming attack in modern times. The fact that the Union frigate was at anchor when attacked was overlooked. Later attempts proved that it was exceedingly difficult to ram a ship in motion, and that such action was dangerous to the rammer. The Confederate ironclad *Albemarle* was nearly pulled under because she had difficulty backing clear after ramming a Union gunboat. Most attempts to ram in the Civil War, even in rivers and other confined waters where conditions were exceptionally favorable, were failures. Yet Rear Admiral Louis M. Goldsborough asserted in a letter to the Union Secretary of the Navy in 1864 that "the value of rams, at this very moment, cannot be overestimated."

It is not surprising that the Civil War witnessed the first full-scale employment of armored vessels. The emphasis that European powers were placing on the construction of ironclads was generally known in American naval circles. Ironically, the Union navy—which previously had to assume an offensive strategy in order to win the war—adopted as its principal ironclad a type of vessel that was basically defensive in nature. Early in August 1861 Congress appropriated $1,500,000 for the "construction or completing of iron or steelclad steamers or steam batteries," and authorized the creation of a board of naval officers to examine proposals and make recommendations. In September the board recommended that contracts be awarded for three vessels: a seagoing broadside type of vessel, *New Ironsides;* a lightly armored wooden vessel, *Galena;* and a revolving-turret vessel, *Monitor.*

While the board of naval officers had been deliberating, the army had already contracted for seven ironclads for service on the Mississippi River and its tributaries. Known as "Pook Turtles" after their designer, Samuel M. Pook, they were similar in appearance to Confederate ironclads with their sloping, rectangular, armored casemates. These vessels came under naval control after they were commissioned.

Three basic types were introduced by the Union navy in its ironclad construction program in the fall of 1861. The Pook Turtles with their light draft, low freeboards, and flat bottoms were designed for river operations; the *New Ironsides* was a more conventional seagoing vessel; and the *Monitor* was primarily a harbor defense vessel. Of these three types, the *New Ironsides* and the *Monitor* represented a fundamental divergence of opinion over the type of warship the navy should employ. The chief engineer, the chief naval constructor, and an undetermined number of naval officers including Farragut and Du Pont were critical of the light armament Monitor type and favored more offensive seagoing cruisers with their guns mounted in broadsides. Nevertheless, *New Ironsides* was the only seagoing armored cruiser to be completed during the war. An improved model, the *Dunderberg,* was laid down but not completed during the war.

The board of naval officers who had recommended the three original armored vessels wrote that "ocean going [armored] cruisers are for the time being impracticable." In 1864 Congress published a *Report of the Secretary of the Navy in Relation to Armored Vessels.* In general, the report was Secretary of the Navy Gideon Welles's defense of the monitor type. But it also included a number of letters from various naval officers critical of the idea

A twin-turret Union monitor. *(Library of Congress)*

of seagoing ironclads. Captain John R. Goldsborough wrote, "If any solid benefit is to be derived from iron plating applied to a sea going vessel it is quite apparent that it is only to be done by limiting its use to her most vitally exposed parts." The Federal Board of Ordnance observed that "upon a balance of advantages and disadvantages, a cruiser intended for sea service had better carry no armor at all."

These opinions may have had some effect on Union policy concerning armored vessels, but the major factors were the influence of Assistant Secretary of the Navy Gustavus Fox and the *Monitor's* designer, John Ericsson, and the impact of the battle between the *Monitor* and the *Virginia* on Northern public opinion.

By coincidence, Fox had been at Hampton Roads on the day of the battle and from then on was an enthusiastic devotee of the monitor design. Even before Hampton Roads the Navy Department had asked Congress for $12 million to construct twenty additional turreted vessels. These were designed by the chief of the Bureau of Construction and Repair and were to mount two turrets along the design of Captain Cowper Coles of the Royal Navy. Although the Coles turret was superior to the one designed by Ericsson, the Swedish inventor successfully prevented its adoption by the

American navy. In fact, one might say that the broadside-vs.-turreted ironclad dispute was not nearly so controversial in 1862 as the type of turret to be used. In addition to the Ericsson and Coles turret, a third one designed by James B. Eads was considered. Eads's turrets were installed on the Milwaukee class of river monitor and were probably the most sophisticated of the three. The guns in the turret were mounted on a steam-operated elevator which dropped them to a lower deck where they were loaded, then hoisted and run out through ports opened by automatic steam-operated shutters. Even the Milwaukee class, however, carried only one Eads turret; the other was of Ericsson's design.

The *Monitor* action in Hampton Roads produced such an intense enthusiasm in the North that a "monitor craze" swept the Union. Three weeks after the battle ten improved Ericsson monitors were contracted—the Passaic class which would see more service than any other class of monitors. Until the end of the war the navy would concentrate on monitor construction. Of the forty ironclads laid down by the Union during the war, thirty-five were of the monitor type.

The monitors had the great advantage of achieving a maximum of impenetrability through two radical factors—low freeboard and the concentration of gun in an armored turret. The guns could be aimed without moving the ship in shallow coastal waters. In confined and sheltered waters they were excellent defensive ships but they had serious defects that affected Union navy operations. A majority of them were essentially floating batteries that had to be towed from port to port. They were unseaworthy and had so little reserve buoyancy that a leak could be fatal. For these reasons they were unsuitable for blockade service, the primary mission of the Union navy. In anything but a flat calm a monitor's deck was awash. The crew had to remain below with hatches battened down. As Admiral Du Pont wrote: "How can such vessels lay off [ports] . . . and protect the wooden vessels."

Even more important was their unsuitability for offensive operations. Loading their guns usually required from six to eight minutes. "This delay," as Admiral Hayes has written, "violated the cardinal principal of naval gunnery, volume of fire." In the attack by the *New Ironsides, Keokuk,* and seven monitors on Fort Sumter in April 1863, only 139 rounds were fired by the combined batteries of the ironclads' twenty-three guns. At the same time seventy-six guns in the Confederate forts rained some 2,206 shots on the Union vessels. As Admiral Du Pont wrote Secretary Welles, "I . . . remind the Department that ability to endure is not a sufficient element wherewith to gain victories, that endurance must be accompanied with a corresponding power to inflict injury upon the enemy . . . that the weakness of the monitor class of vessels is fatal to their attempts against fortifications . . . before which they must . . . receive much more than they can return." A heavy volume of fire brought victory at Port Royal, New Orleans, Fort Fisher, and other Civil War engagements where wooden broadside vessels as well as monitors were employed.

Although seagoing cruisers similar to *New Ironsides* were unsuitable because of the shallow waters surrounding the Southern coast, ironclads such as improved versions of the Pook Turtles or Confederate casemated vessels might have been more suitable for bombardment than the monitor type.

The Navy Department attempted also to develop warships suitable for blockade duty and other services peculiar to the type of war conducted in the South. Double enders—shallow draft boats capable of going with equal facility in either direction—were designed and built for inland waterways. The chief constructor designed large, fast frigates and sloops for blockade duty, but only a few were constructed. Generally naval commanders had to depend upon converted merchant vessels for blockade duty. Ironically, the most effective blockaders were probably captured blockade runners.

While the Union building program through the war emphasized the monitor type, the Confederate program would change from one stressing offensive vessels to one emphasizing defense. Historians generally agree with the late Rear Admiral Bern Anderson that the "task of the Confederate Navy was to break, discredit or circumvent the Union blockade." This was generally true although the defense of key ports, inlets, bays, and rivers dominated Southern naval strategy. As a part of this strategy, cruisers such as the *Alabama, Nashville,* and *Shenandoah* were to attack and destroy Union shipping in order to divert naval vessels from the blockade. Historians also suggest, however, that the ironclad was to be the principal weapon employed by the Confederacy to break the blockade.

On May 9, 1861, Confederate Secretary of the Navy Stephen Mallory wrote in an oft-quoted report: "I regard the possession of an iron armored

Confederate Secretary of the Navy Stephen R. Mallory. *(National Archives)*

ship as a matter of the first necessity . . . inequality of numbers may be compensated by invulnerability; and thus not only does economy but naval success dictate the wisdom and expediency of fighting with iron against wood." That same day the Confederate Congress appropriated $2 million for the purchase or construction of ironclads in Europe. Although the Confederacy would contract for several powerful armored vessels in England and France, initial efforts were unsuccessful. Secretary Mallory then determined to construct ironclads within the Confederacy. In the middle of July 1861 the decision was made to convert the *Merrimack* into the *Virginia*, and six weeks later contracts were awarded for the construction of two ironclads later named the *Arkansas* and *Tennessee* to be built at Memphis; a fourth one, the *Mississippi*, was to be built at New Orleans. In September the *Louisiana* was also laid down in New Orleans. These five initial ironclads were all unusually large and were designed to operate on the open sea as well as on inland waters. These vessels were designed not only to break the blockade, but as Secretary Mallory wrote, to "traverse the entire coast of the United States . . . and encounter, with a fair prospect of success, their entire Navy." In other words, Mallory's initial ironclad strategy was offensive in nature.

By 1862 Mallory gave up his determination to build large seagoing ironclads within the Confederacy and instead concentrated on small, shallow-draft, harbor defense, armored vessels. There are various factors to explain this change in policy: the apparent unseaworthiness of the *Virginia* and the iron-clads built in New Orleans and Memphis, the pressing need for defensive vessels, and the belief that the South would be able to obtain powerful seagoing armored vessels in Europe. Approximately forty of these small, harbor defense ironclads were laid down within the Confederacy and half of them were completed. Like the monitors there were various classes deter-mined by length and other characteristics, and the ones completed late in the war were distinct improvements over earlier vessels. Nevertheless, as small, shallow-draft, defensive vessels their capabilities were limited. When the Confederate navy was unable or made no effort to break the Union blockade with these vessels, they came under criticism that was not justified because they were not designed to raise the blockade. In defense of them Mallory wrote: "Certainly they are unseaworthy, as vessels usually are that are built as these were for harbor defense chiefly. They are not expected to go to sea in the ordinary acceptation of the term."

With the exception of two double-ender ironclads with twin stationary turrets laid down at Richmond and Wilmington, the casemated ironclad remained the standard "home water" vessel constructed within the Confed-eracy. Less than two months before General Lee surrendered at Appomattox Court House, the naval secretary was writing: "For river, harbor, and coast defense, the sloping shield and general plan of armored vessels adopted by us . . . are the best that could be adopted in our situation. In ventilation, light, fighting space, and quarters it is believed that the sloping shield presents greater advantages than the *Monitor* turret."

Ironclads used during the American Civil War were inferior to their European counterparts. For example, the armor plate on Confederate and Union vessels was laminated, usually two inches in thickness, while by 1865 English mills were rolling plate as much as one foot thick. Developments in naval guns also lagged behind, but as with armored vessels, the Union and Confederate navies followed divergent paths in their ordnance policies.

The use of armor on warships reduced the effectiveness of shell guns that had become standard during the 1850's. Nevertheless, the Dahlgren smoothbore shell guns continued to be the most popular gun used by the Union navy during the war. The board of naval officers that reported on armored vessels in 1861 also suggested that smoothbore cannon firing spherical shot were superior to rifled ordnance. This view was reflected in the policies of John Dahlgren, who was appointed chief of ordnance in 1862. Although Dahlgren had experimented with rifled guns prior to the war, he became convinced that the smoothbore was the only weapon that could combat the ironclad effectively. The war did nothing to change his mind. In December 1865 he wrote that "naval smoothbore ordnance will not be superceded by Rifles." Rifled guns were used by the navy during the war, but the standard weapons found on most of the monitors and blockaders were 9-, 11-, and 15-inch Dahlgrens.

While the Union navy adhered to the principle of large smoothbore guns, the Confederate navy focused on the penetration capability of small-bore, high-velocity guns. Mallory and John M. Brooke (an officer in the Bureau of Ordnance and Hydrography) were responsible for this policy. Mallory ordered Brooke in the summer of 1861 to design a rifled cannon for the *Virginia*. The Brooke design was so successful that "Brooke guns," as they were called, became the standard guns used by the Confederate navy. Later as Chief of the Bureau of Ordnance and Hydrography, Brooke conducted experiments and gathered data that convinced him of the "superiority and practicability of rifled guns."

The Brooke guns were not original nor did Brooke claim them to be. They were very similar to the Parrott rifles developed shortly before the war and used by the Union. The major deviation was that Parrott used only one wrought iron band on the breech, whereas Brooke double- and even triple-banded his breech rings.

Brooke claimed that his high-velocity rifles had a longer range, were more accurate, and had greater penetrating power than smoothbores. Smoothbore advocates, however, claimed that rifled guns were far less practical than smoothbores. Cast iron smoothbores were stronger and there-

An artist's rendition of an "infernal machine"—a rudimentary naval mine. *(Library of Congress)*

fore were not as likely to burst as cast iron rifles so frequently did; they had greater initial velocity, and thus at short range—and naval engagements were fought at short range at that time—they could deliver a far more powerful blow than the rifled gun.

Actually no ironclad on either side was penetrated by naval gunfire. That is not to say that monitors and casemated vessels were not seriously damaged by gunfire—they were. Turrets and port shutters were jammed, gun mounts disabled, armored plate shattered, but no shot or bolt actually penetrated the armor.

The difficulty in penetrating armor by heavy guns resulted in experimentation in underwater attacks. As early as July 1861 Confederates were floating cylinders of boiler iron filled with powder down the Potomac River against Federal vessels. These earliest mines, or torpedoes as they were called during the war, accomplished nothing, but the Confederates did ultimately develop an extensive and successful mine program. In fact, approximately forty Union vessels were sunk or damaged by mines, including the destruction of four monitors. Various types were developed and used from simple contact mines to rather sophisticated mines and mine fields detonated by electric current. The Confederates used offensive as well as defensive mines. For example, the commanding officer of the ironclad *Charleston* rigged up a type of "barrel" contact mine to be rolled off the stern of the vessel.

The Confederates also experimented with other means of undersea warfare. Their efforts to develop a submarine culminated with the *Hunley,* which sank the *Housatonic* in Charleston Harbor. The semi-submersible vessels were the most unique and perhaps potentially the most important of the undersea weapons developed by the Confederacy. Known as "Davids," these small cigar-shaped vessels showed only the smokestack, pilot cockpit, and top of the armored hull above water. They carried a torpedo attached to a long pole or spar that would explode upon contact with the hull of a ship. The original *David* damaged *New Ironsides,* but despite efforts to construct a large number of the inexpensive vessels, no other attacks were made. If time had allowed they would have been a threat to blockaders. Spars were also used on ironclads and small steam launches.

The Union navy also utilized undersea warfare. Mines were planted in the mouths of various rivers and inlets where Confederate ironclads were located. Small steam launches were fitted out with spar torpedoes and one of these torpedo boats sank the Confederate ironclad *Albemarle.* The Union navy also commissioned a submarine, the *Alligator,* but she never operated against an enemy vessel.

What effects did Civil War naval technology have on later developments? Steam power was probably the most important technological innovation in the 19th century, yet the war itself had little effect on naval tactics. There are certain similarities in commerce raiding as employed by the Confederates and by the Germans in both world wars, but it is doubtful that the American Civil War was responsible for this. On the other hand, there can be no question about the use of the ram in the war. Despite its limited effectiveness, it was a major factor in capital ship design as well as tactics for some half century.

In ship architecture, the adoption of iron in construction was second in importance to the change to steam. Although unarmored warships were constructed of wood for a number of years after the war, nearly all of the monitors had been built of iron. Progress toward the large capital ships of the 20th century would have been impossible as long as ships were built of wood.

In ship design the U.S. Navy continued its opposition to seagoing armored ships until the 1880's; the Monitor type remained the standard armored vessel primarily because of the emphasis on a strategy of coastal defense. With the advent of the high freeboard capital ship the monitor rapidly declined in importance. However, vessels described as monitors were used in the rivers and coastal waters of Vietnam.

It was not the raft-like monitor, but the large, high freeboard, center line, multiple turret, armored ship that was the forerunner of the modern capital ship. Ironically, the *Roanoke,* the only vessel incorporating this principle built in the United States during the Civil War, was a failure. Modern ship design was primarily a result of developments in Europe.

The submarine, the semi-submersible *David*, which reminds one of the Italian human torpedoes used during World War II, and the torpedo boats may have had some slight influence on developments in the 20th century.

Naval guns used during the war were much closer to those of the Revolutionary period than those of the 20th century. Neither side developed and used a breech-loading, steel-rifled gun. These guns would not appear until the 1880's with the introduction of slow burning powder and the attainment of extremely high muzzle velocities. Interestingly, Brooke was experimenting with slow burning powder in 1863 and had also accidentally discovered and recognized the air space principle which made it possible to increase powder charges significantly without straining the gun. Dahlgren's influence was such, however, that his smoothbores remained as standard armament for twenty years after the war.

In naval technology, then, the Civil War was a period of transition, a proving ground for ships and weapons. It was not the first full-scale modern war since most of the innovations in that field appeared before the conflict, but its utilization of these new weapons presaged what "modern" war would one day become.

5

....

The Yankee Blue Jacket

WILLIAM N. STILL, JR.

On August 26, 1863, U.S. President Abraham Lincoln gave a speech in his home town, Springfield, Illinois. In recognizing the contributions of servicemen in preserving the Union, he said, "Nor must Uncle Sam's web-feet be forgotten. At all the watering margins they have been present. Not only on the deep sea, the broad bay, and the rapid river, but also the narrow, muddy bayou, and wherever the ground was a little damp, they have been and made their traces. Thanks to all."

The Union would not have been preserved without its navy. The ever-tightening Union blockade of the Confederate coast, the many Federal expeditions up Southern rivers, sounds, and bays on the East Coast and Gulf of Mexico, the Yankee operations along the Mississippi River and its tributaries, and the distant Northern squadrons seeking out Confederate cruisers on the sea, all contributed significantly to Federal victory. The actions of the *Monitor,* the *Kearsarge,* the *Hartford,* and other famous Federal warships have been written about often, as have the exploits of famous Federal seamen David Farragut, William Cushing, David Dixon Porter, John L. Worden, and John S. Winslow. But the common Union sailor, the "jack-tar," "blue jacket," or "web-foot," and his Civil War exploits, background, shipboard life, and hardships have largely been ignored. There would have been no navy without "jack"—no victory to cheer about.

A few days after Confederates fired on Fort Sumter in April 1861, President Lincoln proclaimed a blockade of the Southern coastline. This proclamation determined Union naval strategy for the war, a strategy of such magnitude the president could not have envisioned what it would take to make it successful. More than 3,000 miles of coastline, with nearly 200 river mouths, inlets, bays, sounds, and harbors, had to be blocked. Lincoln's later determination to expand the blockade to include the Mississippi River and its tributaries made the labor ahead only more imposing. To carry out this enormous task, in 1861 the Union navy had just ninety vessels—forty of them steamers, the remaining fifty powered by sail. More than half of these were decommissioned or totally unserviceable.

Union naval personnel were equally deficient. There were 1,554 officers in the U.S. Navy as of December 1860. Of that number, 373, or approximately 24 percent, departed in 1861, whether by resigning their commissions or by being dismissed for suspect loyalties. Most of the departed joined the Confederate cause. At the outbreak of the Civil War the remaining majority of loyal officers and their approximately 7,500 enlisted men were on ships stationed abroad. Months passed before they were able to travel to action stations along the Southern coast.

In the war years ahead, the navy's number of ships would grow to nearly 700; its number of officers to more than 7,000; and its number of enlisted men to more than 51,000. The number of men recruited by it during the war would total a staggering 118,044. But throughout the conflict the question of where to find these seamen became perennial. And at the war's beginning the question was asked with a hint of desperation.

In April 1861 there were only approximately 200 men in training or receiving ships and stations waiting for assignment to vessels as they were quickly recommissioned for war service. But experienced sailors were scattered throughout the country, especially in seafarers' towns. Facing the crisis, shortly after calling for volunteers for the army, Lincoln announced the navy would recruit 18,000 men to serve from one to three years. Naval rendezvous and recruiting stations were to be opened in all the principal seaports, and commandants of navy yards were to be authorized to enlist seamen.

Enthusiastically, hundreds quickly volunteered. By July 1861, eighty-two additional vessels manned by approximately 13,000 new blue jackets were in commission and taking up blockading stations off the Southern coast. Encouraged, the navy tried expanding its recruiting, in 1862 concentrating its appeals in the Great Lakes region. But results were unsatisfactory, and the percentage of experienced seamen enlisting rapidly decreased. More and more inexperienced men, many of them recent immigrants, volunteered. For a period of time the navy tried to curtail the enlistment of these "landsmen," as they were called, but the rapid commissioning of ships and the increasing difficulty of obtaining sailors for them led to the decision to take any physically qualified man.

By the middle of 1862 every Union squadron was deficient in seamen. In June, Union Secretary of the Navy Gideon Welles wrote one squadron commander, "more than 3,000 men are now wanted for the ships of war." This situation never improved. In July 1863 the steam frigate *Wabash*, flagship of the South Atlantic Blockading Squadron, was only about half-manned. Many of her officers and men had been detailed to duty on other vessels in the squadron. The *Wabash's* insufficient crew could not take the vessel to sea; this situation forced her commanding officer into anchoring her just outside Charleston Harbor, helpless to chase any blockade-runner observed. In March 1864, Welles mentioned in his diary as many as forty vessels were awaiting crews, and more than 10,000 additional men were needed. Three months later, he wrote "our squadrons are becoming almost paralyzed for defense, offense, or blockading purposes," because of the lack of sailors.

Manning gunboats constructed for western river operations proved to be just as acute a problem. Initially, river operations in the West were managed by the U.S. War Department; the navy provided only officers. It was assumed experienced rivermen could be recruited to man these vessels. In summer 1861 Union Commander John Rodgers opened recruiting offices in Cincinnati, Ohio; St. Louis, Missouri; and elsewhere, and was able to obtain more than 1,000 men. Rodgers, however, was not impressed with his "seamen," considering them an ill-kept, poorly disciplined lot. He vowed to "read the articles of war every Sunday until they know them, and get a parson at them whenever I can so as to break down their spirit—and let their wives come on board to lecture them on week days. With all these helps and hard drill they will have no time to give trouble."

In autumn, Captain Andrew Hull Foote, who replaced Rodgers, informed Secretary Welles only 650 of approximately 1,700 men needed were available for his new vessels. Manpower could not be increased for western river gunboats until seamen were shipped from the east and the army detailed troops to help man the vessels. But many soldiers were revolted at the idea of navy service. On one occasion an entire company under orders to serve on one of the gunboats mutinied and had to be confined in irons. In early 1862 twenty-eight men, arbitrarily transferred to the navy, deserted rather than "serve on ironclads."

During the first two years of the war the number of men the army allowed transferred or loaned to the western navy was less than 1,000. And many allowed to transfer were "undesirables"; Major General U.S. Grant proposed the army detail "some thirty or forty men of intemperate habits" to the navy. A soldier in the 4th Illinois Cavalry wrote on January 31, 1862: "Our Captain did some weeding today. There is a Fleet of gunboats just completing here. Men were wanted to man them. . . . The Captain took it upon himself to detail such men that he would rather spare and told them they had to go, and they went. They were mostly Norwegians and Germans that could hardly speak English. . . . Charles Wash who was under arrest for drunkenness and attempting to kill Lieut. Hopeman, was given the privilege to take service on a gun-boat or stand a court-martial. He chose the former."

Bounty paid for army enlistment was another factor that kept the number of naval volunteers small. Federal bounties for army enlistment attracted large numbers of experienced seafarers. In addition, states were to supply the army with "volunteers." When the army volunteer system proved inadequate, Congress passed a conscription act which divided the country into districts and assigned to each district a draft quota. Naval needs were generally ignored in both the volunteer and draft systems, and thousands of civilian seamen were drafted into the army.

Secretary Welles tried to persuade Lincoln and the Congress to adjust conscription to permit sailors to be drafted into the navy, but not until 1864 was he able to get some concession. In February of that year, Congress amended the conscription laws to allow local draft quota credit for naval recruits. Then on July 1, 1864, navy volunteers became entitled to the same bounty "as if enlisted in the army." This act also permitted seamen in the army to transfer to the navy.

The transfer clauses were vague. The army had just as serious a manpower problem as the navy and continued discouraging transfers to it. Very early in the war, this need of the army's to hang onto its cannon fodder had compelled Welles to sanction the enlistment of Confederate deserters, prisoners of war, escaped slaves, and foreigners. Naval records do not indicate the number of "galvanized yanks"[1] recruited into the Union navy, but one account estimated the number at more than 1,000.

The USS *Fernandina*'s captain understood what it took to man a ship. He wrote in July 1864, "I received . . . a draft of thirty men and boys to fill up vacancies caused by men leaving whose times are out. . . . Some of the men are good seamen who have been transferred from the Army where they have served for two years. The [remainder] . . . are young and thoroughly green." In October he received another draft which he described as "about the greenest specimens of humanity who ever went on board a ship. . . . The worst of it is that these fellows, after having managed to dodge all previous drafts, finding that there would be no chance for them to get clean otherwise, shipped in the Navy, receiving $600 to $700 bounty, while the few real seamen we have, have been serving faithfully for three years on their scanty pay."

Black Americans proved to be one of the Union navy's best sources of personnel. They were common in the antebellum U.S. Navy and during the Civil War freemen from Northern states continued to be recruited. But serious Civil War manpower problems also forced the navy to enlist fugitive slaves, or "contrabands," from Southern states.[2] Welles agreed to allow contrabands to be enlisted as early as July 1861. Later, a restriction was adopted decreeing no more than 5 percent of a ship's complement could be made up of contrabands, but the rule was rarely enforced. And the percentage serving in the navy increased as the war progressed. Union Flag Officer Samuel Du Pont confided to his wife: "Everybody wants contrabands. . . . I always say yes, if you can find them; plenty ashore is the answer."

Not all commanding officers wanted them. Rear Admiral David Dixon Porter, while in command of the Mississippi Squadron, complained of his "difficulties of keeping them" and requested permission "to get rid of some on board" his ships. Then a flag officer, David Farragut informed Welles that sailors of his squadron "disagree with them [contrabands] so much that we are obliged to be very rigid with the sailors in consequence. The contrabands soon desert because of the ill feeling manifested toward them by the sailors."

There is, however, abundant evidence former slaves performed well once they adjusted to navy discipline and were accepted by crews. And a few warships were manned predominantly by Blacks. But generally, they made up a minority of a ship's crew. Statistical studies fill out the picture of their naval service. The USS *Kearsarge,* when she fought the Confederate raider *Alabama* in 1864, had fifteen Blacks on board. Four Blacks won the Navy Medal of Honor during the war. Some 800 were casualties.

From 1813, foreigners, by law, were not allowed to serve on American men-of-war. In practice the law was ignored. Occasionally, U.S. ships visiting far-off ports would fill vacancies in their crews, a practice generally frowned upon by the Navy Department. But during the Civil War large numbers of recent immigrants were enlisted in the Union navy, and as the war progressed agents recruited seamen in a number of foreign countries.

According to historian Ella Lonn's *Foreigners in the Union Army and Navy,* foreign-born seamen constituted from one-fourth to one-half of enlisted Union navy personnel. They came from nearly every country, with Englishmen and Irishmen being the most numerous, followed by Scandinavians and Germans. On the USS *Colorado,* twenty-nine different nationalities were represented; on the USS *Hartford,* twenty-five; and on the USS *Minnesota,* twenty-six. The USS *Florida*'s Paymaster William Keeler told his wife "we have a motley collection for a crew—from all parts of the world—England, Ireland, France, Spain, Portugal, Russia, Austria, Poland, Norway, Sweden, have representatives on board. Beside these we have a Lascar, a Mexican, Sardinian, Italians, one from Maderia, one from Manila, another from Peru, etc." In 1864, 636 Black aliens were enlisted, the majority from Canada and the West Indies. Presumably, many, if not most from Canada were escaped slaves or the descendants of escaped slaves.

A sailor's term of enlistment varied from six months, or the duration of a cruise or operation, up to three years or the end of the war. There was no standard policy followed. Length of enlistment depended upon a variety of factors, such as when a man signed on (those who joined early in the war were able to ship for shorter enlistments than those who came in later), where he signed on (enlistments in the west were usually for a year), and his experience.

Of the approximately 50,000 men serving in the Federal navy at any one time during the war, perhaps a third of them were experienced seamen. The great majority were landsmen; at least 12,000 to 15,000 serving in the blockading squadrons had never set foot on a ship before enlisting. A few ships were able to keep experienced crews, but this was rare. The USS *Colorado* when she returned home from foreign duty, was able to ship nearly her entire crew before going on blockade service. However, a year later, when their enlistments once again expired, most *Colorado*, seamen elected to go North and be paid off; their replacements were, according to one officer, "by no means so fine a body of men."

The USS *Portsmouth*'s boatswain, "very profane," referred to all new enlistees as "farmers." On one occasion, when an officer criticized a sailor's performance aloft, the boatswain responded: "That's a farmer up there, sir; he don't know that he's on the crosstrees, say *haymow* and he'll jump overboard."

Ahead of race and experience, money was the tar's major concern. The pay of enlisted men in the navy, unlike that of Union army volunteers, was regulated by the length of term of service. The pay scale tapered down from seamen, who received eighteen dollars a month, to twelve dollars a month for landsmen and other inexperienced hands (usually called "greenhorns"), to the pittance paid "boys" in the positions of "powder monkeys" and "waterboys." The boys received eight to nine dollars a month and their rations. Contrabands initially were given landsmen's pay regardless of their duties, but in time they did receive comparable pay to freemen and white counterparts.

Paymaster Keeler of the USS *Florida* informed his wife, "A sailor is never paid in full till his time of enlistment expires. I usually pay them 3 to 5 dollars a month as spending money. Sometimes they come to me with a doleful tale of sickness, death or destitution at home and a request for 15 to 20 dollars to send to their families.

" 'You say your wife wrote you that one of the children was dead?'

" 'Yes sir.'

" 'Well, where's the letter?'

"If their tale was a true one the letter is produced and I give them as I think they need—if on the contrary the letter, as is frequently the case, has been torn up or thrown overboard they meet with a pretty abrupt refusal."

New recruits near the end of the war received bounties of $600 to $700, but throughout the conflict the prospect of receiving "prize money"

U.S. Navy sailors, with a boy in the center, pose in a studio. *(Library of Congress)*

was a major attraction to enlist. This was an old English custom adopted by Americans during the colonial period. If a blockade-runner or Southern merchant vessel was captured, it was sailed to a Northern port, condemned in admiralty procedures, and sold to the highest bidder. Half of the money received was retained by the government, the other half was distributed among the officers and seamen of the ship or ships participating in the capture. Although there were many inequities in the system, it provided a strong incentive, especially for crews on blockade duty.

Service on ships engaged in blockading the Southern coastline, despite its monotony, was preferred to service on ships engaged in other activities where the possible remuneration would not be as great. The most popular station was off North Carolina's Cape Fear River, dubbed "the prize money command" because so many blockade-runners were seized there attempting to reach or leave Wilmington, North Carolina. Some enlisted men made considerable sums from prizes. A "boy" on the USS *Nahant* received $176.16 as his share of the $300,000 prize money paid for the captured Confederate ironclad *Atlanta*. On the other hand, the great majority made very little. One tar made just thirteen cents.

Just as important to a common sailor as his pay was another Federal provision, his clothing. Uniforms were issued to enlistees at rendezvous, navy yards, or receiving ships. The uniform for petty officers and crew varied considerably from ship to ship. Dress regulations followed in the Civil War were drawn up in 1852 and slightly modified in 1862. As is true today, blue woolen frocks and trousers were issued for cold weather and white duck frocks and trousers for hot weather. Then, each tar also received either blue or white cloth caps, along with a pea jacket, a black silk handkerchief, two under flannel shirts, and two pairs of woolen drawers—all standard issue. In his memoirs, "A year on a Monitor," one sailor recalled, "I was conducted to the [receiving ship's] outfitting room where I was supplied with a uniform—two blue flannel shirts, socks, etc. in a clothes bag, a hammock with hair mattress and a pair of blankets." However, once a sailor was on board a ship, his uniform was determined by his commanding officer who had wide latitude in what his crew could wear. The result was ships in the same squadron or at the same station often had sailors dressed in both blue and white uniforms and combinations of both at the same time.

A forge aboard a Civil War–era vessel. *(Library of Congress)*

According to the *Florida's* Keeler, his ship's men wore straw hats in the warm months. "They are made on board by themselves from a specie of grass or rather palm leaf. . . . Our man of war has been converted into a straw hat manufactory. Nearly each one of our one hundred and fifty men seated around on various parts of the deck, singly or in groups, each one busy in plaiting or sewing 'sennite braid.' "

In the west, early in the war, it was not uncommon for gunboat crewmen to wear army uniforms or no uniform at all. By mid-1863, however, uniforms in the Mississippi Squadron were nearly universal. There, and at sea, sailors were required to put their name on each piece of their clothing. During inspection any piece not marked was considered stolen and put into the "lucky bag" and later auctioned off.

Recruits frequently were given their initial uniform issue when they reported on board a receiving ship. These were usually old sailing warships stripped of their guns, sails, and masts, and located at different navy yards. There they functioned as floating dormitories. Until assigned to a ship, there the recruit learned the rudiments of navy life. Considerable time was spent drilling recruits in handling sails, small boats, firearms, cutlasses, and occasionally cannon. A recruit might remain on board a receiving ship for several weeks waiting for his ship to be commissioned or recommissioned, but usually his stay was just a few days. Many receiving ships were, as one officer described them, "a floating hell." "There is generally at least a thousand men cooped up on board and they are coming and going every day," he wrote. "A constant thievery is going on all the time which is impossible for the officer to prevent or trace."

In July 1864, thirty replacements arrived on board the USS *Fernandina* from a receiving ship. "Although they have been shipped some four months," the warship's captain wrote, "they are all in debt, their entire pay being swallowed up by their clothing bills. The reason is because they have had all their clothes stolen."

A marine on the USS *Minnesota* informed his parents: "We are now lying in Hampton Roads. . . . Our ship is a receiving ship here. Hundreds of soldiers are coming aboard every day being transferred from the army. They are speedily transferred into sailors by a change of dress and then transferred to vessels in the squadrons who need them. The poor fellows are glad to get rid of the Army."

Many recruits were fortunate enough to be assigned to vessels fitting out in the same yard as their receiving ship; others had to be transported by sea to their vessels on blockade duty. Once a man reported on board his ship, his name and rank (called "rate") were recorded in a muster book. Each section of the ship was numbered and every sailor, in turn, numbered according to his station or location. In order to determine his duties and stations for various drills, he could look up his number on the "station bill" and "quarters bill." Each man was assigned sleeping space according to his number. The space allotted per individual on the berth deck for his hammock was 14 inches.

Once given a rate, a number, and a uniform, a new blue jacket had to confront shipboard life. U.S. warships in the Civil War had a routine that varied little from ship to ship. But, some vessels had reputations of being more strict than others. A sailor on the USS *Lackawanna* recalled, "the ordinary routine of ship life was rigidly observed on board, for we were flag-ship, and must set an example. . . . Our Captain, George F. Emmons, was an officer of the old school, and while scrupulously polite to all hands, and the kindest hearted Commander in the squadron to his men, old 'Pop Emmons,' as they affectionately called him, enforced rigidly every detail of regulation [and routine] . . ." Other commanding officers, especially volunteers, were not as rigid in their attitude toward shipboard duty.

New crew members quickly adjusted to the routine or schedule which governed their lives as long as they were on board that ship. At 5:45 a.m., a marine bugler on large vessels and the boatswains mate on smaller ones would sound reveille. The boatswains, or bo'suns, mate, would begin the day running through the berth-deck shouting "All hands," "All hands," "Rise and roll out," "Get up and Lash-up," or "up all hammocks." Within a few minutes the berth deck was clear of personal effects and the crew turned to cleaning the ship. The berth deck was "saltwater swabbed, swept, scrubbed, and squeegeed," and the spar deck completely holystoned.[3] Guns, gun carriages, and all brass, called "brightwork," topside was cleaned and polished, and aloft rigging and sails were checked and secured properly. The crew then cleaned themselves before being piped to breakfast at around 8:00 a.m., the beginning of the forenoon watch. According to Lieutenant Commander Francis O. Davenport's *On a Man-of-War*, published just after the Civil War, "at 9:30 the drum beats to quarters, whereupon *every man* repairs to his station at the gun, or particular place assigned him. The officer of the division [then] inspects his division."

Except for Sunday and holidays, the crew was daily employed in various drills and exercises. An engineer on the USS *Conemaugh* wrote in his diary, "During the daytime the crew is drilled in many things, such as 'the ship is on fire!' All hands to fire quarters to put the fire out. . . . The gun practice, that is, with cannon, then fencing with sticks instead of swords. . . ." Gun practice started with another roll of the drums and the crew rapidly rushed to their battle stations. Under the watchful eye of the captain and division officers the ship's gun crews practiced loading, running out, and training. Occasionally live ammunition was used to fire at targets. A young volunteer officer of the USS *Tyler* on the Mississippi River wrote, "I have charge of . . . a 30-lb[er] Parrott gun in the stem of the vessel. . . . It is a great difficulty that we cannot muster a drill at the gun to which we belong. It being in the wardroom would ruin the furniture and oilcloth if we drilled there. But if ever we have to use that gun in action, I'll bet the oilcloth etc will pay for [it]. . . ."

The same was true of small arms. Paymaster Keeler wrote in July 1863 from the *Florida:* "This has been a clear still warm day. All hands have been practicing with small arms, at a barrel placed about 300 yds off in the water."

On the western rivers other exercises were emphasized. The crew of the USS *Silver Lake* drilled every day at landing a party. "Every boat had a landing party, to be sent ashore when occasion required, to fight with muskets. Each man aboard the boat . . . was provided with cutlass and revolvers for sidearms. Some were provided with boarding pikes," reported one of the ship's officers. A member of the *Tyler's* crew wrote about practicing general quarters at night, "to prepare them for a surprise." When quarters were sounded at night, crew members turned out under the eerie glow of battle lanterns.

Each crew member was assigned to various stations on deck, at the guns, in the topsails, in a boat, at a mess, and to a watch. As described in *On a Man-of-War,* "each man has to be stationed for 'getting under weigh,' 'bringing ship to an anchor,' 'tacking ship,' 'wearing ship,' 'loosing and furling,' 'reefing top sails' . . . etc." With few exceptions every member of a crew was assigned to a watch, usually port or starboard, on and off four hours each while under way and in port. On gunboats and monitor-pattern ironclads, the various duties associated with sailing vessels were usually eliminated. But gun and boat drills and watches were rigidly enforced.

Saturday afternoons and Sundays were not scheduled for "routine ship's work." Saturday was traditionally a day for sailors to clean and repair items of clothing, purchase needed items, and in general take it easy, unless, of course, they had the watch while under way. The *Florida's* Keeler described a typical shipboard Saturday to his wife: "In the morning each [sailor] . . . brings up his trunk (which is a canvass bag). The contents are taken out and inspected by an officer, who condemns that which he deems unfit for further wear and it is thrown overboard. Articles requiring mending he directs the owner to put in repair."

....

64

Sailors at ease aboard an unidentified U.S. Navy vessel. *(Library of Congress)*

The gunboat USS *Mattabesett*'s surgeon portrayed a typical Saturday on his ship operating with the South Atlantic Blockading Squadron: "The crew are busy mending their clothing and overhauling their bags and ditty boxes [small boxes, sometimes cloth bags, for thread, needles, tape, etc.], it being the day [Saturday] allowed them in the service for that purpose. The spar deck presents more the appearance of a secondhand clothing store than the deck of a man-of-war, the way the pants, shirts, coats, hats, socks, etc. are scattered and hung about the deck. In one part of the ship can be seen the ship's barber, Landsman Pfander, busy shaving the boys as well as cutting the hair of some of them. He has 50 customers at the rate of $0.12 per month or three cents a shave, they finding razor, soap, brush, towel, and strap. . . ."

Saturdays were also wash days for clothing and more than one account mentions the appearance of warships with clothes hung on lines between the masts and over the railings and lines. Not many crews were as fortunate as the *Hartford*'s on blockade duty off Mobile Bay. They had a "washer woman" come on board once a week and take clothes to her home to be cleaned.

Sundays on board a warship were days of rest, relaxation, recreation, and, of course, religion. "Although Jack is usually a profane man ashore, always a rough man, and, frequently a drunken man ashore, the service of the Church had always an excellent influence." This impression by an officer on the USS *Lackawanna* was generally true throughout the navy during the war. Not every ship held divine services. Many, particularly small gunboats, did not have chaplains. On these vessels the commander or an officer was assigned to read passages from the Bible. And on the *Lackawanna* "there were many musical geniuses, and we organized a very good chorus for Sunday services. . . . At ten every Sunday morning the Church pennant was set, and the slowly tolled bell passed forward the invitation to all the men to attend who wished. Presently some two hundred would come aft and cluster in picturesque groups about the guns—the marines, in full dress uniform, drawn up in line to port. Having no chaplain . . . the Captain would read the service." At least thirty ships during the war not only held divine services on Sunday, but daily prayer meetings as well.

A typical Sunday on the USS *Monitor*, according to its paymaster, was "a little more Quiet." "The usual routine of daily work, or men drilling and at quarters, of painting and scraping, etc. is not carried on," he wrote. "After breakfast everything is cleaned up nice and at ten o'clock the men are all 'mustered for inspection.' Each one is expected to be dressed in his Sunday best and at exactly four bells (10 o'clock) the bo'sun's call musters all hands for inspection. The seamen and petty officers are drawn up on one side of the deck, the firemen and coal heavers on the other. Each man answers to his name as the lieut. calls the roll.

"The Captain is then informed that the men are ready for inspection. He passes slowly along in front of the lines of men looking closely at their dress, appearances, etc. —'Jones why are your shoes not blacked?' Jones having no good excuse the Paymaster's steward is ordered to stop his grog for a day or two [this is before grog was no longer issued on U.S. warships] . . . 'Do you belong to this ship?'—'Yes sir.' 'Well you are a filthy beast, a disgrace to your shipmates, the dirt on you is absolutely frightful. If I see you so again I will have the Master at Arms strip and scour you with sand and canvas.' And so the inspection goes on.

"After the men, the ship is inspected by the Capt. to see that all parts are neat, clean, and in order. The men are then released and pass the day as they choose."

This Sunday routine was generally followed throughout the navy. If divine services were carried out, inspection would immediately follow.

Until hammocks were piped down at 8:00 p.m., evenings on board ship for those lucky enough not to have the watch were devoted to rest and recreation. The *Mattabesett*'s surgeon wrote in his diary, "Having occasion to go to the forward part of the ship, I was pleased to see how the crew enjoyed themselves. In one corner might be seen a group of them singing 'The Star Spangled Banner,' another party 'Columbia, the Gem of the Ocean,' one party listening to a yarn which a comrade appeared to be spinning, every now and then bursting out in a laugh. Some of the boys were having a social game of dominoes, whilst another group were watching two of their comrades practicing the 'manly art of self-defense,' or sparring, with a pair of gloves. . . . The last party of them were having a general plantation walk-around, their hornpipes were equal to a Christy, Morris, Sandford, or Mulligan [well-known minstrels]—but the way they danced juba to the patting upon the knee capped the climax. In short, 'joy appears unconfined.' " He wrote a few days later, "the boys on deck are having a fine time 'tripping on the light fantastic toe' and pummelling each other with boxing gloves. . . . Truly they are a jolly set of tars."

In summer 1864 the surgeon recorded, "the crew—that is, part of them—have organized themselves into a Glee Club. There are some fine and splendid singers amongst them. Their instruments consists of violin, tamborine, bones, guitar, etc."

The *Mattabesett* glee club, apparently, did not include all the sailors aboard who could carry a tune. A few days later the diarist mentioned "the crew are having quite a concert tonight under the hurricane deck. The colored portion are on the port side singing camp-meeting hymns, whilst the jolly portion are on the starboard side singing comic, Irish, sentimental and patriotic songs. . . . Both parties are trying to make the most noise."

'He took the anchor on his back,
And leaped into the main ;
Through foam and spray he clove his way,
And sunk and rose again.

" 'Through foam and spray, a league away,
The anchor stout he bore ;
Till, safe at last, he made it fast,
And warped the ship ashore.'

"Such was the tale that was told to me
By that modest and truthful son of the sea ;
For he aint like some of the swabs I've seen,
As would go and lie to a poor marine."

Off-duty sailors aboard the USS *Enterprise*. (*U.S. Naval Historical Center*)

Music may well have been the Union tar's most popular form of entertainment. The Union river gunboat *Cairo*'s paymaster wrote his fiancé, "whenever we have an opportunity we have singing and playing on the flute." Flag Officer Du Pont asked the U.S. Navy Department to "order a band of music to be enlisted for his flagship." On board the USS *Vanderbilt*, officers purchased a complete set of musical instruments. On the monitor USS *Nahant*, "the crew would group just abaft the turret on the main deck, with half a dozen of the best singers in the centre, and song after song would be called for until eight bells."

Plays and other similar performances were also popular with Federal seamen. The USS *Brazileira*'s "theatrical company's" first program was a skit entitled "Stage Struck." This was so well-received by the crew a stage was built on the quarter-deck's port side. The next performance included the "Laughable, Burlesque Opera of Bombashes Furioso" and the "Grand Trial Dance."

Occasionally, minstrels, skits, and plays were presented that were derogatory to blacks and resulted in some shipboard animosity and resentment. One ship put on a play entitled the "Nigger in a Daguerreotype Saloon." The performance led to so much hostility the ship's captain made arrangements to transfer out the blacks on board.

Plays and other forms of organized entertainment were popular but not common. Recreation was usually far less organized and more individual. "We sit about the deck, reading newspapers, magazines, letters, etc." a sailor on the USS *Mound City* wrote. And a few days later he noted, "The evening was pass[ed] in the usual manner on shipboard, in telling yarns, playing checkers and reading." Paymaster Keeler described recreation on the *Florida* as "kill[ing] time the best we can, reading, writing, dominoes." On the USS *Lackawanna,* it consisted of "dominoes, chess, and draughts."

Card playing was generally not permitted on board United States warships but a number of ships had libraries. The monitor USS *Dictator* possessed "quite a nice library of 200 volumes." The library on the USS *Penobscot* included the Bible, the "Constitution of the United States," an English dictionary, James Fenimore Cooper's *Naval History of the United States,* technical books on guns and engineering, and a number of books by storyteller Washington Irving.

Fishing was a universally popular sport with officers and men. Letters, diaries, and memoirs all mention it. Their writings suggest that this activity was engaged in frequently, not only as recreation, but also to provide fresh food. Keeler on the *Florida* mentioned fishing had "become almost a drug" it was done so often. An officer serving on the USS *Valley City* stationed in North Carolina waters wrote, "There are a great many fish in the Chowan River, and [the crew] . . . has often caught shad and herring by the barrel, in a large seine." The crew of the *Nahant* found a seine and a pair of oyster tongs. "Both of these finds were sources of much pleasure to our crew when we were in South Carolina and Georgia waters," recalled one of her crew. He added, "Crab fishing was another one of our sports at this time. Getting an iron hoop from a beef or pork barrel we would make a net by stretching stout fishing line or marline across it. . . ."

On holidays, boat races or regattas were common in all the squadrons. Paymaster Keeler wrote that at Beaufort, North Carolina, a regatta was held in which thirty-one boats "containing about 300 men participated."

Recreation ended promptly at 8:00 p.m. when the night watches were called. Fires and lights were put out on the berth deck, pumps sounded, batteries secured, and an extra anchor readied to let go in an emergency. "From this moment until morning, unless something extra turns up, everything will be quiet . . . quiet as the grave." So wrote a surgeon on duty with the South Atlantic Blockading Squadron. Of course, it was not uncommon for ships to be sighted, and if considered "suspicious," quarters would be sounded, disturbing the quiet.

To American sailors, life aboard any Union ship carrying out routine operations could be irksome and dull; a tar's most fervent wish, frequently voiced, was to get off the ship for a few hours or days. "Liberty," as shore leave is still called, was prized by the sailor because it allowed him a brief period of independence, away from the sharp eyes of officers and petty officers. But, occasionally, there was the old salt similar to the one Keeler mentioned on the *Florida,* who said "when he [got] . . . on shore he always [felt] . . . so lonesome that he [was] . . . glad to get on [the] . . . ship again, it seem[ed] . . . so like home." But most jacks would have agreed with the *Lackawanna* sailor when he wrote, "there were two bright points in our life to be kept well in view—one the chase after the blockade runner . . . the other, an occasional visit to New Orleans for necessary repairs, and perchance to expend some of the money accumulated during months of hermitage at sea."

Liberty for the Civil War sailor was permitted depending upon where he was stationed. If on a ship assigned to a blockading squadron, he would be able to go ashore when his vessel returned to one of the repair and coaling yards at Port Royal, South Carolina; Beaufort, North Carolina; Hampton, Virginia; Pensacola, Florida; or New Orleans, Louisiana. If he was lucky enough to serve on a small vessel operating inshore and in the sounds and rivers, he would be allowed ashore at times to fish, swim, pick blackberries or peaches, or just walk around. On a western river gunboat, he rarely was allowed ashore, except in occupied towns; there, guerrillas were always a danger. Those assigned to vessels operating in distant waters to run down Confederate cruisers were granted liberty infrequently.

The crew of the bark *Fernandina,* on station in St. Catherine's Sound, Georgia, in spring 1864, spent their liberties "wander[ing] about the islands full of rattlesnakes and alligators." Sailors on Charleston blockade duty were permitted ashore on Morris Island after Union troops secured the area. The monitor *Nahant* used an inflatable rubber life raft called "the Catamaran" towed by a cutter to carry liberty parties ashore. Although the blue jackets would occasionally visit captured Confederate batteries "Wagner" and "Gregg," the majority made a beeline for the army's sutler stores where they were able to purchase beer, wine, or grog.

The *Hartford,* Admiral David Farragut's flagship in the West Gulf Blockading Squadron, usually went to Pensacola for repairs and coal. According to a marine private on board "we all . . . have liberty here, a few every day." Not all crews were so lucky. A carpenter on the *Portsmouth,* also in Farragut's squadron, wrote in August 1862, "our men are getting very uneasy for the want of a run on shore. Some have been near a year shipped, and have had no liberty. Rather tough for men who call themselves free . . . think of it, you who live on shore, and then no wonder a sailor runs wild when he gets on shore."

It was not, and is not, uncommon for sailors to get intoxicated and "run wild" on shore after a lengthy period at sea. Robley D. Evans' memoir, *A Sailor's Log,* described what happened when the USS *Powhatan,* of which he was executive officer, sailed into a West Indies port after a long stretch of sea duty. "Our men were kept on board so long, and we were steadily under steam, that they became very irritated and ugly. Fights were of daily occurrence, and some of them serious. . . . Several men lost their lives in this way, and the Admiral finally went to St. Thomas to give shore liberty to the crew.

"When we arrived we found the English Flying Squadron in port, but while the feeling against them was very bitter [for supposedly siding with the Confederates] we did not consider it a good reason why our men should be kept on board; so the Starboard watch, consisting of one hundred and fifty men, were sent on shore for twenty-four hours. It was only a few hours before word came off that there was trouble ashore, and later a letter from the English admiral, saying that our men were rioting with the English sailors, some of whom had been killed. Admiral [James] Lardner directed the Captain to send the other watch on shore. And then there was a fine time sure enough! The Danish garrison was turned out and attempted to arrest some of the leaders; but they were soon driven back into their forts, and the English and our men went at it again . . . just before sundown the general recall was hoisted as a signal for all hands to repair on board, and such boats as we could man were sent in charge of officers to bring the men off. . . . By midnight we had our people on board, and found that three had been killed and many more . . . wounded, while the English were in about the same fix . . . after this our men had no more shore liberty until we got back to the United States."

Although there were other occurrences of brawling and fighting, the type of incident that took place on St. Thomas was rare. Drinking was universal and it frequently led to quarrels, but the usual consequences were black eyes, broken noses, and sore heads.

Another unfortunate consequence of shore leave, particularly in Northern ports and larger occupied Southern ports such as New Orleans, was venereal disease. After a period of liberty, the *Fernandina*'s surgeon found "no less than 28 cases of venereal, both gonorrhoea and syphilis," on board.

Although women were few and far between, alcoholic beverages were available wherever liberty was granted. And "if you want a sailor to work give him his whiskey and he is true to the letter," one jack tar commented in his journal. But drunkenness has always driven naval officers to despair because it deteriorates discipline. Paymaster Keeler, at one time serving on the *Monitor*, reflected the view of many officers: "there are three great evils in both our army and navy . . . the first is whiskey, the second is whiskey, and the third is whiskey."

In the antebellum navy the grog ration (rum or whiskey diluted with water) was nearly as important to the sailors as liberty. However, pressure from the growing temperance movement resulted in Congress passing a bill calling for the end of the spirit ration after September 1, 1862. In its place sailors would receive five cents extra pay per day. The bill passed.

Blue jackets throughout the fleet were incensed at this bill. A number of ship's crews started petitions to have the law repealed. Some called it "an act of tyranny." A carpenter's mate named Philbrick recorded in his diary an event that occurred throughout the fleet and undoubtedly caused heavy hearts: "Yesterday sent all the whiskey that was in the ship on shore, except what is necessary for sickness." The USS *Portsmouth*'s crew lowered the Stars and Stripes to half mast and the ship's paymaster wrote a ballad entitled

"Farewell to Grog." This composition made the rounds in the navy and was recited on board U.S. warships for many years. Its final stanzas summed up the sailors' woe.

Now mess mates pass the bottle round
It is the last, remember,
For our grog must stop, and our spirits drop, on the first day of September.
All hands to 'splice the main brace' call,
But we'll splice it now, in sorrow,
For the spirit-room key will be laid away,
Forever, on to-morrow.

The law, of course, did not affect officers' wine messes, nor did it curb drinking or drunkenness. A volunteer officer on the U.S. gunboat *Forest Rose* wrote in April 1864, "It is very disagreeable to be situated, as I am sometimes, with nearly every officer aboard intoxicated." But every liberty produced drunkenness, and at sea captured blockade-runners were eagerly searched for liquor by U.S. Navy boarding crew members; if any liquor was found, crewmen smuggled it aboard their ship. Off the Cape Fear River in August 1863, the blockade-runner *Kate* was driven ashore, and according to the ubiquitous Keeler, "the officers and men upon getting on board found an abundance of liquor and all hands got drunk and went to fighting among themselves."

Substitutes for commercial alcohol were found if the real thing was not available. "Navy sherry," dispensed as medicine, became popular. At least one ship's crew manufactured its own. Undetermined quantities of "liquor for medical purposes" were stolen or given to crew members by sympathetic surgeons. Rear Admiral John Dahlgren, on the eve of his squadron going into action, ordered six barrels of whiskey from the army to be used "under medical direction" for his ships. Dahlgren was criticized for this action by the U.S. Secretary of the Navy.

Perhaps the most notorious suppliers of liquor were the sutlers, merchants who followed the fleet as they did the army. These "businessmen" usually chartered trading schooners and sold provisions, tobacco, and, of course, liquor to sailors who came on board their vessels. "From early morn until late at night the cry is 'Sutler! Sutler! Sutler!'" wrote a ship's surgeon in 1863. "No sooner had a boat returned from the schooner but what there are others who want something else." The following day, the surgeon mentioned "some of the boys have 'sore heads' today the effects of ale and wine which they managed to get [on] . . . the schooner."

At least one officer complained that the trading schooners serving the South Atlantic Blockading Squadron under permits from the Secretary of the Treasury were "fast becoming . . . more or less floating grogships" retailing "almost poisonous liquors" to the seamen at exorbitant prices. But efforts to stop this practice only resulted in the disguising of intoxicating beverages in cans supposed to contain oysters and "milk drink."

If drinking and liberty were foremost in the minds of sailors, food was close behind. "When breakfast's done, the next thing I look to is dinner, and when that's done, I look for supper time." By an 1842 public law the navy ration was determined in terms of kinds of food (salted pork, bread, vegetables, etc.) and amounts per day. This law, passed in peacetime, was impossible to carry out during the Civil War, a war with enormous logistical problems. But the navy did a surprisingly good job of provisioning its scattered ships. Early in the war, the Navy Department purchased fast steamers to carry beef and other perishables to the blockading squadrons. And it was rare when there was not enough food, although the availability of fresh provisions fluctuated.

When it came to food shortages, the men in Gulf blockading squadrons suffered more than the others because of their distance from East Coast shipping points. Winfield Scott Schley, who served on the USS *Potomac* in the Gulf of Mexico, wrote in his *Forty-Five Years Under the Flag*, "the diet for the rest of the month [after the fresh meat and vegetable supplies had run out] was composed mainly of salted meats, cheese, hard bread, bad butter, inferior coffee and positively bad tea." The *Hartford*'s spring 1864 menu was notoriously monotonous. According to the daily account of a marine on board, on March 14 dinner was "pork and beans," March 15 "bullion beef," March 16 "pork and beans," March 18 "duff again," March 19 "pork and beans," Sunday March 20 "Bullion and coffee," March 21 "pork and beans," March 22 "duff," March 23 "pork and beans," and on and on until April 7, when he wrote, "Got a lot of fresh beef, ice and vegitables [sic]." April 8 continued "fresh grub," but on April 11, back to "pork and beans" again.

The USS *Silver Lake*'s bill of fare rivaled the *Hartford*'s, consisting of pork and beans, salt beef, coffee, tea, rice, sugar, pepper, canned beef, hardtack, and butter—"and such butter," one of the crew wrote. "I have often heard it remarked of butter 'it is strong enough to walk alone,' but the butter of the navy was strong enough to run a sawmill. [The crew] got very tired of pork and beans."

Other items found on various ships included navy bread, flour, dried apples, desiccated potatoes, vinegar, and molasses. For those vessels stationed in salt water estuaries and sounds, oysters, clams, and crabs were often served as part of a meal. And fish was a frequent course on all ships. But some ships were better "feeders" than others. The *Monitor* had a good reputation for meals and so did the ironclad *Nahant,* one of her crewmen recalling, "The food was abundant and good." An officer on the USS *Conamaugh* agreed and wrote, "there is always plenty of food as 'Uncle Sam' is a good quartermaster."

Ships frequently supplemented their provisions with local fresh food. One of the *Nahant*'s crew wrote "small flatboats or dugout canoes, each having a darky man and woman aboard . . . would . . . bring alongside a few eggs, a pair of fowls, or a basket of fresh fish to sell." The *Fernandina*'s surgeon mentioned in his diary, "two contrabands from Sapelo Island . . . made their appearance . . . in a dugout, having sweet potatoes, pumpkins, etc. to sell." In July 1864 he recorded the purchase of watermelons off Edenton, North Carolina. "[Contrabands] have availed themselves of the opportunity to sell to the invaders large quantities of beef, mutton, and vegetables, the owner-ship of which nobody troubles themselves to inquire about," a member of the USS *Alabama*'s crew wrote in December 1861.

Plundering provisions on Southern farms and plantations was at times encouraged. A volunteer officer on the USS *Valley City* stationed in the North Carolina sounds noted: "the fleet anchored off several of the planta-tions along the river and the men were allowed to regale themselves with fresh provisions . . . that were contraband of war."

Sailors on western river gunboats lived off the land even more than their counterparts on the Atlantic and Gulf. The *Tyler*'s paymaster wrote his wife, "yesterday we stopped at Mr. Diamond's plantation [in Mississippi] and helped ourselves to what sweet potatoes and corn meal we wanted and dressed a beef." Six months later, on September 5, 1863, he wrote her that "Since my last letter . . . we have been living at our present anchorage [near Natchez], only leaving it to run down to Mrs. Hunt's plantation to forage. We generally take what beef we want and pay for milk, fruit and vegetables." By then aboard *Forest Rose,* the paymaster wrote, "We require a beef every few days," and confided "whenever they come within convenient range of the vessel, we confiscate one." An officer on the *Silver Lake* described a similar occasion where a herd of cattle were observed on an island. The beef were brought on board "and dressed . . . as we pulled along." He added, "you can imagine how our deck looked an hour after landing on that island."

Griping has been characteristic of seamen throughout the centuries, and the blue jackets on the Union warships were no exception. In their letters, diaries, and journals, and even in their memoirs, usually written many years after the conflict, they complained about their food, work, homesickness, lack of liberty or leave, and in the warm months, the heat. But as historian James M. Merrill wrote in his article "Men, Monotony, and Mouldy Beans—Life on Board Civil War Blockaders," the sailor's most common grievance was monotony. The *Fernandina*'s surgeon in the South Atlantic Blockading Squadron noted in his diary, " 'a life on the ocean wave' is not a very pleasant one unless a person is fond of feasting sumptuously every day on salt junk and hard tack, reading papers a month after they are published, hearing from home once a month, etc., etc." On another occasion he cheerlessly wrote, "Dull! Dull! Dull! is the day. Nothing to do." And a volunteer who spent virtually his entire enlistment on the blockade off the Texas coast recalled, "for the most part a routine life which grew so terribly monotonous." On the *Florida,* stationed off the Cape Fear River, a sailor penned in his diary: "I told her [his mother] she could get a fair idea of our 'adventures' if she would go on the roof of the house, on a hot summer day, and talk to half a dozen hotel hallboys, who are generally far more intelligent and agreeable than the average 'acting officer.' Then descend to the attic and drink some tepid water, full of iron rust. Then go on to the roof again and repeat this 'adventurous process' at intervals, until she has tired out and go to bed, with every thing shut down tight, so as not to show a light. Adventure! Bah! The blockade is the wrong place for it."

Blockade life perfectly fitted the military adage "hurry up and wait." Most of the time was spent in waiting, occasionally to be abruptly interrupted to chase a Southern ship. Upon the sudden appearance of any craft, the Union vessel's cable was slipped, its engines started, all hands drummed to battle stations, and if the spotted vessel could not properly identify herself, the blockader's guns would open fire on her when within range. If, as was so often the case, the vessel proved to be legitimate, a Union gunboat or transport serving the fleet, the order would be given to secure from battle stations. "We go below," an officer on the Union's *Alabama* wrote, "throw ourselves, clothes and all, on the bunk —only to be startled by another gunshot."

Occasionally, the suspicious vessel proved to be a blockade-runner or a Southern vessel engaged in trade. The chase and boarding of such a vessel would create a sense of excitement which would linger on for several days. And a capture might result in a change in diet if the ship carried fresh provisions. Then passengers and members of the captured vessel's crew would usually be brought on board the Union blockader, stirring up curiosity and conversation, particularly when the passengers included females.

Life was not considered so dull on the western rivers. The river gunboats rarely remained on one station, but moved around, either patrolling different areas or operating as units cooperating with the army. And combat was far more of a daily occurrence than in the blockading squadrons. Guerrillas frequently harassed naval river vessels with rifle and cannon fire. But for river men, unlike their brothers on blockade, there was little likelihood of capturing a prize.

Although life on a blockader was monotonous and dull, and wearisome on river gunboats, the most physical discomfort was experienced by sailors serving on the ironclads. Paymaster Keeler, after being on board the blockader *Florida* for a few days, told his wife that he was extremely pleased with his ship, especially after "being 'cabined, cribbed, [and] confined,' on board the *Monitor* for nearly a year." Keeler's opinion was generally shared by those who served on both wooden ships and ironclads. The commanding officer of the monitor-class vessel USS *Chickasaw* wrote his mother shortly after the Battle of Mobile Bay, "these iron-clads are pretty rough on a fellow, they are not and have no comforts." Union Lieutenant Robert B. Ely, who served on the monitor USS *Manhattan* in the same engagement, referred to his ship as "this filthy ironpot," and said, "a man who would stay in an ironclad from choice is a candidate for the insane asylum, and from compulsion is an object of pity." A young volunteer, transferred to a wooden-hulled blockader from the monitor *Weehawken,* told his parents "our life this far has been most exciting and has had a great variety—so different and so much more desirable than a life on one of those *terrible dark* Monitors. " "I'd rather go to sea in a diving bell," wrote the USS *Monitor*'s surgeon, and another sailor exclaimed, "Give me an oyster scow! Anything—only let it be of wood."

Both officers and enlisted men disliked serving on the monitors. Quarters were "damp, dank, and dingy," and in the hot summer months impossible to live in when the hatches were shut. (Hatches were sealed all of the time a monitor was under way because of its low freeboard, near the waterline.) Temperatures below deck became "intolerable." On July 1, 1864, Ely despondently recorded in his diary it was 90° Fahrenheit in the ward-room, and "everything is dirty, everything smells bad, everybody is demor-alized." The following day, he mentioned the thermometer in the fireroom was 135° to 138°.

Because of complaints like Ely's and the monitors' poor reputation, the wages of enlisted men serving on them was increased one-fourth over wages paid to men serving on wooden vessels. Nonetheless, "old salts" disliked them, one telling a seaman on the *Nahant* that the monitors "ain't fit for hogs to go to sea in, let alone honest sailors."

Morale on monitors was not helped by the excessive illness among their crews. Lack of adequate ventilation and excessive dampness produced many medical problems. In summer 1863 an average of 20 percent of the *Nahant*'s crew was hospitalized. Its surgeon wrote, "I have sent some 15 men to the hospital . . . and when hot weather sets in, few of the old crew will be left."

Illness, however, was a serious problem throughout the fleet. Nearly 145,000 disease cases were treated on board naval vessels during the war. Of the 4,588 Union sailors who died in wartime, 2,784 perished from illness. Yellow fever and malaria were constant problems, and in the Civil War sailor's day venereal disease was also quite serious. Surgeon Boyer, during his tour on the *Fernandina,* lanced boils, pulled teeth, and struggled with a whole variety of diseases such as anthrax, cholera, ersipelas, scrofula, and bronchitis. Other surgeons had similar experiences, and many of them could add wounds from combat as sources of business. During the war, 3,266 Union tars were wounded in battle and 1,804 killed.

Considering the heavy influx of volunteers and those detailed from the army, as well as the unglamorous type of service that had to be performed by all sailors, disciplinary problems or desertion were not excessive. Deserters numbered just 4,649 men, or approximately 6 percent of the service, during the war. The overwhelming majority of sailors faithfully and loyally served out their enlistments and were a credit to the Federal navy.

Admiral Farragut wrote after his victory at New Orleans: "We did our duty to the best of our ability, I believe." Undoubtedly, this was the sentiment of the thousands of sailors as they saluted the flag for the last time and, as one wrote, "hoisting my hammock to my shoulder and getting my clothes Bag under the other arm" walked down the gangway and into civilian life.

Notes

Copyright © 1985 Historical Times, Inc.
This chapter first appeared in the February 1985 issue of *Civil War Times Illustrated*.

1. Any Confederate prisoner-of-war who took an oath of allegiance to the Union and accepted Federal military service was referred to as a "Galvanized Yankee." Most of these men entered the army and were sent West for frontier duty.
2. The number of contrabands enlisted in the navy is not known. A recent study of Black sailors in the Civil War suggests approximately 8 percent of all enlisted personnel were Blacks. It does not, however, indicate what percent were contrabands.
3. Sailors scoured wooden decks with blocks of sandstone called holystone.

6

....

The Confederate Tar

WILLIAM N. STILL, JR.

W hen "Johnny Reb" is mentioned, the public thinks of a gray-clad veteran who fought his way from Shiloh to Vicksburg or stood under the Stars and Bars at the First Battle of Manassas or Gettysburg. Americans never think of Johnny Reb as a blue-clad sailor manning a 7-inch Brooke gun on the ironclad CSS *Fredericksburg* or standing the mid-watch on the cruiser CSS *Shenandoah* in the South Pacific. No one remembers the sailors of the Confederate States Navy.

Southerners created a navy when they established the other institutions that made up the Confederate States Government. In February 1861 the Confederate Congress called for all individuals experienced in naval matters to consult with the Committee on Naval Affairs, and in his inaugural address, President Jefferson Davis stated: "I . . . suggest that for the protection of our harbors and commerce on the high seas a Navy adapted to those objects will be required." Two days later, on February 20, the Confederate Congress established the C.S. Navy Department and President Davis appointed Florida's Stephen R. Mallory Secretary of the Confederate States Navy.

Mallory was a secretary without a navy in February 1861. But within a few weeks a miscellaneous assortment of revenue cutters, former slave ships, steamboats, and even tugboats had been obtained; by arming them with a few cannon, they were transformed into Confederate warships. Mallory had more than enough officers for these vessels. Some 343 officers, approximately 24 percent of the 1,554 officers who were serving in the United States Navy as of December 1, 1860, resigned their commissions and joined the Confederate navy. For more than a year there were far more Confederate naval officers than billets available; many of them had to seek service with the army or command land batteries while remaining in the naval service. All, however, later obtained employment of some kind, and additional officers were commissioned.[1]

The Confederate navy had far more difficulty in filling its enlisted ranks. And throughout the war the naval service suffered from a manpower shortage. One reason for this was that the Confederate army's appetite for men was nearly insatiable. Another was that Southern officers in the old U.S. Navy could resign their commissions and follow their political consciences, but Southern enlisted men had "enlisted" for a given period and could not resign. There is no evidence that any of these enlisted Southerners made it into Confederate naval service, even by desertion.

The Southern states were not without seafarers, however. Before the war there were hundreds of sailing vessels and steamboats owned and manned by Southerners. But the Rebel navy apparently was unable to secure the majority of these experienced seamen. Early in the war the few vessels in the small navies established by individual seceding states and in the large Confederate States Navy itself absorbed only a limited number of them; the remainder were swept up into army service. Shortly after the firing on Fort Sumter the C.S. Navy Department established recruiting stations, or "rendezvous," throughout the South. Advertisements calling for naval recruits were run in local newspapers, but few men were obtained. It was soon apparent the usual recruiting methods were inadequate. Early in 1862 the naval secretary advised recruiting officers that a bounty of $50 could be offered to "all persons, except boys, who will enlist for three years or the war." This, again, was not particularly successful, primarily because those who would normally be attracted by this offer were already in the army. As Lieutenant J. N. Barney discovered in December 1861: "it is impossible to get men of the proper kind unless from the Army, and I have applied for the discharge of a number of men who have expressed a desire to enter the Navy."

In January 1862 Confederate naval officer William F. Lynch, in command of Confederate naval forces in the North Carolina sounds, wrote about the consequences: "My greatest difficulty is in the want of men. . . . I have sent to Washington, Plymouth, Edenton, and Elizabeth City [all in North Carolina] for recruits without success . . . to meet the enemy I have not more than a sufficient number of men to fight half the guns."

The navy then tried to persuade the army to allow men to transfer to the naval service, but with limited success. On February 10, 1862, Captain Franklin Buchanan wrote, "The *Merrimack* [*Virginia*] has not yet received her crew, notwithstanding all my efforts to procure them from the Army." Eventually, 200 volunteers were recruited from Major General John B. Magruder's command at Yorktown to fill out the approximate 260-man crew of this famous ironclad.

The first Confederate conscription act, passed April 16, 1862, provided that "all seamen and ordinary seamen" who had been conscripted and who requested naval service were to be transferred to the navy upon application to the Secretary of the Navy. This act was implemented by a War Department general order which provided that applications for transfer would be forwarded through supervising officers who would certify whether the applicant was or was not a seafarer. In October 1862 another act was passed which permitted men subject to conscription to enlist in the navy, but "naval officers sent to conscript camps had little success in recruiting." In May 1863 Congress agreed on another piece of legislation which, in effect, said that any individual in the army could transfer to the navy if so requested by the Navy Department. In apparent defiance of these acts, the War Department continued to allow unit commanders to determine whether men could transfer or not. Considering the ever-present army manpower shortage and given this latitude it is not surprising few men were able to transfer.[2]

Under these acts the navy secretary as well as many of his officers repeatedly requested transfers from the army with little success. When Lieutenant Isaac N. Brown sought men for the ironclad CSS *Arkansas* being completed at Yazoo City, Mississippi, he received six of twenty-five soldiers who requested transfer. Forty-eight hours before he was to go into action, in desperation he appealed to an army commander who agreed to detail sixty artillerists to man the vessel's guns. These men were on loan, however, and three days later, after the ship had run through the Union naval force above Vicksburg, Mississippi, they returned to their army unit. Brown, with too few men to man the guns, agreed to take volunteers from the army to serve on board for terms of a week. One officer wrote rather bitterly, "It is a shame for the Department to keep us here, half manned with green soldiers . . . [when] there is a good crew of sailor men, the *Virginia's,* in a shore battery near Richmond." (The *Virginia* was scuttled May 9, 1862, and its crew given shore duty.)

In Mobile, Alabama, Buchanan, later a Confederate admiral, complained frequently of his inability to obtain men from the army. For example, on April 6, 1863, he wrote, "I am much in want of men and unless the Secretary of War and the Generals are more liberal toward the Navy in permitting transfers from the Army to the Navy we cannot man either the gun-boats or floating batteries." He told a local reporter that of 650 applications to the War Department for seamen in the army to be detailed for naval service, only twenty had been approved. Eventually about 150 men were detailed from a Tennessee unit to serve on Buchanan's ironclad flagship the CSS *Tennessee.*

Up the Red River in Shreveport, Louisiana, the ironclad CSS *Missouri* was being completed. In December 1863 the ship's commanding officer wrote Secretary Mallory, "my only hope [of acquiring men] is from the Army." He requested 60 seamen, 12 firemen, 1 carpenter, and 1 blacksmith from Lieutenant General Kirby Smith, but only a handful of men were transferred. He searched for seamen in military units in Texas and persuaded thirty-two men to apply for naval service. Major General Magruder, their commanding officer, at first refused, but later agreed to detail them for temporary duty. Within weeks, however, Magruder asked for their return, writing, "I hear the *Missouri* can never be of any use." Major General Richard Taylor sent thirty-six artillerists to the ironclad, but after a taste of shipboard life and naval discipline all but twelve decided to return to their units. The *Missouri's* commander continued trying to fill his ship's complement of enlisted men from the army. By early 1865 he had enough men, but wrote most of them were "wild Texans and men who have never seen a gun or a ship."

On March 20, 1864, the Confederate Congress passed a general conscription law, and Adjutant General Samuel Cooper directed the major army commanders to release a total of 1,200 men to the navy. Naval station commanders and ship officers scoured the enrollment camps, and 960 men, many of them experienced seafarers, were enlisted in the navy. Subsequently, the navy reached its manpower peak in 1864. By the end of that year there were 3,674 enlisted men on active duty, and still ships were short-handed. Courts then sentenced a number of criminals to serve out their sentences on board warships, with the approval of the C.S. Navy Department.

In comparison to vessels stationed in home waters, ocean-going Confederate cruisers had little difficulty in attracting qualified seamen. When the first cruiser, the CSS *Sumter,* left New Orleans in June 1861, Commander Raphael Semmes, her captain, said the majority of his crew was composed of men taken from the merchant marine. "New Orleans was full of seamen, discharged from ships that had been laid up, and more men were offering themselves for service than I could receive." And like most of the other cruisers, nearly all the *Sumter's* crew were foreigners. Semmes wrote in *Memoirs of Service Afloat,* "although I had sailed out of a Southern port, I had not half a dozen Southern born men [in] . . . my crew. They were mostly foreigners." He added, "I had two or three Yankees on board." A British visitor to the ship when it put up in Gibraltar in early 1862 noted that the crew "are of all nations—even the Irish brogue was among them."

When Commander John Taylor Wood fitted out the cruiser CSS *Tallahassee,* in summer 1864 he was able to hand-pick a crew of 120 officers and men, volunteers from the Confederate navy's James River Squadron. Wood had been naval aide to President Davis and was on good terms with many Confederate officials, including Secretary Mallory; this may well explain why he was able to recruit volunteers from the naval force defending the nation's capital, a force with its own manpower shortage.

The cruisers obtained in Europe were manned by foreign sailors. When the most famous Rebel cruiser, Raphael Semmes' CSS *Alabama,* or the "290" as she was known then, sailed from Liverpool, England, in 1862 "about sixty persons [were] . . . picked up promiscuously about the streets of Liverpool," Semmes wrote in his memoirs. He added, "My little kingdom consisted of 110 of the most reckless sailors from the groggeries and brothels of Liverpool." They included English, Dutch, Irish, French, Italian, and Spanish seamen. And the *Alabama,* as well as the other cruisers, would enlist men from captured vessels. The CSS *Shenandoah* shipped a number of Germans from a seized merchant ship, and later a number of Americans, including several from New England. But according to the American minister to England, the *Shenandoah* was manned by English subjects. The CSS *Rappahannock*'s crew was principally English with a few Dutch. Later sixteen Belgians enlisted.

A large majority of those who agreed to serve on a Confederate cruiser did so not out of loyalty to the Southern cause, but for mercenary reasons. Semmes recognized this when he wrote, "with rare exception a common sailor has no sense of nationality. He commences his sea-going career at so tender an age, is so constantly at sea, and sails under so many different flags, that he becomes eminently a citizen of the world." James T. Waddell, commanding officer of the *Shenandoah,* wrote in his memoirs, "Seamen, as far as our service was concerned, were merchantable articles with a market value. It was necessary to pay the price demanded or dispose with their services and abandon the cruise. It was felt, therefore, that if, in the exercise of my discretion it became necessary to go beyond the established pay allowance, the Navy Department would take steps necessary to legalize the act." A seaman who deserted from the *Rappahannock* informed a United States diplomatic official that the ship's captain in a speech told his crew that they were to fight for money "and he was going to fight for his country and his home."

The cruiser's commanding officers followed merchant marine practice of paying wages high enough to persuade men to ship. Prize money was always emphasized. Equally important, by special permission from the Navy Department, they were allowed to pay their crew in gold. Arthur Sinclair wrote in *Two Years on the* Alabama that in recruiting, the items "most alluring—double pay, *in gold,* generous rations; tobacco *ad libitum,* grog twice a day and in generous quantity, [and] prospective prize money. . . ."

Semmes recalled in his memoirs how he persuaded seamen to ship: "Finally I came to the finances, and like a skillful Secretary of the Treasury, I put the budget to them, in its very best aspect. As I spoke of good pay, and payment in gold, 'hear! hear!' comes up from several voices. I would give them, I said, about double the ordinary wages, to compensate them for the risks they would have to run, and I promised them, in case we should be successful, 'lots of prize money!' " But in spite of the attractive wages and other incentives, the cruisers were frequently short-handed. The CSS *Florida*, commissioned a Confederate man-of-war in Nassau, the Bahamas, could attract only twenty-two men there. John Newland Maffitt, her commanding officer, had to sail to Mobile, Alabama, risking capture by a blockader, in order to fill his ship's complement of 130 men.

Semmes, Waddell, Maffitt, and the other cruiser commanders all mentioned that they also had difficulty retaining seamen. Desertion was a major problem. Semmes wrote, "I had a precious set of rascals on board—faithless in the matter of abiding by their contracts." In every port men disappeared and had to be replaced. Frequently, the local United States diplomatic official or "spies" were blamed for "luring" crew members into deserting. Paymaster Douglas Forrest of the *Rappahannock* noted in his diary, "Captain refused to let men go on liberty . . . the Captn. in view of the frequent desertion even of appointed officers is unwilling to give an opportunity to the men to do likewise."

An undetermined but apparently large number of foreigners also served in the home water vessels. Confederate naval vessels on the New Orleans, Charleston, Mobile, and Savannah stations all had a considerable number of foreign seamen. An officer reporting on board the CSS *Morgan* in the Mobile Squadron was shocked at her crew. "To call the *Morgan's* crew sailors would be disgracing the name," he wrote with a touch of xenophobia. "Out of a hundred and fifty not one is even *American,* much less a Southerner. We have Irish, Dutch, Norwegian, Danes, French, Spanish, Italians, Mexican, Indians, and mutezos [sic]—a set of desperate cut throats. But worst of all their loyalty is doubtful . . . I could go into the country and get *ten Southerners* and teach them more in one week about seamanship and gunnery than these fellows will learn in twelve months." Not surprisingly, Admiral Buchanan wrote, "There are on board . . . these vessels some of the greatest vagabonds you will ever read of . . . one or two such hung . . . would have a wonderful effect."

Of course not all foreigners serving in the Confederate navy were, as one officer put it, a "disgrace to the service." An Englishman noted the crew of the *Virginia II* (commissioned for James River service late in the war) "were truly magnificent specimens of bone and muscle—mostly foreign-born, from the merchant navy . . . reminded me much of what I had seen in the British navy." The Charleston Squadron, which included a large number of foreign seamen, was well-trained and well-disciplined. Lieutenant William H. Parker in his *Recollections of a Naval Officer* wrote that the crew of the CSS *Beaufort,* which he commanded in 1861, was "composed of Englishmen, Danes and Swedes. I had never sailed with a better one [crew], and I never knew them to fail in their duty; indeed I used to wonder at their eagerness to go into battle considering the fact that they knew nothing at all about the cause of the war." His crew included "two splendid specimens of men-of-war men" who had trained on the British gunnery ship HMS *Excellent* and had the Crimean War medal. One of these fellows was mortally wounded during the Battle of Hampton Roads in March 1862. Parker mentioned that after the battle he visited him "and asked him what I could do for him. He said he would like a cup of tea and a pair of clean socks, which were given him. He died at 8 o'clock, quietly and resignedly."

There were also blacks, both free and slave, who served on board Confederate warships, but we know little about them. Many of them were servants to the officers and also performed other duties. Some were cooks. The ironclad CSS *Chicora* in South Carolina's Charleston Squadron had three free Negroes "regularly enlisted" as seamen.

By 1864 the majority of seamen serving on board the river and harbor defense vessels were transfers from the army or conscripts. On January 12, 1864, Commander William W. Hunter, in command of Georgia's Savannah Squadron, reported three of his vessels, the ironclads *Savannah* and *Georgia,* and a wooden gunboat were "manned with conscripts." In April a sailor on the *Fredericksburg* in Virginia's James River Squadron wrote his father, "the crew is very mixed up—about half of us have just come from the army . . ." Raphael Semmes, when he took command of the James River Squadron early in 1865, discovered that "its personnel was drawn almost entirely from the army." And in the spring of 1864 the ironclad CSS *Neuse* was completed far up the winding Neuse River in North Carolina. The vessel's crew was obtained from nearby army units. "Long, lank, *Tar Heels* . . . from the Piney Woods," one officer described them. "You ought to see them in the boats," he said. "They are all legs and arms and while working at the guns their legs get tangled in the tackles and they are always in the wrong place and in each other's way."

Robert Watson was one of sixteen enlisted men in the Army of Tennessee transferred to the Savannah Squadron. He considered himself most fortunate and was always willing to aid in getting friends transferred. On April 1, 1864, he mentioned in his diary that "Lieut. Carnes . . . asked me if I knew of any seamen in Johnston's army. I told him that I would give him a list of names in the morning." When one of his friends later deserted, Watson wrote. "I am greatly surprised at his desertion from the navy where he had plenty to eat and little to do."

"Plenty to eat and little to do" were certainly reasons why, given the chance, soldiers would willingly become sailors. Soldiers have always envied and frequently resented what they considered were sailors' plush living conditions—good food and plenty of it, warm dry quarters, clean beds, and rarely having to risk their lives in battle. This was certainly true in the Civil War. In addition, pay was not a factor. The base pay of sailors and soldiers was similar, except for those serving on the cruisers; probably this was not common knowledge in the Confederate armies.

Seamen shipped for the cruisers were paid more than seamen in the home water vessels and stations. The home water sailors were also not paid in gold, but in the Confederate currency that became increasingly worthless as the war and the inflation rate escalated. A young engineer on the CSS *North Carolina* complained to his brother: "Everything is awful high in Wilmington [North Carolina] in two months our pay will hardly pay our washing Bill for one month." Seaman Watson wrote in his diary, "The crew was paid off during the day but I got no money and don't expect to get any for the next six months for it takes nearly all my wages to pay for soap and tobacco. Soap is $8.30 per bar and tobacco is $3.00 per pound . . . Some of the men have been on board over a year and this is the first time they have drawn any money." The normal pay scale ranged from $12 a month for landsmen and other inexperienced hands, to $14 a month for ordinary seamen, and $18 a month for seamen. Watson was rated a seaman, drawing $18 a month. A seaman of the CSS *Georgia* requested transfer to the army "as my pay is two [sic] small for my support."

The having "little to do," mentioned by Watson, was not entirely correct. Watson, himself, would later change his mind about his duties. Daily routine for seamen on board a Confederate warship was generally the same regardless of whether it was a cruiser or a home water vessel. This routine was virtually the same as that followed in the Union navy; this is not surprising considering that nearly all the commanding officers had served in the United States Navy. But there was some variation from ship to ship, depending on the captain. Some commanding officers always had church service and inspection on Sunday, others would hold inspection on Saturday and allow liberty on Sunday. Reveille was usually at 3 a.m. After hammocks were lashed, the crew washed down the decks. On most ships the berth and gun decks were scrubbed down with saltwater and the spar deck holy-stoned.

Seaman Watson talked frequently about this: "Sat. 26th [1864] . . . all hands at work holy stoning the deck, scrubbing paint work and hammocks." On June 18 he wrote: "After breakfast took the covering off the spar deck on shore and holystoned it. This covering is made of inch boards put together in sections and is laid on the spar deck which is iron clad. Scrubbed gun deck, berth deck, and everything else that could be scrubbed." A Confederate States Marine officer on board the *Savannah* wrote, "Every Sat. the ship is scrubbed out from top to bottom, and today being Sat. all hands are washing away and the decks are flooded with water. You can imagine how cheerless and uncomfortable everything is."

After breakfast, the ship's crew was drilled. Watson almost daily wrote in his diary, "Drill in morning," or "Drilled at B.S. [broadside] gun in morning and at small arms in afternoon." On the CSS *Albemarle* and a number of other ships the crews exercised at the guns twice a day. Lieutenant George Gift on the gunboat CSS *Chattahoochee* told another officer, "Our routine is very strict. We drill a gun crew for 45 minutes during the forenoon until all crews are drilled. At 7 bells—½ pass three—all hands to quarters and have half an hour drill, then fire quarters. . . . I am endeavoring to bring them to *regular* man-of-war style."

On the river and harbor defense vessels most of the emphasis was put on drilling with the heavy guns. Occasionally, sailors practiced firing live ammunition. Watson mentioned in his diary several times that the *Savannah* "got up steam and went down the river and fired three shots out of each gun at a target." Emphasis was placed, as it had been since the introduction of muzzle–loaders, on improving speed in loading and running out the guns. But the cruiser captains put less emphasis on drilling and firing the guns. Semmes, when in command of the *Alabama,* would allow his gun crews to practice on captured ships before burning them. Subsequently, gunnery on the *Alabama* was not good, as was evident in its doomed 1864 fight with the USS *Kearsarge,* where very few shots hit the Union vessel.

In addition to exercising the guns, the crew usually drilled with rifles, cutlasses, and sidearms. They were called away to general quarters several times a week. An officer on the Charleston Harbor ironclad CSS *Palmetto State* wrote: "One drill I introduced on board here . . . Every officer and man had his appointed port or hatch to escape by in case of the vessel's suddenly sinking . . . the first man who reached the deck immediately took off the iron grating without waiting to be told. At the order, 'clear the ship,' all hands would assemble on the [casemate's] roof in less than a minute."

The men had other responsibilities depending upon whether they were on sailing ships, ironclads, or small gunboats. On all the ships they had to stand watch, whether in port or operating. At sea or while operating, except during general quarters, the ship's crew was divided into port and starboard watches. On the ironclads the crew was constantly caulking and pumping. These ships' bulkheads were constructed primarily out of green timber and leaked incessantly. An engineer on the CSS *North Carolina* wrote his sister, "our ship is not worth much . . . she is beginning to leak badly." He later wrote that "she leaks so badly that we have to keep steam up all the time" to work the pumps. An officer on the CSS *Atlanta* recorded in his diary: (December 17, 1862) "3 inches water in the ship"; (December 18) "pumps steadily at work—7 inches water in the ship"; (December 19) "Pumps well attended to—9 inches water in the ship"; (December 22) "pumps regularly attended to." Another officer on that ironclad complained, "if a person were blind folded and carried below and then turned loose he would imagine himself in a swamp, for the water is trickling in all the time . . ." Crew members frequently jumped out of their hammocks at reveille only to find themselves standing in cold water.

On the cruisers daily work included scrubbing the decks, drilling the guns and other exercises, as well as the typical work of an ocean-going warship in the days of sail. Arthur Sinclair in *Two Years on the* Alabama wrote, "we have settled down once more to the ordinary routine of ship duties. .

. . The plane or adz of carpenter Robinson is smoothing or trimming a timber; gunner Cuddy and mates, pots and pans in hand, are polishing up the battery; sailmaker Alcott is mending a rent in the awning; Jack, seated on deck . . . is painting a main brace. . . . On the yard-arms and rigging, top men here and there, under the supervision of boatswain McCaskey, are securing chaffing gear on the yards and rigging." Accounts written about the cruisers also mention that small boat drills were carried out whenever possible.

When "knock off ship's work" was piped late in the afternoon, all but those on watch had the rest of the day to themselves. "Jack Tar," as the sailor has traditionally been called, found a variety of ways to amuse himself while on board ship. As with most sailors during the 19th century, dancing was a favorite amusement with Confederate sailors. Semmes, in his memoirs, wrote that on the *Alabama*: "after the duties of the day were over, they [sailors] would generally assemble on the forecastle, and, with violin, and tambourine—and I always kept them supplied with these and other musical instruments—they would extemporize a ballroom, by moving the shot-racks, coils of rope, and other impediments, out of the way, and, with handkerchiefs tied around the waists of some of them, to indicate who were to be the ladies of the party they would get up a dance with all due form and ceremony; the ladies, in particular, endeavoring to initiate all the airs and grace of the sex—the only drawback being a little hoarseness of the voice, and now and then the use of an expletive, which would escape them when something went wrong in the dance, and they forgot they had the aprons on. . . . On these occasions, the discipline of the ship was wont to be purposely relaxed, and roars of laughter, and other evidence of the rapid flight of the jocund hours, at other times entirely inadmissible, would come resounding aft on the quarter-deck."

On a number of ships minstrel shows or theatricals were staged. On other occasions "yarn-spinners" would occupy an evening's entertainment. And amusement took other forms. Semmes permitted his men to purchase monkeys and parrots. Reading books was rare among enlisted men, but letter writing was surprisingly popular—apparently Confederate sailors were fairly literate. Fishing was common, and in season oystering was popular with crew members in the home water vessels. When the *Shenandoah* crossed the equator, the traditional "King Neptune" ceremony was carried out, an informal initiation rite all sailors undergo the first time they cross this line. Captain Waddell later wrote, "tar and soap . . . and water from a donkey engine which threw a stream two inches in diameter over the unlucky victim is the ordeal through which each one passed upon his introduction to the line where Neptune is supposed to hold his court."

Unquestionably, the most popular pastimes on board ship were eating and drinking. Confederate tars ate well—certainly in comparison to their army counterparts serving in northern Virginia and elsewhere in the South. A former soldier aboard the *Fredericksburg* wrote his father, "We get plenty to eat and of that which [is] tolerably good we get near twice as much as we did in camp." Watson wrote in his diary shortly after going on board the *Savannah,* "Got dinner, pork, peas and hard bread, good living to what we've been use to in the army." But sailors and marines serving in land batteries and shore facilities were at times not as well off. A marine mentioned that at Drewry's Bluff, Virginia, he "had eaten beef and ship biscuit or 'hard tack' as we call it, for weeks without a change." And as conditions deteriorated in the Confederacy, particularly in transportation, the rations for ships' crews were also affected. In May 1864 the *Virginia II*'s crew petitioned for an increase in their bread ration. It was forwarded to the Navy Department where it was turned down. "The supply [of bread] is small. . . . If the present ration (10 oz) is weighed to the men it be found to average over three biscuits per day."

As food became increasingly scarce in Richmond late in the war, the James River Squadron was put on half rations. Squadron officers agreed "the scanty rations" were the principal reason for the demoralization and desertion rampant among their hands during the last months of the war. And although apparently not as bad in the other home water squadrons, there nevertheless was a noticeable decline in the quantity and quality of food for these James River sailors. A midshipman on the *Albemarle,* stationed at Plymouth, North Carolina, in June 1864, could commiserate with Virginia compatriots, writing, "We are living the same monotonous sort of life here as usual, nothing to eat scarcely and no amusements." Little could be done to change these affairs. Subsequently, sailors in the James River Squadron and on the Wilmington station were allowed to go foraging for provisions.

Conditions within the Confederacy generally had little or no effect on rations for cruiser sailors. They had full rations at times and at other times were on short rations. John McIntosh Kell, the executive officer of the *Alabama*, wrote his men "lived almost entirely on our prizes." To some degree this was true of other cruisers as well.

On July 14, 1862, Union President Abraham Lincoln signed into law a bill abolishing the spirit ration in the United States Navy. Unlike the Union navy, however, the grog ration was continued in the Confederate navy. Enlisted men were entitled to one gill of spirits or a half-pint of wine per day. This was generally followed throughout the navy. Only the redoubtable Semmes is known to have doubled his men's grog ration at times. Memoirs, diaries, and correspondence from those who served on the cruisers mention grog and liquor far oftener than the accounts written by "home water" sailors. This is probably because the cruisers included a large number of "blue water" sailors, men used to the grog ration, and because liberty was not a weekly occurrence. As Semmes wrote, "I caused a regular allowance of 'grog' to be served out to the crew, twice in each day. I was quite willing that Jack should drink, but I undertook to be the judge of how much he should drink." Supply rarely matched demand, and it was far from uncommon for sailors to smuggle liquor on board. Semmes mentioned that he had an entire ship load of captured distilled spirits destroyed to keep his men from getting their hands on it.

A large percentage of ship commanders were troubled by efforts to smuggle liquor on board their ships, for even the best sailors could not be trusted where spirits were concerned. Watson mentions in his diary that on Christmas night 1864, a group of sailors on the *Savannah* broke into the "spirit room" and got drunk and rebellious. "The officers armed themselves and came among them to stop their noise, but this made them worse. . . . They were all put in irons and kept on the spar deck for several days and nights and it was bitter cold." Worse, both the *Alabama* and *Shenandoah* had "mutinies" that were instigated by smuggled liquor.

Far more liquor was consumed by sailors on liberty than on board ship. It was by far the principal reason that sailors went ashore. There are occasional references to going to get a good meal, to attend the theater, and, of course, women, but as Semmes wrote, "unless Jack has his periodical frolic, he is very apt to become moody and discontented." And to Jack a "frolic" is to try "and drink dry all the grog shops." "Poor Jack," Semmes added, "how strong upon him is the thirst for drink!"

Watson described a "frolic" that was typical not only of the Confederate sailor, but the sailor throughout history to the present: "I and my chum Alfred Lowe went on shore after [quarters] . . . and I am sorry to say we got most gloriously drunk. When we went on shore we met our 1st Boatswain's Mate and our Yeoman, both very fine men and we went to a bar room and took several drinks together, each treating several times, then we took a cruise about the city, went into several houses of doubtful character and then got to drinking again. I spent $55.00 which was all the money I had . . . for liquor is $2.00 per drink."

The following day he wrote: "Felt very sick all day from the effects of the bad liquor I drank yesterday and must say that I feel heartily ashamed of myself for making such an ass of myself." Finally, he wrote remorsefully the next day, "I feel much better today and have made up my mind to go on no more sprees during the war." Watson's diary does not mention any more "sprees," which, if correct, was an exception to Jack's habits.

Not every ship allowed its crew to go on liberty, out of fear that they might desert. This was true of the *Rappahannock,* the vessels in the James River Squadron, and other ships at different times. And these fears were justified. Virtually every ship had men desert during liberty. The *Tallahassee* lost more than twenty men during a brief stay in Halifax, Nova Scotia, leaving the cruiser short-handed. Stopping liberty did not prevent desertions, however. Picket boats frequently lost men. "Sometimes an entire boat's crew would run off, leaving the officer to find his way on board the best he might," Semmes wrote of the James River Squadron after he assumed command. On a number of occasions, men disappeared from their ships presumably by climbing over the side at night and swimming ashore.

Why did they desert? Was it because of inadequate compensation (pay and prize money), or conditions on board ship (food and other essentials, discipline, danger from illness or combat)? It is difficult to generalize. Various factors—such as the ship and its commanding officer, whether a crew member was a Southerner or not, the period of the war, as well as compensation—all at one time or another persuaded men to "jump ship."

As mentioned earlier, a sailor's pay was generally satisfactory on the cruisers, but not on home water vessels. Inflation seriously affected the value of Confederate money and doubtless contributed to desertion. An impressive number of prizes were taken by the cruisers, and prize money was promised to their crews, but this money was to be paid *after* the war. This led to considerable discontent, and according to testimony given to American diplomatic officials, some of the foreign-born sailors, convinced that they would never receive it (or so convinced by American agents), left their ship at the first opportunity.

The morale of the Southern people, like that of the army, held up well until the summer of 1863 (the summer of Gettysburg and Vicksburg), then fluctuated for the next year, and rapidly deteriorated after the autumn of 1864. This defeatism inevitably affected the navy. A sailor on the *Fredericksburg* wrote an uncle in fall 1864 that "on board this ship there are numbers of men who are for peace on any terms. I am really sorry to write it but it is the truth." Seaman Watson, who ended up at Wilmington after he lost one ship at Savannah and another at Charleston, described in his diary the declining morale of his officers. On January 27, 1865, he wrote, "Officers are drunk and drilling us for their amusements. If these things continue much longer I shall certainly desert." Two days later he noted, "officers fiddling, dancing and drinking whiskey all day and nearly all night." Although this sailor did not desert as he threatened, hundreds of his fellow seamen did in those last weeks. Semmes mentions in his diary that "boat loads" defected from the James River Squadron.

Conditions aboard ship varied from vessel to vessel. Food was generally adequate, at least until late in the war in the home water vessels. But during those final months food, according to one officer, was a major factor in desertion in the James River Squadron. "In the squadron . . . the scanty ration was the principal cause of their leaving. A man shut up in an iron-clad with nothing to do after the morning drill, broods over his hunger."

No information has been located to determine whether similar ration problems existed on other ships and at other stations. But they probably did not. It is more than likely sailors in the James River Squadron suffered more from food shortages than sailors stationed elsewhere in the Confederacy.

Discipline was not usually harsh on Confederate vessels. Flogging was not practiced; punishment usually consisted of being confined and placed in irons, the same discipline as practiced on Union warships. Only the *Shenandoah* was accused of being a "hell ship" with a tyrannical commanding officer, but evidence of this is, at best, dubious.

Usually, Confederate sailors were adequately clothed, and certainly better clothed than many soldiers in the army. Upon entering the navy, an enlisted man was issued a pea jacket, a cloth jacket, flannel woolen jumper and trousers, deck canvas jumper and trousers, hats, shoes, and socks. A man was given a clothing allowance against which issues were charged. Replacements for garments worn out or lost were to be paid for out of his wages. Uniform regulations issued by the navy's Office of Provisions and Clothing called for gray in the winter and white in the summer. The uniform was to be similar to that worn by sailors in the British navy.

Despite the directions, uniforms did vary. The *Virginia's* men wore blue uniforms captured at Norfolk. The *Alabama's* and *Rappahannock's* crews were clothed in blue uniforms in winter and white duck in the summer. In fact, all Confederate sailors wore white duck in the summer. Evidence suggests they wore blue in winter. There is no mention of gray uniforms for enlisted personnel on any Confederate ship. And at the beginning of the war nearly all Confederate naval officers wore the blue uniforms they had used in the United States Navy.

The order adopting gray uniforms was not popular. "Who had ever seen a gray sailor, no matter what nationality he served," wrote a former Confederate naval officer in his recollections. Except for the Mobile station, the regulation concerning gray uniforms was not strictly enforced. On all stations and ships, officers wore blue, gray, and even an occasional black uniform at times. But at Mobile, Admiral Franklin Buchanan issued an order requiring all officers to wear "at all times when on duty" the prescribed gray uniform. Buchanan was indignant when, as he wrote Commander John E. Mitchell, one officer "reported to me for duty in a *black coat,* said he had no uniform and *had* never had one since he received his appointment." One officer, who until the uniform order had greatly admired Buchanan, wrote, "A week or more since the remnant of the crew of the Arkansas arrived here, Admiral Buchanan . . . [informed] the officers that he had no use for them, as they had no uniforms! . . . I have heard it said that with some ladies a sleek coat . . . with brass buttons has a wonderful effect, but I was not prepared to believe that with a man who claimed to be a warrior of age (there is no doubt of that) . . . from this, I deduce that a fashionable tailor can do more to make a good officer in the estimation of old Buchanan than the great creating Prince of Heaven."

By 1864, throughout the Confederacy it was becoming difficult to replace worn-out uniforms. Blue and gray cloth was extremely scarce and other items of apparel were not attainable. In October 1864, the commanding officer of the James River Squadron wrote the paymaster, "The greatest portion of the crews of the vessels under my command are without pea-jackets. . . .An adequate supply of winter clothing is all important at this time to make the men comfortable and unless they are made so they must become discontented and unreliable in health and loyalty. It should be remembered that exposure to bad weather on shipboard is worse than in camp life, where the men can have the advantage of exercise and cheerful fires." There is no record that this request was fulfilled, and it may well have contributed to the high rate of desertion in that squadron during the 1864–65 winter.

Although the naval commander's statement that sailors suffer more when exposed to the weather than soldiers can be strongly debated, there was considerable sickness in the Confederate navy during the war. An abstract from quarterly reports of sick from January 1 to October 1, 1863, revealed 6,122 cases treated and 59 deaths. Flag Officer John K. Mitchell, when he commanded the James River Squadron, reported on August 22, 1864, that 226 men from his squadron were on the sick list. The *Fredericksburg* alone had sixty-one incapacitated by illness. And the ironclads appear to have had far more sickness than the wooden vessels. Living and working conditions on board the vessels were almost intolerable, particularly during the summers and whenever the enemy was being engaged. Ventilation was primitive or nearly nonexistent, and there is no evidence that blowers were ever fitted. The only fresh air came from the gratings on top of the casemate and from ports along the sides. The excessive heat, dampness, and lack of light resulted in a high rate of illness, low morale, inefficiency, and desertion among the crews. Lieutenant James Baker was disgruntled about the habitability of the CSS *Huntsville:* "She is . . . terribly disagreeable for men to live on."

Various remedial measures were tried. Raphael Semmes, when in command of the James River Squadron, ordered his captains to send their men ashore a few at a time to exercise. Later, a board of naval surgeons visited the squadron and recommended that, in addition to the grog ration, a whiskey ration be issued to the crew every morning with their coffee. The general practice, however, was to seek quarters outside of the ships. The crews of the CSS *Tuscaloosa, Huntsville,* and *Savannah* (and probably others) slept in warehouses during the "sickly season." The *Tennessee's* crew was quartered on a covered barge anchored near the vessel. The *Albemarle's* men slung their hammocks under a shed, leaving only a watch on board at night, and tenders were used by the Wilmington squadron and the *Missouri* and the *Arkansas* on western waters. Whether this helped reduce the sickness on ironclads is not known. But illness on the wooden vessels, both the cruisers and home water gunboats, was not unusually high.

Nearly all Confederate warships were involved in some kind of engagement with enemy forces, at one time or another. But some of them were heavily engaged, such as the ironclads *Virginia, Albemarle, Arkansas,* and the cruiser *Alabama.* The majority of them, however, saw only limited combat. Compared to earlier and even later wars that the United States was involved in, as well as land engagements during the Civil War, casualties in ship actions were relatively light. During the five-hour battle fought in Hampton Roads, March 8, 1862, the four Confederate vessels involved, including the ironclad *Virginia,* suffered fewer than sixty killed and wounded. In the Battle of Mobile Bay Confederate ships lost only twelve killed and twenty wounded. The *Alabama* in her final battle with the *Kearsarge* off Cherbourg, France, lost nine men killed and twenty-one wounded. There is no known tally of all Confederate sailors killed in combat on board ship during the war, but it was likely somewhere between 6 and 8 percent of those enrolled in the Confederate States Navy.

In battle the Confederate sailor was just as courageous as his Northern counterpart or his fellow Rebels in the army. He fought well; Union naval commanders admitted it. And perhaps no group of them fought harder than the *Alabama's* crew. Nearly all foreigners, they assailed the *Kearsarge* until their own ship sank under them. They offer the greatest tribute to the Southern seaman—a man who performed creditably during the war, a man who only lost when his nation conceded defeat.

....

Notes

1. The maximum number of Confederate naval officers on active duty at one time (April 1864) was 727. The need for trained junior officers led to the establishment of a practical naval academy on the training ship CSS *Patrick Henry*.

2. J. Thomas Scharf in his *History of the Confederate States Navy* wrote that the "transfer laws were . . . almost entirely disregarded."

7

The Overblown *Trent* Affair

JOHN M. TAYLOR

The U.S. Government's foreign affairs at the time of the Civil War consisted largely of relations with Britain, France, and to a lesser extent, Mexico. Britain and France were not only the two most powerful nations in the world but also the primary consumers of cotton, America's principal export. When Abraham Lincoln's administration took office, it inherited no critical problems in foreign relations. But the issue of recognition of the Confederacy held considerable potential for friction, and Washington knew that its adversaries would make maximum use of "King Cotton diplomacy."

Because it was the world's greatest maritime power, and because its Canadian provinces bordered the United States, Britain was the most important power with which the North had to deal. Although most Britons were opposed to slavery, the ruling class was distrustful of democracy and wary of republican influence on British society. A collapse of the brash republic to the west would be welcomed by much of the British aristocracy, particularly because the Lincoln administration was slow to take the moral high ground, that is, to make a commitment to the eradication of slavery.

The Confederacy, meanwhile, had diplomatic objectives of its own, the most important of which related to the high seas. Survival of the Confederacy depended on a continuation of the trade that permitted the export of cotton and the import of military matériel. The trade question was closely tied to that of diplomatic recognition. Recognition of Confederate independence would not stop Yankee bullets, but it would strengthen the peace movement in the North and perhaps even provide access to European financial markets.

Even before the attack on Fort Sumter, Confederate President Jefferson Davis had sent emissaries to Europe in search of recognition and trade concessions. The warm welcome accorded a delegation led by William L. Yancey in London generated concern in Washington, and not without reason. On May 13, 1861, the British government issued a proclamation of neutrality that effectively recognized the Confederacy as a belligerent. Under international law, such status gave the Confederacy the right, among others, to purchase arms and commission warships. For the seceded states, which the Lincoln administration dismissed as "insurgents," to be given any legal standing, was galling. Instructions from Secretary of State William H. Seward to U.S. envoys emphasized that the United States would regard any move to recognize the Confederacy as an unfriendly act.

The cordial welcome accorded the Yancey delegation in Britain was short-lived. Nevertheless, Davis decided to upgrade the Confederacy's diplomatic representation in Europe. In August 1861 President Davis named James Mason of Virginia and John Slidell of Louisiana envoys to Britain and France, respectively. The pompous Mason had been a vociferous defender of slavery when in the U.S. Senate; he was not an inspired choice to represent the Confederacy in a sensitive post. Diarist Mary Chesnut wrote, "The English can't stand chewing [tobacco]. Yet they say at the lordliest table, Mr. Mason will turn round halfway in his chair and spit in the fire."[1] But if Mason was something of a caricature, his colleague was not. Both U.S. Secretary of State Seward and Charles Francis Adams, the U.S. minister in London, viewed John Slidell as an able intriguer and a formidable diplomatic foe.

The new Confederate commissioners seemed in no hurry to depart for Europe, but by mid-October they were in Charleston, South Carolina, Mason with a male secretary, Slidell with his wife and three children. They chartered a fast, shallow-draft steamer, the *Theodora*, with which to dodge Federal blockaders offshore. On the night of October 12 the *Theodora* made her escape through the still-forming Federal blockade, and two days later

Captain Charles Wilkes of the USS *San Jacinto*. *(U.S. Navy Imaging Center)*

she dropped anchor at Nassau. There the emissaries discovered that they had missed the mail packet for Liverpool and would have to wait three weeks for another.

The Confederates were not the only people waiting. In the placid waters of the Bahama Channel, the Federal steam sloop *San Jacinto*, commanded by Charles Wilkes, lay in wait. The tall, spare Wilkes was one of the best-known figures in the Old Navy. From 1838 to 1842 he had led an expedition to survey and chart the South Pacific. He and his flotilla surveyed some 280 islands and charted some 1,600 miles of the coast of Antarctica.

For all his ability, Wilkes was a man of few friends. Within weeks of his return from the explorations that made him famous, Wilkes requested courts-martial for several of his officers. He himself was found guilty of excessively punishing several sailors—a remarkable achievement in a navy in which flogging was routine. In the words of one historian, Wilkes's egotism "led him to make decisions often based on impulse and ambition, [and] to ignore naval etiquette when regulations or orders contravened what he defined as the proper course of action."[2]

By all rights Wilkes, now age 62, should have been deemed too old for sea duty by 1861, but there was no navy retirement system, and the navy needed experienced officers. Secretary of the Navy Welles put Wilkes in command of the *San Jacinto* and gave him the mission of seeking out the *Sumter*, the first Confederate commerce destroyer to reach the high seas. Cruising the Caribbean, Wilkes called at Havana, where he learned that Mason and Slidell were in Nassau awaiting passage to Europe. At the residence of Robert Shufeldt, the U.S. envoy in Cuba, overlooking Havana harbor, Wilkes discussed the propriety of his intercepting the next British steamer and seizing the Confederate commissioners he expected to find on board. The Confederates would be carrying dispatches. Might not such dispatches constitute contraband of war? Shufeldt was supportive. He and Wilkes exchanged farewells and Wilkes took the *San Jacinto* to sea.

The morning of November 8, 1861, dawned warm and bright in the Caribbean. Wilkes remembered it as a beautiful day, with the breeze scarcely ruffling the waters of the Bahama Channel. At 11:30 a.m. his lookout spied smoke. Wilkes, who had informed no one of his intentions, called for his executive officer, Donald Fairfax, and gave him orders. He was to board the British packet, by then known to be the *Trent*, and request to see her papers. This was standard procedure—the right of a belligerent to stop and search a neutral was well established in international law. What was to follow, however, was extremely controversial. Fairfax was to ascertain that Mason and Slidell were on board and, if they were, to seize them and convey them to the *San Jacinto*.

The seizure of passengers from a neutral vessel had no sanction in international law. Indeed, Britain's practice of impressing American sailors had brought on the War of 1812. Fairfax had the temerity to tell his captain as much, but Wilkes was not to be dissuaded. He did not think that Fairfax would have to use force, and he expected Fairfax and his boarding party to conduct themselves "with all the kindness which becomes the character of our naval service."[3]

When his ship was about a mile from the *Trent*, Wilkes showed his colors and fired a shot across her bow as a signal to heave to. When the packet showed no sign of complying, Wilkes fired an exploding shell close by, which brought the *Trent* dead in the water. Her angry captain demanded through his trumpet by what right his ship was being stopped. No captain liked to be halted and searched, belligerent prerogatives or not.

As boarding officer, Fairfax was all too aware of the delicacy of his position. He was met by an officer at the ship's ladder and taken to her angry skipper, James Moir, who was surrounded by a group of excited passengers. When Fairfax told Moir that he knew that Mason and Slidell were on his ship, there was no attempt at deception. Slidell promptly stepped forward and identified himself. So, then, did Mason, and the emissaries' two secretaries.

The air of restraint that marked these proceedings evaporated when Fairfax announced that his orders were to take the Confederates to the *San Jacinto* as prisoners. Other passengers were so outraged that Fairfax had to ask Moir to maintain order. The Federal officer was the lone Yankee on the *Trent*, and the commotion on deck brought his boarding party up the accommodation ladder. When it was clear that Fairfax was not in danger, the sailors returned to the cutter. Mrs. Slidell asked who had ordered the arrest of her husband. "Your old acquaintance, Captain Wilkes," Fairfax replied, for Wilkes had known the Slidells socially in Washington. "Really!" she replied, adding with some prescience, "Captain Wilkes is playing into our hands."[4]

Despite Fairfax's urging, the four Confederates refused to come peacefully. The minutes slipped away, and Fairfax sent to the *San Jacinto* for help. Wilkes sent 25 armed sailors and marines, and Fairfax led four men to Mason's cabin, where the Virginian was seized and led to the cutter alongside. Slidell had retreated to his own cabin, with his wife and daughter, and warned Fairfax that he would not go quietly.

The scene in and about Slidell's stateroom was one of shouting and confusion. Following his return to England, a British officer on the packet reported that Rosina Slidell, daughter of the envoy, had slapped Fairfax, denouncing him as a "cowardly poltroon."[5] Raphael Semmes's postwar memoirs would speak of "the screams of Miss Slidell, as she had been gallantly charged by the American marines, commanded, for the occasion, by an officer bearing the proud old name of Fairfax."[6] Considering that Fairfax appears to have behaved very correctly throughout this tension-charged episode, charges that Slidell's family were treated with other than consideration may be viewed with skepticism.

The envoys and their entourages were transferred to the *San Jacinto*, and the *Trent* was allowed to proceed. In the excitement of the capture, neither Wilkes nor Fairfax appears to have remembered to seize the Confederate dispatch box, the one item of baggage that might have been

Confederate commissioners James Mason and John Slidell being removed from the British mail steamer *Trent* (left) by boarding parties from
the USS *San Jacinto*. *(U.S. Naval Historical Center)*

regarded as contraband. Nor was the *Trent*, in being allowed to proceed to
England, treated in accordance with international law. Historian Allan
Nevins would write,

> [Wilkes] had a perfect right to search any suspected ship for . . . con-
> traband of war, and to take a vessel carrying contraband into port to
> await the verdict of a prize court. But he had no right to decide the
> question of a violation of neutrality by fiat on the spot, without judicial
> process. Moreover, it was extremely doubtful whether persons, as distin-
> guished from goods, could ever be deemed contraband.[7]

The *San Jacinto* and her prisoners reached Hampton Roads on November 15; the *Trent* reached Britain 12 days later. The reaction in London
was one of indignation. The *Times* predicted that Lord Palmerston's cabinet
would fall if the insult to the flag went unrebuked. The *Illustrated London
News* asserted that the British public would not permit the forcible removal

of passengers from a British vessel. These journals were an accurate reflection of government sentiment; the prime minister reportedly told his colleagues, "You may stand for this, but damned if I will!"[8]

In America, Wilkes's action was cheered on both sides of the Mason-Dixon line, but for very different reasons. The North had found little to cheer in news from the battlefield; now, the press cheered an action that appeared both a setback to the Confederacy and a thumb in the eye to a traditional enemy, Britain. Secretary of the Navy Welles—no friend of the irascible Wilkes—put out a statement praising his firmness and approving his action. Northern newspapers greeted with glee an act that appeared to be fitting retribution for Britain's recognition of Confederate belligerency. The House of Representatives voted him a gold medal. The *San Jacinto* proceeded, first to New York and then to Boston, where the prisoners were incarcerated in dank Fort Warren.

Confederate sympathizers, meanwhile, could hardly believe their good fortune. Diarist Mary Chesnut wrote that something good was bound to result from such a foolish Yankee blunder. Secretary of War Judah P. Benjamin smilingly told an associate that he thought it was the best thing that could have happened for the Confederacy.

Fortunately for the North, Britain and the United States were each represented in the other's capital by men of judgment and common sense. Charles Francis Adams, 54, was the third member of his famous family to serve as U.S. minister to Britain. As a member of the House of Representatives he had worked closely with Seward in the years leading up to the war. In patience and imperturbability, Adams would prove more than a match for his British hosts.

Adams's counterpart in Washington was Richard Pennell, Lord Lyons. A ruddy, humorless bachelor of 44, Lyons was a veteran in the foreign ministry, but his record was so undistinguished that President James Buchanan had taken offense at his appointment. Lyons considered America an acquired taste. He found Washington a dreary post, lacking as it did clubs, good restaurants, and a decent theater. But the British envoy was diligent and observant. He was also opposed to slavery, and felt none of the elation that many of his compatriots had experienced at the disruption of the Union.

On the official level, the Palmerston government moved resolutely, but in a manner calculated not to inflame the situation. On November 30,

Foreign Secretary Russell sent a dispatch to Lyons demanding the return of Mason and Slidell and an apology by the United States. In an accompanying letter, Lyons was told that he should allow just seven days from the time he delivered the message for the U.S. response, and if no satisfactory reply had been received by that time he should request his passport and return to Britain. At the same time, Russell instructed Lyons to call on Secretary Seward, and to brief him on the contents of the note before formally presenting it. Thus, the administration could consider its reply before Lyons presented his note and started the seven-day "clock."

Although Seward had a reputation as an anglophobe, no one was more interested in resolving the *Trent* affair than he. When Lyons, on December 19, advised him of his government's position, Seward expressed appreciation at London's forbearance; he promised to consult President Lincoln and report back within 48 hours. Seward found the president very reluctant to give up the Confederate emissaries, but the secretary was firm. He warned the president that his choices were to surrender Mason and Slidell or face a real possibility of war with Britain, "and war means the instant defense of New York, Boston and Philadelphia."[9]

Forty-eight hours, however, were not enough. Lincoln was looking for a peaceful solution—he was first inclined toward international arbitration—but he had to deal with inflamed public opinion in the North. Seward, on his part, had the daunting task of convincing Lincoln that the prisoners must be given up. Seward knew his international law. He remarked to his son Frederick, who served as his secretary, that London was demanding no more in terms of freedom of the seas than the United States had asked in its early decades as a republic.

On Christmas Day a four-hour cabinet session that began at 10:00 a.m. was devoted entirely to Seward's draft reply to Lyons. Lincoln had taken the unusual step of inviting Charles Sumner, chairman of the Senate Foreign Relations Committee, to join him and his cabinet. As the meeting began, only Sumner and Postmaster General Blair were prepared to join Seward in recommending that the prisoners be released. The discussion was heated, but inconclusive; as it broke up, Lincoln told Seward that he was inclined to draft a paper of his own, a brief explaining why the prisoners should not be returned.

What conversations may have taken place later that Christmas Day are lost in the mists of history. The cabinet met again on December 26, and in a much shorter session adopted Seward's reply to Lyons, without enthusiasm, but without audible dissent. After the meeting Seward remarked to the president that he had not produced a competing draft. Lincoln smiled and shook his head, remarking that he had found he could not produce a convincing counterargument.

Seward's reply to Lyons was a long, polemical document, masquerading as international law. The secretary addressed the questions of whether Wilkes was justified in stopping and searching the *Trent*, whether Confederate emissaries might properly be regarded as contraband, and whether Wilkes had carried out his search in a proper manner. All these questions he answered in the affirmative. He then raised questions of procedure, and concluded that the captives should not have been taken because the *Trent* itself was not taken to a U.S. court for adjudication. It was a virtuoso performance, one that freed the prisoners on a technicality.

As a cold dawn broke over Provincetown, Massachusetts, on New Year's Day, 1862, the residents were treated to the sight of a British sloop, the *Rinaldo*, at anchor in the harbor. Word spread quickly that the arrival of the vessel was somehow related to the *Trent* affair. Late that afternoon a tugboat from Boston brought the two Confederate emissaries from their prison at Fort Warren. Mason, portly and bald, and Slidell, slim and taciturn, were transferred with their baggage to the *Rinaldo*. The *Trent* affair was over, and with it went the South's best hope for foreign intervention. The captain of the *Sumter*, Raphael Semmes, wrote from Gibraltar early in 1862, "The whole British nation were so frightened in their late quarrel with the Yankees . . . that I am afraid we shall never bring them up to the mark again."[10]

In part because the press commentary was so extreme on both sides of the Atlantic, the *Trent* affair has sometimes been considered a greater threat to Anglo-American relations than it really was. In fact, neither Britain nor the United States had any incentive to go to war with the other. The Lincoln administration, although angered by Britain's assistance to the Confederates and by France's moves to establish a protectorate in Mexico, had a policy of "one war at a time." The Palmerston government, although angered by Wilkes's rash deed, was all too aware of Canada's vulnerability in the event of hostilities with the United States.

The arrival of the Confederate emissaries in Europe proved anti-climactic. Their welcome was cool, and neither proved able to gain any

LOOK OUT FOR SQUALLS.

Jack Bull. "YOU DO WHAT'S RIGHT, MY SON, OR I'LL BLOW YOU OUT OF THE WATER."

A cartoon that appeared in the British weekly *Punch* at the height of the *Trent* affair. *(Author's collection)*

significant concession on behalf of their cause. As for Wilkes, he continued to be a thorn in the side of the Navy Department, but, like some of Lincoln's incompetent generals, he had too great a popular following to be forced immediately out of his position. In August 1862 he was placed in command of a newly formed flotilla on the James River, and subsequently he returned to the Caribbean in command of a squadron dedicated to capturing destructive Confederate commerce raiders such as the *Alabama* and the *Florida*. His failure to apprehend any enemy cruisers resulted in an acrimonious correspondence with the Navy Department, and in July 1863, Secretary Welles did what he should have done long before: he removed him from command of the squadron and from active duty.

The British, despite their bias toward the Confederacy, handled the *Trent* affair with great skill, giving the Lincoln administration time to adopt a face-saving formula for returning Mason and Slidell. Seward showed considerable courage in putting himself out in favor of an unpopular, but necessary, decision. In the end, the Lincoln administration compensated for Wilkes's bad judgment, with considerable assistance from London.

Notes

1. C. Vann Woodward, ed., *Mary Chesnut's Civil War*, 520.
2. Geoffrey S. Smith, "Charles Wilkes" (James C. Bradford, ed., *Captains of the Old Stream Navy*, Naval Institute Press, Annapolis, MD).
3. Ivan Musicant, *Divided Waters* (New York: HarperCollins, 1995), 112.
4. Ibid., 113–14.
5. Frank J. Merli, *Great Britain and the Confederate Navy* (Bloomington: Indiana University Press, 1970), 77–78.
6. Raphael Semmes, *Memoirs of Service Afloat During the War Between the States* (Baton Rouge: Louisiana State University Press, 1996), 515.
7. Allan Nevins, *The Improvised War* (New York, 1959), 390.
8. Ibid., 79.
9. John M. Taylor, *William Henry Seward* (Washington, DC: Brassey's, 1996), 183.
10. *Official Records (Navy)* Series II, vol. 2, 148–49.

8

Porter . . . Is the Best Man

WILLIAM N. STILL, JR.

On October 9, 1862, 49-year-old David Dixon Porter was chosen to command the Mississippi Squadron with the rank of acting rear admiral. Porter, only a lieutenant the year before, was passed over more than eighty officers—commanders, captains, and commodores—to become the second admiral in the United States Navy. Years later he wrote, "I was not a flag officer, with the title of Acting Rear Admiral. Let those laugh who win. I won in spite of many obstacles, and enjoyed my victory immensely." And to his mother he reflected, "How proud my old Father would be if he could see me an Admiral. Yet it gives me pain to be hoisted over the heads of those old veterans who have so long considered the Navy as belonging to them. It seems somewhat like the Justice of Providence who takes this method of mortifying them for their treatment of my Father."

His father was Commodore David Porter, one of the most controversial officers in the United States Navy, a man who was, as his biographer wrote, courageous, intelligent, and dedicated, and at the same time impulsive, hot-tempered, conceited, "sometimes vicious, and finally paranoiac." The younger Porter took after his father in many respects.

The third of ten children born to the Commodore and Evalina Anderson Porter, David Dixon was born in Chester, Pennsylvania, on June

8, 1813. His early years were spent in Chester and Washington, D.C. In 1826, after a controversy culminating in a court-martial, Commodore Porter resigned his commission and took service in the Mexican Navy. He took with him two of his sons, 10-year-old Thomas and 13-year-old David Dixon. Appointed a midshipman in the Mexican Navy, David Dixon saw his first combat service against the Spanish ships off Cuba. In an encounter with the Spanish frigate *Lealtad*, Porter's vessel, the *Guerrero*, was taken, and David Dixon spent several months as a prisoner in Havana. Upon returning to the United States, the 16-year-old veteran was appointed a midshipman in the United States Navy.

Porter's career in the years before the Civil War was varied. Tours of sea duty were followed by service in the Coast Survey and on board merchant vessels. He spent most of his time as a midshipman in the Mediterranean Squadron, where he gained the reputation of being undisciplined and a troublemaker. In 1836 he was posted to the Coast Survey and spent the next six years making hydrographic surveys along the Atlantic coast. In 1839, he married George Ann Patterson, the daughter of Commodore Daniel Patterson, whom he had met during one of his early cruises. He was promoted to lieutenant in 1841 and shortly afterward returned to active service in the Navy.

During the Mexican War, as first lieutenant and later captain of the small side-wheel steamer *Spitfire*, he participated in a number of engagements and gained recognition as a "brave and zealous officer." After the end of the war, Porter returned to the Coast Survey. He commanded the survey vessel *Petrel* while surveying Hell Gate and Buttermilk channels in New York Harbor. He then obtained a leave of absence from the Navy to command the merchant steamer *Panama*, and later the *Georgia* and an Australian steamer, the *Golden Age*. He became widely known as a captain of steamers that broke various speed records.

He returned to the Navy in 1855 and immediately undertook the most unusual assignment of his career. In command of the storeship *Supply*, he made two trips to the eastern Mediterranean to bring back camels for the Army to use as pack animals in the West. For the next three years he was first lieutenant at the Portsmouth, New Hampshire, Navy Yard. The duty was boring and Porter, a middle-aged lieutenant of 48 with more than thirty

The USS *Powhatan*, Porter's command early in the war. *(U.S. Naval Historical Center)*

years in the service, decided to resign and accept employment with the Pacific Mail Steamship Company. Fate, however, intervened; Porter was at his home in Washington, D.C., when the threatening Civil War demanded his services.

On April Fool's Day, 1861, Porter was ushered into the office of the newly inaugurated President, Abraham Lincoln. The occasion was Secretary of State William H. Seward's scheme to relieve Fort Pickens in Pensacola Harbor. Porter had discussed such an operation with Army Captain Montgomery C. Meigs, a member of a politically influential family, who had apparently approached Seward with such a proposal. Lincoln agreed to allow a secret expedition to be sent with Porter in command of the sloop-of-war *Powhatan* and Meigs in command of the relieving troops. Though it was clearly a naval operation, Secretary of the Navy Gideon Welles was not informed, and the two commanders even drew up their own orders. Later, Welles learned of the affair and persuaded the President to cancel the order. But it was too late. The order rescinding the operation was received by Porter shortly after the *Powhatan* had left the navy yard in New York City and was anchored off Staten Island. However, it was signed by Seward and his original orders by the President, so he ignored it. Although Porter was probably aware that he was disobeying orders, he was confident that when Fort Pickens was relieved—and he had no doubt about that—the order would be conveniently forgotten.

The *Powhatan's* arrival at Pensacola was something of an anticlimax. Fort Sumter had fallen while the sloop-of-war was steaming southward; Meigs had arrived with reinforcements for Fort Pickens before Porter arrived; and the cautious policy followed by the senior officers present effectively blocked Porter's eagerness to attack the Confederates in the city. After a frustrating six weeks, the *Powhatan* was ordered to blockade the Mississippi River.

Porter's initial success came as the *Powhatan* was under way for the Mississippi's mouth; a schooner was overhauled and seized as a prize. This was his only success for months, however. The *Powhatan* had too deep a draft to pass over the bar into the river, and there were simply too many passages for the Union force of two vessels to effectively guard. Among the Confederate vessels that successfully evaded the blockade was the *Sumter*, Raphael Semmes's small raider. A few weeks after Semmes's escape, Porter captured a vessel and uncovered information on the Sumter's whereabouts from captured documents. He immediately gave chase. Three months and 10,000 miles later he still had not caught up with the elusive raider. Early in November 1861 the *Powhatan*, badly in need of overhaul, arrived in New York and Porter, recently promoted to commander, left for Washington.

In his *Incidents and Anecdotes of the Civil War* Porter presents a highly colored and dramatic account of how he conceived the idea and developed the plan for the capture of New Orleans. He is, however, less than accurate in his presentation. The basic plan was conceived in the fertile mind of the Assistant Secretary of the Navy and Porter's friend, Gustavus V. Fox. Porter did contribute to the plan, however. Shortly after arriving in Washington, he was questioned by Welles and Fox about the approaches to New Orleans. His answers, supported by the assistant secretary's endorsements, persuaded Welles to outline the plan to him. Porter favored it and added the idea of a flotilla of mortar boats to bombard the forts below the city. He also warmly recommended Captain David G. Farragut as commander of the main fleet. Farragut (raised by Porter's father as a foster son) received the command, and Porter that of the flotilla.

By the middle of April 1862 Farragut's fleet, accompanied by Porter's mortar flotilla of twenty schooners and six shallow-draft gunboats, had passed the bar into the Mississippi River. On the 17th—Good Friday—the mortar schooners were in place and began the bombardment of the forts. For six days they kept up an almost continuous fire, each mortar firing every ten minutes and doing heavy damage to both forts. On April 24 Farragut's fleet, supported by fire from the mortar schooners, ran past the forts and ascended the river to receive the surrender of New Orleans. Porter, left in command of the lower river, demanded the surrender of the forts, but they did not capitulate until they were reduced practically to rubble by the mortars. Major General Benjamin F. Butler, in command of the troops on the expedition, disparaged Porter's claims that the forts were seriously damaged. Porter resented this, a resentment that would simmer and later explode into actual dislike.

After the United States flag was raised over the forts, a wearied but jubilant Porter wrote to Fox, "You may put the rebellion down as 'spavined,' 'broken-backed,' and 'wind-galled'. . . . It will take me ten years to rest and recover from the exhaustion caused by vexation of spirit, in the last year. My liver is completely turned upside down. . . . One more slap at the Rebels through Mobile and I will be satisfied."

He would get his "one more slap" and others as well, but not at Mobile. In preparation for such an operation, Porter early in May went to Mobile Bay to locate sites for the mortars and to buoy channels for Farragut's ships when they appeared. Although Pensacola was reoccupied, Farragut did not appear. Under orders from the Navy Department, Farragut had ascended the river as far as Vicksburg. In June Porter followed with his mortar schooners. While Farragut and Flag Officer Charles Davis, in command of the Union squadron that had come down the river, conferred on attacking the city, Porter's vessels rained shells on the Confederate bastion. On the night of July 9 Farragut received telegraphic orders to send Porter and twelve of his mortar schooners to Hampton Roads at once.

Porter arrived at Norfolk in late July, ill with fever and exhaustion. For two months he remained inactive. On September 22 he was called into Secretary Welles's office and there informed that he would relieve Davis in command of the Mississippi Squadron, with the rank of acting rear admiral. The appointment was a surprise. For Welles to select a junior commander over the heads of all the captains (more than eighty officers were over him) was unprecedented. Nor was Porter one of the secretary's favorites, having incurred his displeasure on more than one occasion. Porter was convinced that Lincoln had a hand in it, although it is more likely that Welles simply considered Porter the right man for the job.

Rear Admiral Porter relieved Davis at Cairo, Illinois, on October 15. The Mississippi Squadron at that time consisted of more than thirty vessels, the nucleus being the ten ironclads completed during the year. Before the fall of Vicksburg more than fifty additional vessels (ironclads, wooden gunboats, mortar boats, etc.) would be added, including the steamer *Blackhawk*, the future flagship.

Porter's primary responsibility was cooperation with the Army. The question was—which army? Before leaving Washington he was informed that Major General John A. McClernand, a political general, was to raise an army to cooperate with him on the Mississippi. After he arrived in the West, however, he discovered that Major General Ulysses S. Grant was already planning to move on Vicksburg. Porter was determined to participate. He did not trust the Army (i.e., West Pointers). He told Fox that Grant was trying to take Vicksburg without the Navy. But he found both Grant and William T. Sherman, who commanded part of Grant's army at Memphis, cooperative. While awaiting McClernand's arrival, Porter worked with Sherman in sending warships up the Yazoo River and in an attack on Arkansas Post.

In February 1863 Grant was in sole command of Union forces assembled to take Vicksburg and was once again above the city. Porter moved his squadron to within a few miles above the Confederate stronghold. During the following weeks the Mississippi Squadron cooperated in a number of expeditions designed to seal off Vicksburg.

While Porter was thus occupied above the city, Farragut once again ascended the river. Passing the batteries at Port Hudson, his vessels anchored below Vicksburg. However, his stay was short; after he left, Porter passed vessels below the city to assist Grant. Grant had moved his troops down the Louisiana side of the river and, under the protective umbrella of Porter's warships, crossed to the Mississippi side. While the army fought its way to

Vicksburg by way of Jackson, Porter's vessels continued patrolling the river above and below the city. On the 18th of May, Union forces reached the hills just north of the Confederate fortifications and the Siege of Vicksburg began. Porter's warships moved into position and bombarded the city until an armistice was signed on July 3. Porter's dispatch announcing the victory reached Washington on July 7—the first news of it. For his part in the campaign, Porter's rank of rear admiral was made permanent.

In August Porter's command was extended to New Orleans. However, outside of guerrilla activities there was little trouble in keeping the rivers opened. During the winter of 1863–64 Porter made preparations to cooperate with Major General Nathaniel P. Banks in an expedition up the Red River. Such an operation had been originally urged by Secretary of State Seward, who was concerned by Maximilian's imperial designs in Mexico. Texas needed to be occupied, and Banks was given this responsibility. It was decided that Shreveport, Louisiana, would be the first objective, followed by a drive into Texas.

By the beginning of March 1864 Porter had assembled a naval force of fifteen ironclads and four wooden gunboats at the mouth of the Red River. The warships were accompanied by transports bearing a corps from Sherman's army under then Brigadier General Andrew J. Smith. Alexandria was captured on the 16th by Porter's gunboats. Banks's troops arrived there ten days later. On April 2 the combined Union force started up the river—the troops along nearby roads while the gunboats passed through the rapids above the city with considerable difficulty. Porter was later criticized for sending his heaviest vessel, the *Eastport*, through first. She struck on the rocks, and nearly three days were lost while the sailors sweated and swore to free her. With several of his lighter, faster vessels, Porter passed through Grand Ecore—about halfway between Alexandria and Shreveport. A few days later they were coming back down the river. On April 8 Banks was beaten by a Confederate force near Pleasant Hill, Louisiana, and retreated rapidly toward the Mississippi.

With the river falling and under harassment by advancing Confederate troops, Porter's vessels slowly retired. He only narrowly avoided a disaster at Alexandria. There was only about four feet of water in the rapids, and the gunboats needed a minimum of seven to pass through. He and his vessels were saved by an engineering officer and former logger who commandeered more than 3,000 sailors and soldiers to construct a dam [see *Civil War Times Illustrated*, October 1975]. All of the vessels escaped but the *Eastport*. The retirement continued until they reached the river's mouth. Two months later Porter was ordered East.

Wilmington, North Carolina, was a port of enormous value to the Confederacy. With the capture of Norfolk early in 1862, it was the closest port of any size to Richmond and the Army of Northern Virginia. Although Union authorities recognized this, they could do little about it. Because of the peculiar geographical conditions along the North Carolina coast, it was almost impossible to successfully blockade the mouth of the Cape Fear River. In addition, the Confederate defenses were unusually strong. Fort Caswell guarded the southwest point to one entrance and Fort Fisher, considered by many to be the most powerful fort in the Confederacy, guarded the northeast point of the other. (There were two inlets separated by Smith's Island.) The only feasible way to seal off Wilmington was by an amphibious assault. Unfortunately, troops for such an assault were not available until the summer of 1864.

Farragut was the first choice for the naval command, but he declined it. "Porter is probably the best man," Welles wrote, "but his selection will cut Lee to the quick." Rear Admiral Samuel P. Lee was the commander of the North Atlantic Blockading Squadron whom Porter was ordered to relieve. Porter assumed command on October 10 and immediately began to assemble what was to be the most formidable fleet to be used during the war.

Grant assigned Major General Godfrey Weitzel to command the troops, but as North Carolina was a part of General Butler's department, Butler decided to accompany the expedition and in reality assume the command. The antipathy between Porter and Butler engendered during the New Orleans Campaign appeared again and lingered on for years.

The planned attack was delayed because the troops were slow in arriving and also because of a scheme by Butler to blow up Fort Fisher with a ship loaded with gunpowder. Although he would later deny it, Porter was enthusiastic about the project. On the night of December 23, 1864, the ex-warship *Louisiana* was loaded with over 200 tons of powder, run in close to the fort, and exploded. The explosion was spectacular but did no damage.

Admiral David D. Porter aboard one of his vessels. *(Library of Congress)*

For the next two days Porter's fleet bombarded the fort, firing more than 20,000 shells. Porter claimed that the fort suffered extensive damage, but in reality it suffered very little. He became furious when Butler refused (wisely) to attack with his troops. On the day after Christmas the troops were withdrawn and returned to Norfolk. Porter complained to Grant about Butler's action and requested that a second expedition be organized.

Grant agreed and assigned Major General Alfred H. Terry to the command. On January 12, 1865, Porter's fleet was again off Fort Fisher. Forty-four warships, including several ironclads that closed to within 700 yards of the fort, opened a devastating and deliberate fire on selected targets. On the 13th and 14th some 8,000 troops landed under the fire of Porter's guns. On Sunday the 15th, 2,000 sailors and Marines landed and attacked the seaward face of the fort while Terry's troops assaulted from the land. Although the seaward attack failed, it did draw attention away from Terry's assaulting columns. The fort fell after his troops broke into the fortifications. Within a few days Fort Caswell was captured and the river was closed.

Following Fort Fisher's capture, Porter's activities were confined primarily to the James and York rivers. During the last week in March, President and Mrs. Lincoln visited City Point on the James, which had become the headquarters and supply depot for the Army and Navy. Lincoln accepted a cabin on Porter's flagship, the *Malvern*, and they ascended the river to newly captured Richmond. After touring the former Confederate capital, Porter returned to City Point and was there when news was received of Lee's surrender at Appomattox.

Porter's career during the Civil War was spectacular. Unlike Farragut's, however, his spawned considerable controversy. Porter's rapid rise in rank probably made this inevitable, but his nature also contributed to it. He was ambitious and self-confident to the point that he irritated his seniors and many of his contemporaries. One newspaper correspondent wrote that he was "vain, arrogant and egotistical to an extent that can neither be described nor exaggerated." He was politically minded and was the most publicity-conscious naval officer during the war. He had no compunction about undercutting his fellow naval officers, including Farragut. He clearly was jealous of his "adopted half-brother" and on one occasion tried to persuade the Navy Department to retire him because of age. Secretary Welles recorded in his diary that "I did not always consider David to be depended upon if he had an end to attain, and he had no hesitation in trampling down a brother officer if it would benefit him." The secretary also wrote that Porter "is impressed with and boastful of his own powers, given to exaggeration in everything relating to himself."

Yet the perceptive Welles recognized under the pretentiousness a man who combined daring with "great energy, great activity and abundant resources." Porter was intelligent, enterprising, and an extremely competent, if not brilliant, officer. Junior officers universally admired him, many of them considering him to be the most capable officer in the Navy—not excepting Farragut.

Porter's relationship with army officers was mixed. He disliked political generals such as Banks and Butler but got along well with Grant and Sherman. Grant admired him and in his *Memoirs* compared him to Lord Nelson. Porter was chagrined that Grant gave the Army more credit than the Navy for certain operations, yet he was by far the most successful officer in the Union Navy in joint operations with the Army. John Milligan writes in *Gunboats Down the Mississippi* that during the Vicksburg Campaign "Porter was largely responsible for . . . harmony," and Bern Anderson in *By Sea and By River* said that the capture of Fort Fisher was one of the "best co-ordinated and conducted joint operations of the war."

The most widespread criticism of Porter during and after the war concerned his hunger for prize money, particularly contraband cotton. During the Red River Campaign thousands of bales were seized, branded with painted letters "U.S.N.," and loaded on gunboats for shipment to prize courts. Confederates bestowed on Porter the nom de guerre "Thief of the Mississippi," and he even had to assure his mother that his cabin was not, as she had heard, "full of silver taken from the plantations." Although there can be no question that Porter, in the words of one authority, "seldom . . . overlooked a bale of cotton," it was legitimate booty. Even Welles with his New England conscience defended him.

Nevertheless, Porter was extravagant both professionally and personally. He certainly retained the amenities of life while on active service. His pantry was always well stocked. His meals were popular and sought after even by hard campaigners such as Grant and Sherman. On his flagship *Blackhawk*, Porter carried a cow, several hunting dogs, a number of saddle horses, and a buggy. Every day after dinner he expected his guests to join him in a ride— the buggy was for those who preferred driving to riding.

Porter's star continued its rise after the Civil War. He spent four years as superintendent of the Naval Academy, and in 1869 President Grant installed him in the Navy Department as the "advisor" to Secretary Adolph Borie. In reality he ran the department for more than a year. In 1866 he had been promoted to vice admiral, and upon the death of Farragut in 1870 he inherited the fourth star of an admiral. Although he would remain the highest ranking officer in the Navy, he had little actual power for the last twenty years of his life. He was subordinated to the bureau chiefs, seldom entered the department, and spent most of his official time inspecting ships and yards. He bitterly resented this anomalous position. During these years he spent much of his leisure time in writing. Though most of his parables and poems were never printed, his historical works and a number of novels were published. Porter died in 1891 and was buried in Arlington Cemetery.

9

At Semmes's Hand

Norman C. Delaney

One of the best known Civil War naval engagements is the contest between CSS *Alabama* and USS *Kearsarge* off Cherbourg, France, June 19, 1864. Every Civil War enthusiast knows the outcome of that encounter—the end of the famous Confederate raider. Less well known, however, is the fact that the *Alabama* encountered, fought, and defeated a Federal warship, USS *Hatteras,* in open ocean 17 months earlier. Although the *Hatteras* was not an equal of the powerful *Kearsarge,* neither was she the customary prey of Confederate Commander (later Captain) Raphael Semmes, who prowled the seas in search of unarmed Northern merchant ships. The men of the *Hatteras* fought well with what they had—and lost.

One hundred and sixteen years after her sinking, the *Hatteras* is again making news. Dr. Paul Cloutier, Professor of Space Physics and Astronomy at Rice University, located the vessel in 1976, 20 miles off Galveston, Texas, using a magnetometer of his own invention. Items already salvaged from the *Hatteras* provide a fascinating glimpse of a Civil War blockader.

On January 11, 1863, five vessels of a Federal squadron stood several miles outside Confederate-held Galveston. The sea was calm and visibility good when, at about 3 p.m., Lieutenant Commander Homer C. Blake, commanding the steamer *Hatteras,* received a signal from the flagship *Brook-*

lyn: "An unidentified vessel has been sighted." Blake ordered that the *Hatteras* build up steam and head southeast. When a sail was finally sighted, Executive Officer Henry O. Porter was the first to voice his suspicions. He said to Blake, "That, sir, I think is the *Alabama.*" Porter's belief was well founded. Since her launching in August 1862, the *Alabama* had already gained a reputation as a notorious raider by taking twenty-six prizes. Her commander, Raphael Semmes, was well known for audacity and unpredictability. On December 7 he had captured the mail steamer *Ariel* in the Windward Passage between Cuba and Santo Domingo. It was logical, therefore, to assume that the *Alabama* might turn up in the Gulf of Mexico. "What shall we do?" Porter asked. Blake's answer was decisive: "If that is the *Alabama* we must fight her." He signaled to the *Brooklyn,* "The vessel is suspicious," then prepared to give chase.

For more than three hours the *Hatteras* steamed in pursuit. Finally, the stranger disappeared from sight and for a time seemed to have eluded them. But, reappearing, she suddenly seemed to reverse the chase. Now the stranger was approaching the *Hatteras.* This maneuver seemed ominous because the *Hatteras* was by this time about 20 miles from the Federal fleet and entirely out of its sight. It was about 6:30 p.m. and midwinter darkness was quickly closing in as the two vessels reached hailing distance, approximately 50 yards apart. After cutting his ship's engine, Blake shouted, "What ship are you?" and received an answering shout, "Her Britannic Majesty's Ship *Petrel!*" He failed to catch the name of the ship. From the stranger came the question, "What steamer is that?" and Blake identified the *Hatteras.* Still wary, Blake then called out that he was sending a boat over. A gig with five men aboard was lowered, but as they shoved away from the *Hatteras* the stranger suddenly began moving closer. A voice boomed out of the darkness, "This is the Confederate States Steamer *Alabama!*—Fire!"

Homer C. Blake, a 40-year-old New Yorker, had assumed command of the *Hatteras* only two months earlier, in November 1862. It was his first command. The iron side-wheel steamer, 1,126 tons and 210 feet long, appeared to be a lucky ship. Under her previous commander, George F. Emmons, she had captured fourteen blockade runners, half at Cedar Keys, Florida, and the other half off Mobile, Alabama. One of her prizes, the small pilot boat *Poody,* was renamed *Hatteras, Jr.* and converted into a blockader.

Commander Homer C. Blake, who had the misfortune of encountering the *Alabama* with an inferior vessel, the paddlewheel steamer USS *Hatteras*. *(From* Harper's Pictorial History of the Great Rebellion*)*

But in spite of her excellent record, the *Hatteras* had severe limitations. Built in 1861, she had served as the passenger ship *St. Mary* on the Delaware River before being purchased by the United States Government for conversion to a warship. Her engines, although in good condition, remained unprotected, and her boilers were only partially shielded by a coal bunker on both sides. Although equipped with fore and aft sails and a jib, she was nevertheless unsuited for sailing. Her sails were useful only to keep her steady. Also, she was lightly armed: four 32-pounders, two 30-pounders, one 20-pounder, and one 12-pound howitzer. But when Blake took command, her most serious deficiency was her slowness. The accumulation of barnacles on her hull cut her normal speed of 13 knots in half.

In December, Blake was ordered to bring the *Hatteras* from Mobile to New Orleans for repairs and a thorough cleaning of her hull. He had just arrived at New Orleans when news came of the capture of Galveston by Confederate forces. Blake was ordered immediately to join the Federal squadron. There was no time to clean the hull. With a crew of 107 men and 16 officers, the *Hatteras* joined Commodore Henry H. Bell's squadron, which was engaged in shelling Galveston. However, since the *Hatteras* lacked long-range guns, Blake brought her to a position about half a mile from the flagship. The 3,000-ton, heavily armed *Brooklyn* was indeed a formidable ship, but the futile shelling of Galveston ceased soon after the *Hatteras* arrived. Of the squadron, the gunboat *New London* was, like the *Hatteras,* lightly armed. The 900-ton *Clifton* was a slow side-wheel steamer like the *Hatteras,* while the 324-ton *Sciota* had been intended to serve as a sunken harbor obstruction.

Immediately following the shout, "Fire!" from the *Alabama,* a shell passed directly over the *Hatteras.* The *Alabama*'s other guns then opened up a "tremendous volley" which could be heard aboard the ships of the Federal squadron. The men on the *Hatteras* were already at their guns as Porter sang out, *"Alabama,* boys, now give it to her!" Blake put his helm to starboard and had the gong sounded for full steam. Although he tried to close in for boarding, the *Alabama*'s superior speed prevented him from doing so. However, the two ships were close enough for musket and pistol fire to be exchanged between them. The air resounded with the pounding of shot against the iron hull of the *Hatteras.* Standing on the hurricane deck near the wheel, Blake was unable to see his men, but he could hear shouts of encouragement from his forward division: "Give it to her, boys!" "Stand by the captain!" "Don't give her up!"

Not all the officers and crew stood at their posts, however. Unseen by Blake, one officer threw himself flat on the deck after the second broadside. The captain of the forecastle, standing only six feet away, was unable to recognize the man in the darkness but could discern the gold band on his cap. He lunged at the officer, kicking and cursing him until the man sprang to his feet and ran aft. The sailor fired a shot from his revolver in the direction he took.

Elsewhere, several sailors, believing themselves to be severely wounded, rushed to the sick bay where they fell on the deck groaning. Surgeon Edward Matthews noted that their injuries were "mere scratches" and shouted that they were all right and must return to their posts. Astonished, the men responded, "We will!" and went without protest. Although the surgeon thought that these men had truly believed themselves to be seriously wounded, there were cases of panic among a few others. Ensign John Butman struck several skulkers with the flat of his sword and shouted at them to return to their posts. But most of the men were at their stations. Even the ship's paymaster, Henry Conkling, was busy passing shell to the men of one division. A Confederate officer aboard the *Alabama* later described the action:

> Twas a grand though dreadful sight to see the guns belching forth, in the darkness of the night, sheets of living flame, the deadly missiles striking the enemy with a force that we could feel. Then, when the shells struck her side, and especially the percussion ones, her whole side was lit up and showing rents of five or six feet in length.

Although numerous shot and shell from the *Alabama* were striking the *Hatteras,* the most devastating were 110-pounder shells fired from the Confederate vessel's Blakely pivot gun. One of these entered the *Hatteras* just above her water line and tore into the sick bay, shattering bottles of turpentine. Another shell struck the walking beam, moving the engine out of line and causing it to vibrate so badly that it became increasingly unmanageable. As he hurried to the engine room, Porter observed entire plates knocked off their port side and portions of the paddle wheel driven into the hull. But even more serious, another shot hit the steam chest and cylinder, completely disabling the engine. The resulting steam became so thick that the engineers were forced to evacuate the engine room. When the steam had cleared somewhat, Engineer Abraham Covert returned to inspect the damage and found that he could no longer manage the steam. He raised the safety valve to let the pressure off the boiler. He then discovered that plates had been knocked off of the *Hatteras* at water level, and he tried unsuccessfully to plug one of these holes with hammocks.

Back on deck, Covert admitted to Porter, "We are pretty near played out, I think." Then came cries of "Fire! Fire!" The spilled turpentine had ignited, and flames were spreading to the port bunkers and foreholds. It was dangerously close to the ship's magazine. Porter made a futile attempt to go below deck, burning his shoes in the effort. He reported to Blake that the fire was out of control and that he had put the hatches on. Blake then ordered Porter to drown the magazine quickly. Since this was above the water line, it could be flooded only by pumping, and several men managed to pump in two feet of water.

Whatever they did made no difference in the fate of the *Hatteras.* Blake could hear water rushing in and feel her listing to port. Realizing the hopelessness of his situation, he concentrated on saving lives. Already, two men—a fireman and a coal heaver—had been killed in the coal bunker. Blake ordered Porter to fire a lee gun as a surrender signal. When there was no acknowledgment, a second and finally a third distress signal were given. After Blake's third signal, the *Alabama* ceased firing and passed out of sight. Turning to his captain with a look of astonishment, Porter asked, "Is it possible that that fellow is going to leave us in this way?" Equally alarmed, Blake replied, "I don't know!"

By this time the ship was listing to port so badly that Porter had the entire battery on that side pushed overboard, causing the vessel to right herself. Meanwhile, all hands were preparing to abandon ship. The wounded men had been brought on deck, and the officers were stationed at each of the boats. Then, a voice from the *Alabama* hailed them, offering assistance. Blake replied immediately and had his five wounded men placed in the first boat to leave the *Hatteras*. Three *Hatteras* boats and three sent from the *Alabama* made several trips before all the Federals were brought aboard the *Alabama*. Blake and Porter, the last to leave, attempted to go below for a final check but were driven back by smoke from the raging fire. Before leaving his sinking ship, Blake threw overboard his heavily weighted signal book and watched it sink quickly in nine fathoms. About 40 minutes had elapsed from the firing of the first lee gun to the removal of all survivors from the *Hatteras* to the *Alabama*. The action itself had lasted only about 13 minutes.

Stepping aboard the *Alabama*, Blake, highly mortified, surrendered his sword to Confederate Commander Raphael Semmes. Semmes smacked his lips with delight at his victory. His own ship had suffered no permanent damage, and only one of his seamen had been slightly wounded. The crew of the *Hatteras,* now prisoners, were placed in irons, but not the officers. After learning that all would be released if they signed a parole, Blake and his officers did so, rationalizing that this would be the quickest way to get back into service again. Once the sailors were released from their irons, all were well treated, and the wounded were given prompt attention. The crew of the *Alabama* gave up their places on the berth deck to their prisoners, while the Federal officers were accommodated, according to rank, in the wardroom and steerage. Semmes gave up his own quarters to Blake.

Early the next morning, as Blake came on deck, he recognized Executive Officer John McIntosh Kell of Georgia. Saluting Kell, he remarked, "How do you do, Mr. Kell? Fortune favors the brave, sir." Thanking Blake, Kell added, "We take advantage of all fortune's favors." The officers of the *Alabama* had, indeed, been fortunate. The damage to their ship could be quickly repaired, and—although one shell from the *Hatteras* had come close to wiping out an entire gun crew—the one casualty aboard the *Alabama* was only slightly wounded by a shell fragment.

As Semmes hastened to reach Jamaica to discharge his prisoners, several *Hatteras* seamen asked the Confederate officers whether they could enlist aboard her. Lieutenant Kell refused their requests, suspecting that they were motivated solely by their desire for the twice-daily grog ration. The custom had recently been discontinued in the United States Navy.

Although most of the Federal officers felt the sting of defeat, Paymaster Conkling took the recent events in a jocular vein. As he entered the *Alabama's* wardroom soon after coming aboard, he exclaimed, "Well, boys, I'll be damned if we hadn't a cast iron atmosphere in our engine room! I was stationed there, and shell after shell exploded until the air smelt of iron fragments!" The Federals were annoyed that Conkling's remarks obviously amused and pleased the Confederates. He complained that he was tired of a war that was almost "played out." But Surgeon Matthews, although disgusted with Conkling, felt that his remarks were more the result of a "weak intellect than practical disloyalty."

On January 21 the *Alabama* arrived at Port Royal, Jamaica, and Blake was allowed to go ashore to arrange for the disposition of his men. Back in the United States, a naval court of inquiry concluded that Blake had acted "in an efficient and praiseworthy manner" during the fight and that his conduct afterward was both "commendable and proper." Only one officer—Conkling—and one sailor were judged to have conducted themselves improperly either while aboard the *Alabama* or later after being released at Jamaica.

For the rest of the war Blake commanded the steamer *Utah* and participated in naval operations off Malvern Hill and Trent Reach, Virginia. Promotion was slow in coming, and Blake was not promoted to commander until 1866. He became a captain in 1871, after his participation in the Korea

Expedition, and had just been promoted to Commodore at the time of his death in 1880.

For Raphael Semmes and the other officers of the *Alabama*, the sinking of the *Hatteras* was the high point of their 22-month cruise. Semmes's orders were to avoid engagements with enemy warships, and he undertook this fight only because he felt so strongly that he could win. His success in so easily sinking the *Hatteras* undoubtedly influenced his decision to fight the *Kearsarge* off Cherbourg, France, 17 months later. The victory off Galveston greatly strengthened both the confidence of Semmes and the reputation of the *Alabama*.

To veteran naval officer Rear Admiral David D. Porter, the lesson of the *Hatteras-Alabama* encounter was simple: "Never send a boy on a man's errand. Had Commodore Bell sent two gun-boats instead of one, the 'No. 290' or 'Alabama' would probably have ended then and there." But Porter forgot that the *Alabama* could make up to 13 knots and that Semmes would probably have avoided a fight with two adversaries. Nor would he have taken on a ship with the armament of the *Brooklyn*.

The *Hatteras-Alabama* engagement was a naval first—the first time a steam warship had been sunk by another steam warship. The battle indeed represents a dramatic episode in American naval history.

10

....

A Naval Sieve:
The Union Blockade
in the Civil War

WILLIAM N. STILL, JR.

A navy imposes a blockade in order to isolate the enemy, or some part of his territory, from the rest of the world. In most wars the side with the stronger fleet tries to blockade the other side. Thus, the British Navy has blockaded, among others, France, the United States, Germany, and most recently the Argentine forces in the Falkland Islands. The United States Navy has blockaded Mexico, the Confederacy, the Spanish forces in Cuba, Japan, and, briefly, North Vietnam.

Blockade has been hailed by those who have used it, or wish to employ it anew for some current conflict; it has been reviled by its victims. When we look at its results we find that it has been useful. However, it has not always had the influence with which it is often credited. The American Civil War in 1861–1865 is a good example.

Historians generally agree that the Union navy's major task in the Civil War was the establishment and maintenance of the blockade. This was determined on 19 April 1861, when President Abraham Lincoln proclaimed a naval blockade against the seceded states. His navy's secondary tasks included the protection of American foreign commerce and the support of land operations. Both the blockade and support of land operations would necessitate combined operations, including amphibious operations, against the Confederate states. In his first annual report, for 1861, the Union Secretary of the Navy, Gideon Welles, listed these tasks:

1. The closing of all the insurgent ports along a coast of nearly three thousand miles, in the form and under the exacting regulations of an international blockade, including the naval occupation and defense of the Potomac River. . . .
2. The organization of combined naval and military expeditions to operate in force against various points of the southern coast, rendering efficient naval cooperation with the position and movements of such expeditions when landed, and including also all needful naval aid to the army in cutting intercommunication with the rebels and in its operations on the Mississippi and its tributaries; and
3. The active pursuit of the piratical cruisers which might escape the vigilance of the blockading force. . . .

These tasks determined Union naval strategy for the war.

Although this strategy is obvious, the results of it are not so clear. In fact, historians continue to debate the Union navy's effectiveness in the war. This has been particularly true of the blockade. What makes this issue highly significant is the emphasis placed on the blockade. An impressive number of historians consider it a major factor in the Confederacy's ultimate collapse. They hold that the ever-tightening blockade strangled both the import of vital war material and essential necessities of life from Europe, and the export of cotton, the Confederacy's most acceptable collateral to European ports; that is, the blockade was instrumental in stimulating the economic chaos that ultimately shattered the Confederacy's will to fight as well as its means. For example, E. Merton Coulter in *The Confederate States of America 1861–1865* wrote, "Without a doubt the blockade was one of the outstanding causes of the strangulation and ultimate collapse of the Confederacy," and Rear Admiral Bern Anderson in what is probably the best one-volume naval history of the war, stated, "Without the relentless pressure of Union sea power economic disintegration could not have been achieved. The blockade was the active instrument of that sea power, and it was one of the major factors that brought about the ultimate collapse and defeat of the South."[1]

Charles P. Roland wrote that "The silent grip of the Federal navy grew tighter and the number of captures among blockade-runners steadily mounted. Still more significant, Southern ports were avoided altogether by the major cargo vessels of the world. By 1864 the blockade was strangling the Southern economy."[2]

Roland's statement implied that the Union navy expanded until it was powerful enough to close the 189 inlets and river mouths scattered along the more than 3,000 miles of Southern coastline as well as provide support for operations on the Mississippi River and its tributaries. From approximately 90 warships in 1861, the navy expanded to more than 700 by April 1865.

James R. Soley, one of the first writers to accentuate the Union navy's role in defeating the Confederacy through the blockade, wrote that "The number of prizes brought in during the war was 1,149 of which 210 were steamers. There were also 355 vessels burned, sunk, driven on shore, or otherwise destroyed, of which 85 were steamers; making a total of 1,504 vessels of all classes. . . . Of the property afloat, destroyed or captured during the Civil War, the larger part suffered in consequence of the blockade."[3]

There can be no question concerning the economic exhaustion within the Confederate states. A host of writers have graphically described it: the sufferings and hardships of civilians and soldiers; the impact it had on both the means and the will to continue the struggle. Students of the war overwhelmingly agree that this economic collapse was a major factor in Confederate defeat. The question is, however, the role that the Union blockade played in the collapse. Was it a principal reason as Anderson, Coulter, Soley, and others have suggested? There is considerable evidence that it was not. If the blockade was not a major factor in the Confederacy's economic exhaustion, why not? This certainly was the objective of the blockade. Was it because the blockade was ineffective and, as Frank L. Owsley wrote, a "leaky and ramshackled affair?"

Some fifty years ago, Owsley's monumental study *King Cotton Diplomacy* was published. In a chapter entitled, "The Effectiveness of the Blockade," Owsley evaluated the Union blockade in terms of numbers of violations along with the increase in Confederate cotton exports and the successful delivery of huge amounts of cargoes to the South. For example, in the last four months of 1864, more than 90 percent of the cotton shipped out of the Confederacy managed to get through the blockade. More than 80 percent of the ships carrying munitions to the Confederacy in 1862–1864 reached their destinations.[4]

Owsley's conclusions concerning the blockade were not generally accepted by historians, but in later years other studies appeared that substantiated his work. By far Marcus W. Price's series of articles published in *American Neptune* have been the most important. In an article entitled "Ships That Tested the Blockade of the Carolina Ports, 1861–1865," he estimated that out of 2,054 attempts to run past the blockading vessels off Wilmington, North Carolina, 1,735 succeeded. They amounted to an average of 1.5 attempts per day with 84 percent of them getting through. In a second article he analyzed the blockade off the Gulf ports. Between 20 April 1861 and 4 June 1865, according to his calculations, 2,960 vessels attempted to slip through the blockade, a daily average of two. As with the Carolina ports, in 1861 very few vessels were taken. But in 1862 and 1863, the blockade was tightened. During that period the percentage of successful runs into and out of these ports was 65 percent and 62 percent respectively. He attributes the lower percentage of successful runs to the larger number of sailing vessels used in the Gulf. In 1864 and 1865, however, the picture changed dramatically, particularly in steam-propelled vessels challenging the blockade. Eighty-seven percent in 1864 and 94 percent in 1865 of vessels that challenged the Gulf blockade got through. Although there is reason to believe that Price exaggerated his statistics on successful runs by including so-called violations that were not, he nevertheless clearly suggests that the blockade was quite porous.[5] It certainly was off Wilmington, North Carolina, which became the most important port in the Confederacy for blockade running. One recent student estimates that 230 runners entered the port in 1863–64, and 15 more slipped in before the port was taken early in 1865.[6]

Frank Vandiver in several of his books recognized the ineffectiveness of the blockade. In a study of blockade running through Bermuda which was published in 1947, he wrote, "It must be apparent that the blockade was, from the Union point of view, far from a completely effective measure . . . it is not too much to say . . . that the amount of supplies which did arrive through the blockade enabled the Confederate armies and people to carry on appreciably longer than would otherwise have been possible."

Over thirty years later he remained convinced of this: "The task of sealing off the South with its vast coastline was super-human; not even the Federal navy could meet the challenge."[7] A recently published study by Richard L. Lester, a British historian, agrees substantially with Vandiver.[8]

Because the blockade was the major Union naval strategy, it has been assumed by many historians that the major strategy of the Confederate navy was to destroy the blockade. As Anderson wrote, the Union blockade "automatically made attempts to thwart that blockade the primary task of the Confederate Navy."[9] This was not true. From the beginning Stephen Mallory, the Confederate Secretary of the Navy, viewed defending the harbors and rivers as his navy's major responsibility. This, of course, fits in well with Jefferson Davis' overall strategy of defense.

It is true that Mallory wanted to challenge the blockade. A principal reason for the assault on Union shipping by cruisers such as the *Alabama* and *Florida* was to force the Federal navy to weaken the blockade by drawing off ships to protect Northern shipping. Also early in the war the Secretary ordered the construction of armored vessels both at home and abroad to attack blockaders.

Neither idea was successful. The Union navy did not weaken its blockade despite losses among Union merchant ships, and only one of the armored ships built in Europe, the *Stonewall,* actually reached Confederate hands. She was too late to have even challenged the blockade. Mallory also tried to build five large ironclads within the Confederacy capable of going to sea, but of these only the *Arkansas* and the *Virginia* were completed, and they were not seaworthy.[10]

Historians in general consider the Confederate naval effort a failure. This is particularly true of the ironclad program. They base this on the erroneous assumptions that the ironclads were built to challenge the blockade and that only a few were commissioned. Out of approximately fifty armored vessels laid down within the Confederate states, twenty-two were completed and placed in operation. With the exception of the five initial vessels, the ironclads were built as harbor and river defense vessels.[11]

Confederate officials wrote surprisingly little about the blockade in their official correspondence. Much of what was written concerned the international implications of the blockade rather than the blockade itself or its effects. President Davis had little interest in naval affairs and generally left them in the capable hands of Secretary Mallory. His few references to the blockade indicate concern from an international point of view; that it was a paper blockade, clearly illegal and should be ignored by other nations.[12]

In January 1865, Davis issued one of his few directives concerning naval operations when he ordered the Confederate naval squadron at Charleston to attack Union forces off the harbor; not, however, because of the blockade, but in order to prevent if possible a link-up between the warships and the approaching army of Major General William T. Sherman.[13] Even Mallory in his reports and correspondence rarely mentions the blockade. This suggests that many Confederate officials did not consider the blockade to be very effective or a serious threat to the Confederacy. This does not mean to say that they ignored the existence of the blockade; but from their vantage point it was never damaging enough to require a change in strategy. It is often asserted that Confederate officials ignored it during the early months of the war, but as its effectiveness increased, they became more concerned. In fact the blockade was being broken more frequently in 1864–65 than at any time previously and Confederate officials were aware of this.[14]

A major factor in explaining their attitude was the industrial revolution experienced by the Confederate states. In order to have a chance to win, the Confederacy had to industrialize. This transformation from an agrarian to an industrial economy has never been completely told, but in recent years several writers have examined aspects of it. Vandiver in his biography of Josiah Gorgas, Confederate ordnance chief, recounts his success in developing an arms industry. Goff does the same with the quartermaster stores, while Still tells of the creation of a naval shipbuilding industry. Although self-sufficiency was not obtained, the Confederacy made extraordinary progress. As Raimondo Luraghi wrote, "Never before in history had anything like this been seen. A backward agricultural country, with only small preindustrial plants, had created a gigantic industry, investing millions of dollars, arming and supplying one of the largest armies in the world. . . . "[15]

This does not mean to say that supplies from abroad were not vital—they were. What it does say, however, is that the economic collapse of the Confederacy cannot be blamed on the blockade, but on its internal problems, primarily the breakdown in transportation and inadequate manpower resources.

Although the Confederate government would nationalize industry, it generally allowed blockade running free rein until early 1864. Even when it finally established trade regulations on blockade running, it only required ships to reserve one-half of their cargo for government shipments. During the first years of the war the evidence strongly suggests that, to those involved in the blockade-running business, what sold well was far more important than the needs of the war effort. As late as November 1864, only a few months before the final collapse, a Wilmington, North Carolina, firm was writing to its agent in Nassau not to send any more chloroform as it was too hard to sell. The firm requested perfume, "Essence of Cognac," as it would sell "quite high."[16] Cargo manifests found in port newspapers and elsewhere suggest that this was not an isolated incident.

In describing efforts by the Union navy to enforce the blockade, historians usually emphasize the numerical increase in warships on blockade duty during the course of the war, suggesting that at some point there were enough ships on station in Southern waters to retard blockade running significantly. The evidence does not substantiate this. One recent study points out that although the number of blockaders on the Wilmington station steadily increased, the number of blockade runners captured or destroyed remained approximately the same.[17] Squadron commanders were constantly appealing for additional vessels. Because of the shortage of vessels for both blockade duty and combined operations, vessels had to be shifted from one point to another. Although this was a normal naval procedure, it did affect the blockade's efficiency. This would frequently result in a noticeable increase in shipping activities at the port from which blockaders were withdrawn.[18]

Union squadron commanders encountered extremely difficult logistical problems in their efforts to enforce a tight blockade. The use of steam-powered vessels theoretically helped the efficiency of a blockade, but this was largely offset by problems of maintenance and supply. As early as 1862 the four blockade squadrons required approximately 3,000 tons of coal per week, and the amount needed grew as the number of blockaders increased.[19]

Robert Browning's recent study of the blockade off Wilmington, North Carolina, clearly demonstrates that the naval force on that station, by 1863 considered the most important, was frequently and seriously weakened by the inefficiency of the vessels deployed there. Many of them were too slow or were poor sea boats. A large number were converted vessels, without the qualities necessary to operate at sea for long periods. Carrying heavy guns, for which they were not designed, in numerous cases had a detrimental effect on their performance. Breakdowns in machinery were all too often normal occurrences resulting in vessels having to leave their station for repairs without being replaced. Browning suggests that repairs kept from one-third to two-fifths of the vessels constantly away from the station. At one time ten vessels from the Wilmington station were in the yards undergoing repairs.[20]

Although the blockaders replenished some provisions and supplies while on station, coal and ordnance stores usually could be obtained only by leaving the station. Beaufort, North Carolina; Port Royal, South Carolina; and Pensacola, Florida, became the most important supply depots for the various squadrons in the Atlantic and the Gulf. Even the depots were frequently short of coal, resulting in delays for vessels returning to their station. The coal shortage also affected their readiness while on station. In September 1863, Rear Admiral Samuel P. Lee, in command of the North Atlantic Blockading Squadron, wrote to the force commander off Wilmington: "You may find it expedient not to keep more than one of the little vessels in moving about at a time, even at night."[21] If logistical problems and vessel inefficiency were the same throughout all the blockading squadrons, and they probably were, the effectiveness of the blockade was seriously affected.

How effective was the Union blockade? It would be an oversimplification to say that it was either effective or not effective. It was both. In general, its effectiveness increased as the war progressed. Nevertheless, no Confederate port was completely closed until it was captured by Union forces.

Perhaps a more important question would be what effect did the blockade have on the war's ultimate outcome? Was it an important factor, as various writers say, in Confederate defeat? In this case, the answer is no. It was not a major factor in the collapse of the Confederacy.

Obviously, imports could at best provide the Confederates with only a small percentage of the material they needed to fight the war. In fact, a substantial percentage of the imports consisted not of war materials, but of clothes, liquors, and other items that would bring high profits. In order to fight, the Confederacy had to industrialize and did so. There was never a serious shortage of guns, munitions, and other war material. In fact, no Confederate army lost a major engagement because of the lack of essential supplies and arms.

The Union navy might well have contributed more to victory by concentrating on combined operations along the seaboard and the inland rivers. The blockade absorbed hundreds of ships and thousands of men, and generally had little effect on the war's outcome.

Notes

This chapter first appeared in the May/June edition of *Naval War College Review*.

1. E. Merton Coulter, *The Confederate States of America 1861–1865* (Baton Rouge: Louisiana State University Press, 1950), p. 294; Bern Anderson, *By Sea and By River* (New York: Knopf, 1962), p. 232.

2. Charles P. Roland, *The Confederacy* (Chicago: University of Chicago Press, 1960), p. 137.

3. J. Russell Soley, *The Blockade and the Cruisers* (New York: Scribner, 1890), pp. 44–45.

4. Frank L. Owsley and Harriet C. Owsley, *King Cotton Diplomacy: Foreign Relations of the Confederate States of America* (Chicago: University of Chicago Press, 2nd ed., 1959), pp. 229–267, 392.

5. Marcus W. Price, "Ships That Tested the Blockade of the Carolina Ports, 1861–1865," *American Neptune,* July 1948, pp. 196–241; "Ships That Tested the Blockade of the Gulf Ports, 1861–1865," ibid., October 1951, pp. 262–297; "Ships That Tested the Blockade of the Georgia and East Florida Ports, 1861–1865," ibid., April 1955, pp. 97–132.

6. Richard E. Wood, "Port Town at War: Wilmington, North Carolina 1860–1865," Ph.D. dissertation, Florida State University, 1976, pp. 183–184.

7. Frank E. Vandiver, ed., *Confederate Blockade-Running through Bermuda, 1861–1865: Letters and Cargo Manifests* (Austin: University of Texas Press, 1947), p. xli; Vandiver, *Their Tattered Flags: The Epic of the Confederacy* (New York: Harper and Row, 1970), pp. 233–234.

8. Both Lester and Richard Goff say, however, that the war might have been won by the Confederacy if the blockade had been destroyed. They imply that the Confederates were unable to create a naval force powerful enough to challenge Union sea power and break the blockade. In fact, the Confederate government never gave priority to challenging the Union blockade. Richard I. Lester, *Confederate Finance and Purchasing in Great Britain* (Charlottesville: University Press of Virginia, 1976), pp. 49, 165, 168, 177, 197, 199; Richard D. Goff, *Confederate Supply* (Durham, N.C.: Duke University Press, 1969), p. 139.
9. Anderson, p. 288.
10. William N. Still, Jr., *Iron Afloat: The Story of the Confederate Armorclads* (Nashville: Vanderbilt University Press, 1971), passim.
11. For the Confederate ironclad program, see ibid.
12. Dunbar Rowland, ed., *Jefferson Davis, Constitutionalist: His Letters, Papers, and Speeches* (10 vols., Jackson, Miss.: Little & Ives Company, 1923), v. V, p. 405.
13. Davis to Tucker, 15 January 1865, *Official Records of the Union and Confederate Navies in the War of the Rebellion* (31 vols., Washington: US Govt. Print. Off., 1894–1927), Series I, Vol. XLVII, Pt. 2, p. 1014.
14. Raimondo Luraghi, *The Rise and Fall of the Plantation South* (New York: New Viewpoints, 1978), p. 136; Goff, pp. 145, 247.
15. Luraghi, p. 128.
16. Wood, p. 178.
17. Robert Browning, "The Blockade of Wilmington, North Carolina: 1861–1865," MA thesis, East Carolina University, 1980, pp. 176–177.
18. Goff, p. 141.
19. Robert E. Johnson, "Investment by Sea: The Civil War Blockade," *American Neptune*, January 1972, pp. 53–54.
20. Browning, pp. 58–59.
21. Lee to Ludlow Case, 4 September 1863, *Official Records of the Union and Confederate Navies in the War of the Rebellion*, Series I, Vol. IX, p. 191.

11

Admiral Goldsborough's Feisty Career

WILLIAM N. STILL, JR.

In September 1861 the United States Navy Department divided the Atlantic Blockading Squadron into two squadrons: the North Atlantic Blockading Squadron, which would have the responsibility for the Atlantic coast between Cape Henry, Virginia, and the dividing line between North and South Carolina; and the South Atlantic Blockading Squadron, which would have the responsibility from that point to Cape Florida. Flag Officer Louis Malesherbes Goldsborough was ordered to the command of the North Atlantic Blockading Squadron. Secretary of the Navy Gideon Welles wrote Goldsborough: "It is essentially necessary that the Navy should at this time put forth all its strength and demonstrate to the country and to foreign powers its usefulness and capability in protecting and supporting the Government and the Union." At that time Goldsborough had been in the navy 49 years, having entered as a midshipman at the extraordinary age of 7. He received the command in spite of a law retiring officers after 45 years' service.

He was born in Washington, D.C., on February 18, 1805, the son of Charles W. Goldsborough, chief clerk of the Navy Department and the author of *The United States' Naval Chronicle*. Although a midshipman during the War of 1812, he saw no active service. In 1825 he received a lieutenant's commission and spent the next 5 years in Europe, part of the time on leave and part with the Mediterranean Squadron. In 1831 he married Elizabeth Gamble Wirt, daughter of William Wirt, who ran for President on the Anti-Masonic Party ticket that year. Goldsborough shortly afterward left the navy to lead a band of German immigrants to his father-in-law's plantation in Florida. During the Seminole War he commanded a steamboat expedition and later a company of mounted infantry.

In 1841 he returned to the navy as a commander. During the Mexican War he commanded the ship-of-the-line *Ohio* on blockade duty in the Gulf of Mexico and led an attack on the inland port of Tuxpan. After the war he performed a variety of duties including serving on a commission which explored California and Oregon; superintending the Naval Academy, 1853–57; and commanding the Brazil Squadron for 2 years before the outbreak of the Civil War.

Shortly after assuming command of the North Atlantic Blockading Squadron, Goldsborough proposed seizing Roanoke Island off North Carolina. The idea was ignored, however, until Major General George B. McClellan developed his Peninsula Campaign and realized that the capture of Roanoke Island would provide a base of operations to cut Confederate communications. On February 7, 1862, some 10,000 troops under the command of Brigadier General Ambrose E. Burnside joined Goldsborough's force of seventeen shallow draft gunboats in assaulting the island. Under the protective umbrella of the Union warships, Burnside's troops landed in waves similar to the patterns employed in the Pacific in World War II. In addition to providing the assaulting troops with fire support, Goldsborough's active vessels defeated a small force of Confederate gunboats and bombarded two forts until they were effectively neutralized. Two days after the initial landing the island was secured.

The capture of Roanoke Island was an important victory. It played no small role in McClellan's Peninsula Campaign by opening the way to the capture of Norfolk and its large naval base. The Confederates' loss of this base was followed by the destruction of the CSS *Virginia*, which had successfully held the mouth of the James River and blocked the river route to Richmond. The island's capture also contributed to the Union blockade along the Southern coastline. As one Confederate officer wrote: "It lodges the enemy in a safe harbor from the storms of Hatteras, gives them a rendezvous, and large, rich range of supplies, and the command of the seaboard from Oregon Inlet to Cape Henry." Finally, it led to the occupation of eastern North Carolina and its important ports, canals, railroads, and river arteries. By the summer of 1862 Burnside's troops, convoyed and supported by Goldsborough's vessels, were in control of most of the area, leaving only Wilmington and the southern corner of the state in Confederate hands. Although these achievements won Goldsborough the "thanks of Congress" and the consequent right to 55 years' service before retirement, he was criticized by Welles and others for spending too much time in North Carolina waters.

Much of this criticism came about because of the flag officer's absence from Hampton Roads when the Confederate ironclad *Virginia* [*Merrimack*] attacked units of his squadron there. Admittedly, Goldsborough had been apprehensive over the Confederate ironclad. Throughout the fall of 1861 and early 1862 he frequently forwarded news of the armorclad's progress. Nevertheless, Secretary of the Navy Welles was unfair when he wrote that Goldsborough was "purposely and unnecessarily absent, in my [opinion] . . . through fear of the *Merrimac*." The flag officer recognized the importance of the operations in North Carolina waters. He gave instructions to the senior officer present in Hampton Roads regarding what action should be taken if the armorclad sortied, and he left what he believed to be adequate forces to meet such a threat. He returned immediately upon the receipt of news of the March 8–9 engagements.

On March 10 Welles sent a telegram to his assistant, Gustavus V. Fox, who had hurried to Fort Monroe: "It is directed by the President that the *Monitor* be not too much exposed, and that in no event shall any attempt be made to proceed with her unattended to Norfolk." Goldsborough agreed with this when he arrived. "It will not do," he wrote, "in my judgment, to count too largely on [the *Monitor's*] . . . progress. She is scarcely enough for the *Merrimac*." Because of the presence of the *Virginia* General McClellan decided to concentrate his troops on the York River for the Peninsula operation. Goldsborough's responsibility was to keep the *Virginia* from threatening McClellan's line of communication on the York. This meant following a defensive strategy until the Confederate armorclad was removed.

On April 11 a small squadron led by the *Virginia* entered Hampton Roads with the objective of attacking the Union gunboats and transports in the York River. The *Monitor* was observed in the channel off Fort Monroe, and the remainder of Goldsborough's force just beyond. The Confederate commander, Josiah Tattnall, decided not to attack the *Monitor* in the channel for fear that the *Virginia* would be trapped by the Union vessels steaming just beyond the *Monitor*. According to the *Monitor*'s paymaster this was Goldsborough's strategy: "His object is to get the *Merrimac* in deep water where the large steamers fitted up as rams can have a chance at her." Throughout most of the day the two protagonists steamed back and forth within sight of each other, but outside of each other's range. Flag Officer Tattnall's cautious policy was based on the realization that, if the *Virginia* were damaged or lost, Norfolk and the control of the James River would be jeopardized. That night, after the Confederate naval force had disappeared around Craney Island, the ever-feisty Goldsborough wrote his wife: "Had the *Merrimac* attacked the *Monitor* where she was and still is stationed by me, I would instantly have been down before the former with all my force. . . . The salvation of McClellan's army, among other things, greatly depends upon my holding the *Merrimac* steadily and securely in check and not allowing her to get past Fort Monroe and so before Yorktown. My game therefore is to remain firmly on the defense unless I can fight on my own terms."

Goldsborough continued to follow this cautious policy during the following weeks. Although this policy was approved of and in fact ordered by the Navy Department, he, nevertheless, came under increasing criticism from the public, as well as his own subordinates. The New York *Herald* wrote: "The public are justly indignant at the conduct of our navy in Hampton Roads." Even the *Monitor*'s paymaster complained that "It is a great mistake that superannuated old men are given the control of such important measures."

On May 5 Abraham Lincoln and members of his cabinet paid a surprise visit to Fort Monroe. Three mornings later, while the President was still there, a deserter brought information that Norfolk was being evacuated. Lincoln then ordered Goldsborough to bombard Sewell's Point to ascertain whether the Confederates had abandoned that post and also to draw out the *Virginia* if possible. Six warships, including the *Monitor*, steamed near the point and opened fire. The *Virginia* was then in the yard at Norfolk, but she got under way quickly and entered Hampton Roads, standing directly for her old antagonist. Once again, the *Monitor* retired under Goldsborough's orders, hoping to draw the Confederate ironclad into a position where she could be attacked by the entire Union force. The *Virginia* refused to be drawn into the channel, and after steaming in the Roads for more than 2 hours, she withdrew. The Union flag officer complained to his wife that night, "She kept more in reserve than ever and would not even give me half a chance to run her down." Nor would he have another chance, because two days later the Confederates themselves destroyed the *Virginia.*

The *Virginia's* destruction opened the James River, and Goldsborough immediately ordered units of his squadron to ascend the river toward Richmond. On May 15 the *Monitor,* the ironclad *Galena,* and three wooden gunboats reached Drewry's Bluff in a bend of the river about 8 miles below the Confederate capital. The Confederates had placed obstructions across the river and placed a number of heavy guns on the bluffs above. For 4 hours the vessels withstood a terrific bombardment from the guns before retiring down river. This repulse again brought public censure upon Goldsborough's head.

Throughout the summer months of 1862 Goldsborough remained in Virginia waters. During May his flagship was anchored in Hampton Roads or up the James River; in June his headquarters was Norfolk. His squadron by this time comprised nearly sixty vessels scattered from the York River to Wilmington, North Carolina. The flag officer was anxious to mount an attack on the forts guarding the Cape Fear River, the entrance to Wilmington; and with the approval of the department, he began withdrawing vessels from the North Carolina sounds for this purpose. He was unable, however, to make final plans for the operation until General McClellan had taken Richmond. McClellan's advance on the Confederate capital had been checked during the last week in June, and after the Battle of Gaines Mill on June 27, he decided to base his army on the James River under the protection of Goldsborough's vessels. Commander John Rodgers was given the responsibility of directing naval operations up the James, but the flag officer insisted that all communications between McClellan and the naval vessels in the river go directly through him. Goldsborough was also sensitive regarding what he considered to be the peremptory tone of the army's communications. He replied to one telegram, "Its wording was so manda-tory that I desire to ask you if it is intended as an order?" Nevertheless, cooperation was generally satisfactory, and McClellan's base at White House Landing and line of communications on the James were well protected.

On July 6, 1862, Goldsborough was informed by Welles of the creation of the James River Flotilla and the assignment of Captain Charles Wilkes to his command. The naval secretary made it quite clear that Wilkes was to operate independently and report directly to him. More than a third of Goldsborough's squadron was turned over to the new Commodore. The flag officer was incensed at what he considered evidence of the department's dissatisfaction with his conduct of affairs. This was certainly true of Welles who called Goldsborough "inefficient,—had done nothing effective since the frigates were sunk by the *Merrimac,* nor of himself much before." Yet the secretary's decision to create the flotilla was not because of dissatisfaction with Goldsborough (although there was dissatisfaction), but to placate the public, to whom Wilkes had become a hero since the *Trent* affair. Wilkes, however, was 62 years old and had a well-deserved reputation for insubor-dination and an ill-temper. He was also incompetent, and this became quite obvious during his brief tenure on the James River. He fouled up things so badly that within weeks the flotilla was abolished and the Commodore was ordered elsewhere. By that time Goldsborough was no longer in command of the North Atlantic Blockading Squadron.

A week after the flotilla was created, Goldsborough asked to be relieved of his command, as Wilkes's assignment had exposed him to "the most scurrilous and unmerited attacks." The press, which had blamed Goldsbor-ough for the destruction of the two warships in Hampton Roads by the *Virginia,* had not let up with its criticism afterward. The Wilkes decision simply convinced Goldsborough that he no longer had the respect of the department or the public. As Flag Officer Samuel F. DuPont wrote, "when people got over their own fright and panic a thousand miles away, then they looked for a scapegoat." Goldsborough considered himself to be that scape-goat, and he probably was. Ironically, the day after he asked to be relieved, he was promoted to rear admiral, second in line to David G. Farragut.

From September 1862 until April 1865 Goldsborough performed administrative duties for the Navy Department in Washington, D.C. "He is what we call a 'handy billy' for the Department," DuPont told his wife, "whenever things go wrong they fall back upon men of his cleverness and rank, but they never consult him nor anyone like him who are at hand to prevent such wrongs, only to get relieved by them from the consequences of their own blunders." In June 1864 another member of the navy's staff in Washington wrote that Goldsborough was "busy with the allowance books and matters relating to organization and discipline." However important these duties were, Goldsborough desperately wanted an active command again. He successively applied for command of the *Monitor* shortly before she started her ill-fated cruise that ended off Hatteras, North Carolina; for command of the Pacific Squadron in 1864, but was told that he could not be spared from the department; and for command of the Fort Fisher expedition, which was finally tendered to Admiral David Porter. He even volunteered his services when Confederate Major General Jubal Early threatened Washington in July 1864. Goldsborough's personal life during this period was little better. His oldest son died in 1863, and his only daughter, whom he adored, had failing health.

In February 1865 the Navy Department decided to reestablish a squadron in European waters. The old Mediterranean Squadron had been discontinued at the war's outset, and only individual ships in search of Confederate raiders occasionally cruised off the shores of the Old World. By the second month of 1865 only two major ports, Wilmington, North Carolina, and Galveston, Texas, remained in Confederate hands; and Wilmington would fall before the end of the month. Secretary of the Navy Welles considered the few Confederate warships still afloat in Southern waters to be less dangerous than the raiders. At that time the *Rappahannock, Shenandoah, Tallahassee,* and the powerful ironclad ram *Stonewall* were believed to be somewhere in European waters. The devastating successes of the *Alabama* and other Confederate cruisers in preying on Union shipping convinced Lincoln's government that the raiders must be destroyed. This was to be the primary objective of the European Squadron, and Goldsborough was given the new command. At first glance Goldsborough's appointment is surprising. Welles had little respect for him. The naval secretary mentioned in his diary that Goldsborough "had not a single qualification, but size, belly, and lungs." Yet there was little choice. Farragut was probably the first choice, but the hero of Mobile Bay was recuperating from physical fatigue. Of the other senior officers, only Goldsborough and DuPont were available, and Welles (and his assistant, Fox) considered the former more capable. Finally, Goldsborough had political influence and was not averse to using it.

Although the appointment was made in late February, Goldsborough did not sail until June and did not arrive in European waters until July. By then the Civil War was over. Nevertheless, the *Shenandoah* was still at large (although far from European waters by that time); and the *Tallahassee* and *Rappahannock* were at Liverpool, England. Goldsborough was ordered to "seize and send into port any of the rebel vessels that you may find out of neutral waters." His squadron consisted of the flagship *Colorado* and four smaller vessels.

The squadron spent the summer of 1865 cruising off the southern coast of England, but seized no former Confederate vessels. The two in Liverpool were interned by the British government and were joined there by the *Shenandoah* in November. Goldsborough then took his squadron to the Mediterranean.

Goldsborough commanded the European Squadron for two years. After the internment of the former Confederate vessels, his tour became a typical one of showing the flag. His squadron rarely cruised as a tactical unit; instead, individual vessels followed a port to port routine, occasionally being ordered to a specific place where American interests needed to be protected. On Bastille Day, July 14, 1867, Goldsborough relinquished the command to Farragut and sailed for home.

The European tour had not been a happy one for Goldsborough. The war ended before he could repair his tarnished reputation. Also, he had hoped his family could join him, but his daughter's failing health and subsequent death shattered this expectation.

In 1867 the admiral was 62 years old, with 55 years of naval duty; he had served longer than any active officer. He was ready for retirement, or so Secretary Welles thought. Much to the secretary's astonishment, however, Goldsborough asked to be retained on active service on the dubious grounds that he had not received orders for sea until 4 years after his appointment. Despite Welles' strong disapproval, President Andrew Johnson

Admiral Louis Goldsborough, commander of the North Atlantic Blockading Squadron. *(Library of Congress)*

permitted the admiral to remain four additional years on active service.
Goldsborough's wife, Elizabeth, was apparently instrumental in persuading
the President to do this. DuPont once wrote of her, "She has . . . much
sense, one of those people whose minds never *pause,* and I now understand
how she injured her husband at the Department when he came [home] . . .
from the sea. "

Goldsborough's final years in the navy were spent in Washington,
performing various administrative functions for the department. Four years
after his retirement in 1873 he died.

Goldsborough, or "Old Guts" as he was called by the sailors, was a well-
known figure in the navy partly because of his immense size (6 feet, 4 inches
in height and weight estimated from 300 pounds up) and "red, red beard,"
but also for what one officer called his eccentricity in deportment. To junior
officers "his manners [were] somewhat rough, so that he would almost
frighten a subordinate out of his wits." One well-known story concerned

a classic remark he made when a group of midshipmen set fire to his backyard privy while he was superintendent of the naval academy. He allegedly roared, "I'll hang them! yes, I'll hang them! So help me God, I will." Another tale is told that on a Sunday morning while his flagship was at anchor, the chaplain began his sermon by bowing his head and saying "The Lord is in his Holy Temple," when Goldsborough violently flung open his cabin door and bellowed, "Hold on chaplain, hold on. I'll have you to understand that the Lord is not in his Holy Temple until I get there." Even his good friends wrote disapprovingly of his intemperate nature. "He seems . . . to have wanted patience and amenity with officers; they complain very much of his imperious temper," DuPont informed his wife.

Goldsborough was a competent officer. His conduct of the Roanoke Island expedition was excellent and the conquest of the North Carolina sounds and their tributaries, although without fanfare, was well done. Even his actions during the Peninsula Campaign (including the *Virginia*'s successes) do not discredit him. He was wrongfully blamed by the press and public for the failure of the Union Navy to destroy the Confederate ironclad. Yet it was Lincoln and Welles who insisted on a cautious policy. In a sense Goldsborough was also caught up in McClellan's failure. If the Union general had succeeded in taking Richmond, Goldsborough probably would have been lauded by the press. Instead he was maligned. Goldsborough received little or no support from Welles, who wrote that the admiral had "wordy pretensions . . . some capacity, but no hard courage." Most of his contemporaries, however, agreed with DuPont that Goldsborough was "an able officer. . . . There is no one who . . . could aid the government more in all those matters connected with the national defense of the country than he."

12

....

Corpus Christi:
The Vicksburg of Texas

Norman C. Delaney

For the residents of coastal Texas it was an oppressively hot summer. The region was suffering from a severe drought, bringing even more misery than usual at that season. And, since it was the peak of the hurricane season, there loomed the possibility of yet another of nature's violent phenomena. But in the summer of 1862 it was man and not nature that posed the greater threat. The "hurricane" that threatened Corpus Christi was a Yankee naval officer who, with fewer than a hundred men aboard a task force of a steamer, a yacht, and two captured sloops, had entered Corpus Christi Bay and trained his guns on the city.

John W. Kittredge deserved his reputation as "a bold and daring officer." A career merchant officer, the native New Yorker had volunteered his services to the Union when war came. Appointed an acting lieutenant in August of 1861, he was assigned command of the bark *Arthur*, a former merchant ship which carried a crew of eighty and was equipped with one Parrott and six 32-pounder guns. Because of his familiarity with coastal waters from Galveston to Brazos Santiago, Kittredge was assigned to blockade the Texas coast from Pass Cavallo to Aransas Pass.

On January 25, 1862, near Pass Cavallo, he captured the schooner *J. J. McNeil*, carrying a cargo of cotton. Reluctant to part with her, Kittredge nevertheless sent her on to Ship Island, Mississippi, for disposition. His own ship's 14-foot draft prevented Kittredge from crossing the shallow channels that connected with the intracoastal waterway, and he realized that his blockade would be effective only by acquiring the same "light Aransas vessels" used by the Confederates. Confederate Major Caleb G. Forshey, supervising coast defenses, understood the threat posed by the blockader. Federal control of the waterway would deprive the Confederacy of salt from the lakes below Corpus Christi as well as lead and coffee imported from Mexico. It would also interfere with the outbound cotton and sugar that the Confederacy needed to sell in order to help finance the war. The Federals, too, were well aware that the waterway was the major avenue along which supplies were shipped from Matamoras for distribution throughout Texas and Louisiana. If the passage were closed, it would leave only "miserable roads" as alternate routes to the Confederates.

Following his capture of the *McNeil*, Kittredge began his active blockade. He raised United States flags on St. Joseph's Island and on the lighthouse at Harbor Island. He regularly probed the sparsely settled outer islands, gained information on enemy positions, and kept the *Arthur* stocked with fresh beef and mutton. However, Kittredge's activities in the Matagorda area were limited by the Confederates' Fort Esperanza at Saluria, which guarded Pass Cavallo. Occasionally Kittredge parlayed with the Confederates ashore. Kittredge warned the Southerners that although his orders were to stop their trade rather than fight them, he would not hesitate to retaliate if fired upon. After meeting the Yankee, Confederate Major Daniel B. Shea warned military authorities: "If this man is not stopped immediately . . . he will command our whole western coast." Shea believed that "a small party of good men" might succeed in capturing the Yankee officer. He understood his adversary's penchant for taking chances; indeed, on April 22 Kittredge and a party of sailors narrowly escaped capture on St. Joseph's Island. In a hasty retreat to the sand dunes, the Federals abandoned three of their prizes with prisoners aboard, and even their own two launches. The exultant Confederates who were involved in the affair later presented one of their trophies—an "elegant" compass—to Commodore William H. Hunter, naval commander of Texas.

After five months of apparent failure to check the main avenue of coastal traffic, Kittredge's fortunes changed abruptly. In June of 1862 the shallow draft yacht *Corypheus* was sent to him from New Orleans. Arming her with his Parrott gun and a 12-pounder howitzer, Kittredge brought the yacht across Aransas Bar on July 7. He captured the sloops *Reindeer* and *Belle Italia,* both carrying cotton, but was cheated of still another prize, a schooner beached and set afire. Kittredge was pleased to learn from his shoeless prisoners how effective his blockade had been after all. Not only was there a shortage of basic goods, but whiskey, the staple commodity, was selling at $10 per gallon when available. The two captured sloops were converted into gunboats. Kittredge now controlled the Shell Bank (Corpus Christi Bayou), which had been abandoned, and he was prepared to "rake and control the ship channel from Aransas to Corpus Christi Bay." As he planted his colors over the works on Shell Bank, Kittredge dramatically announced that the flag would continue to wave there.

Realizing the danger, Major Shea ordered that all vessels at Matagorda be detained there. Equally alarmed, Colonel Xavier B. Debray, commanding at Houston, ordered that all slaves, cotton, corn, and cattle be removed to the interior. Debray's orders included the threat, "If patriotism does not dictate this course to the citizens, force must be resorted to . . . to prevent the enemy from receiving aid and comfort."

On July 14 Kittredge publicly stated his intention to attack Corpus Christi. Landing at Lamar, he told the residents there that after the arrival of a light steamer he would proceed "with the first fair wind . . . and demand the surrender of the place." When, on July 29, the steamer *Sachem* arrived, Kittredge felt ready. In addition to his patriotism, he was motivated by a driving ambition. He would one day admit that during his naval service he had "proudly sought to win glory for himself."

Writing to Secretary of the Navy Gideon Welles before moving against Corpus Christi, Kittredge boasted: "I drove the enemy's force of 150 men from their battery at Corpus Christi Bayou . . . I have cut off the trade entirely passing through the bayou from Matagorda to Point Isabel, a distance of 180 miles." Although his force of about a hundred men was too small to occupy Corpus Christi, a victory there could result in political changes within the city. The city's mayor was a firm Union man, and Kittredge knew from his contacts ashore that there were other loyalists ready to support him. He may have learned, too, of the panic and confusion within the city and of the doubts by some citizens as to whether Corpus Christi could be defended. Because of other officers' reluctance to assume command, Colonel Charles G. Lovenskiold, the city's provost marshal, did so. As commanding officer, he moved quickly and decisively, impounding and distributing shoes, clothing, and gunpowder to the men of the volunteer companies defending the city. He had all remaining supplies, along with cotton and tobacco, sent into the interior. Lovenskiold also had three small schooners loaded with concrete and sunk in the ship channel to block the enemy's entrance into Corpus Christi Bay. The defenders' morale received an added boost with the arrival on July 20 of Major Alfred M. Hobby and the 300 men of the 8th Texas Infantry Regiment.

On the morning of August 13, 1862, Lieutenant Kittredge landed by launch at Corpus Christi. Only the day before, he had accomplished the "impossible." Using the *Sachem*'s steam power, Kittredge raised the vessels that had been sunk in the channel. Once inside Corpus Christi Bay, the *Corypheus* overhauled and captured the schooner *Breaker,* which had been stationed to observe the Federals. That vessel thus became the fifth of a small but formidable "mosquito fleet" preparing to move against Corpus Christi.

Although Kittredge displayed a white truce flag, two of his vessels moved close by. Standing on the wharf ready to challenge the Federals were Hobby, now commanding all military forces at Corpus Christi, and Henry A. Gilpin, a local rancher-merchant and chief justice of Nueces County. As they stood facing each other, the antagonists took each others' measure. Kittredge—short, looking younger than his 45 years—already had a reputation as a resourceful enemy. In the seven months since his arrival on the Texas coast, he had created near panic among the area's residents. And now he threatened the citizens of the largest coastal city south of Galveston.

Standing on Ohler's Wharf, Kittredge spoke as one accustomed to command. Distrusting the Confederate recognition of his truce flag, he let it be known that his vessels' guns offered him protective cover. His orders, he said, required him to inspect all United States government buildings and property. Hobby demurred, insisting that no such buildings existed in Corpus Christi. Nor did he recognize what Kittredge referred to as the "national ensign." He would allow the Federals to proceed no further. Angry now, Kittredge belligerently demanded that the argument be settled by combat and offered a twenty-four hour truce for the evacuation of women and children. Civilians could remain in the city, he said, as he would respect their lives and property. When Hobby insisted that more time was needed for civilians to evacuate, Kittredge agreed to forty-eight hours on condition that the Confederates made no further military preparations. He returned to the *Sachem* only to make a second visit ashore in the afternoon to again assert his right to inspect government property. Perhaps, as one observer declared, he was a "braggart and blusterer" who deliberately goaded the Confederate officers. In any case, the only point settled was that the forty-eight hour truce would begin at 5 o'clock that afternoon, when all discussion ceased.

The next day Kittredge maneuvered his ships for combat. He knew that the defenders had no guns to match his own for range and power, and he had his Parrott gun, with a range of over four miles, fired across the bay as a demonstration of what awaited those who opposed him. Four guns were kept on both the *Sachem* and *Corypheus,* leaving one gun each for the *Reindeer* and *Belle Italia*. The *Breaker,* with several sick sailors aboard her, would serve as "hospital ship." Earlier, the *Arthur* had been sent to New Orleans for supplies, but even had she remained, she would have been of little use to Kittredge outside the bay.

Major Alfred Hobby, commanding several hundred untrained and untested volunteers, prepared for his own first fight. Only three months earlier, 26-year-old Hobby had resigned a seat in the Texas legislature in order to raise and command the 8th Regiment, a unit made up largely of south Texas farmers and ranchers. Originally from Macon, Georgia, he arrived in Texas in 1857 and established a general store at St. Mary's in Refugio County. In addition to his business and legislative responsibilities, Hobby was active in the Knights of the Golden Circle chapter he had helped organize at St. Mary's. He was also a pro-secession delegate to the 1861 Texas convention, as was one of his officers, Captain John Ireland, a future governor of Texas. Hobby, a published biographer and poet, has been described by Refugio County historian Hobart Huson as "a mature scholar, a brilliant orator, and man of letters."

Hobby was preparing to defend a city mixed in its war sentiment. Although Corpus Christi had raised seven companies for the Confederate cause, there were a number of residents whose sympathies were with the Union. Mayor Henry Berry, a native Ohioan, was the most prominent Unionist, but a sizable minority of the city's residents shared his views.

During the truce, Corpus Christi was evacuated by most of its civilian population. Old and sick people, women, and children left by horse, mule, and oxen, by wagon or by foot, carrying with them food and water and even furniture and cooking utensils. Many refugees believed that nearby settlements at Nuecestown, Banquete, or Flour Bluff would be safe havens, while others left the county entirely. The rest set up improvised tents—in some cases blankets stretched on poles—or crawled under their wagons at locations they believed secure from attack. But because of the region's "long continued draught," the refugees suffered greatly from heat, thirst, and the relentless insects. Not all the civilians left Corpus Christi. There were some, especially among the Unionists, who believed that Kittredge would be true to his word and respect lives and property. Some citizens vowed to remain in their homes regardless of what happened.

Untrained in the use and disposition of artillery, Hobby positioned his three smooth-bore cannon—one 18- and two 12-pounders—at the old Kinney stockade on the bluff that overlooked the bay and the business section of the city. Hobby's choice of the bluff for his defense was an unfortunate one because it endangered the numerous civilian homes located there. According to a story later reported in Corpus Christi, Hobby's decision was influenced by a stranger who, it was later claimed, was a spy sent by Kittredge.

Cannons were scarce in Corpus Christi. According to local tradition, Hobby's two 12-pounders were "condemned" cannon left behind by General Zachary Taylor's army in 1846. Possibly, however, the guns pre-date Taylor's arrival. Kinney's fort is known to have had two pieces of artillery, and these were probably 12-pounders. The guns might also have been left behind by a United States army detachment stationed at Corpus Christi until 1857. In any case, Hobby was indeed fortunate to have them. But he was handicapped by a lack of trained artillerists. Lacking powder for target practice, the men of Captain Benjamin F. Neal's Battery, Sea-Coast Defense, now serving under Hobby, had been unable to learn the proper use of their two 6-pounder guns. Mexican War veteran Felix Blucher understood the use of artillery, however, and he was eager to assist. Another competent artillerist was Billy Mann, who had recently seen action at Island No. 10 on the Mississippi. Mann was the 22-year-old son of the widow Esther Mann of Corpus Christi. Despite the "shattered state of his health from exposure at Island No. 10," Mann was the only soldier on the scene with recent combat experience. He strongly advised Hobby to move the cannons from their position on the bluff. Mann believed that the best place for a defense was the fortifications on the water's edge at the northern end of the city. These had been constructed of solidly packed sand and shells by the American army in 1845 or 1846. Although he found Mann's arguments convincing, Hobby knew that it was too late. The truce was scheduled to end at 5 p.m., and the move could not be accomplished in time.

When the truce deadline arrived, the *Sachem* and *Corypheus* were moved close to shore. But, when there was no attack, Hobby realized that he had his chance. That night the Confederates began moving their guns to the beach fortifications. As they worked, communicating by hushed whispers, they could see the two Union ships silhouetted on the water about 400 yards from shore. The lights of ships' lanterns were plainly visible. At 2 a.m. the work of moving the guns was completed, and Hobby concealed his main force of cavalry and infantry behind the earthworks and in the nearby ravines. A Confederate flag—hastily stitched by local women the day before—was positioned at the battery.

By daybreak the Texans were ready. From either Blucher or Mann came the order—"Fire!"—and the guns roared. The surprised Federals were literally "thunderstruck." Both *Sachem* and *Corypheus* were hit. A shell penetrated the hull of the *Sachem,* and one sailor was slightly injured by a flying wood splinter. The return fire was indiscriminate. The *Reindeer* and *Belle Italia,* both becalmed, were ineffectual in their fire because they were too far to find the range. According to one account, "Many shells . . . were thrown from the fleet in every conceivable direction to and within one and one-half miles about the City, in hopes of finding the locality of our troops." The Confederates' position was finally targeted, and shot and shell began to strike the earthworks, but without serious effect. Other shells struck homes and even splintered grave markers at the Bayview Cemetery overlooking the city. A shell crashed into William Shaw's saloon, striking the counter and smashing bottles of liquor. It struck and killed Shaw's pet Newfoundland dog before passing through another wall.

In the Dix home overlooking the bay, old John Dix sprang into action. Carrying his American flag, he hurried to the stairs leading to the roof. He knew that the flag, which revealed his true allegiance, was the best insurance for property and occupants alike. But Dix never reached the roof. Suddenly, he was confronted by his daughter-in-law, Cynthia, armed with a shotgun aimed directly at him. Forcefully, she exclaimed: "While I am here, if you attempt to raise that flag over this house, over my head, I will shoot you off the roof!" Not wishing to test her resolve, Dix backed off. Many Corpus Christians would nevertheless contend that the Dix home was exempt from enemy fire, despite its exposed position, because of the old man's "treasonous" actions. They believed that he and other Unionists had been earlier signaling the fleet with lanterns.

The heavy shelling continued, but the only fatalities were Shaw's dog and three cows belonging to Maximilian Dreyer. The walls of Dreyer's house, constructed of shell concrete, remained standing despite numerous hits. Among the civilians who had refused to leave the city was James Bernard. But Bernard was suffering from painful rheumatism, and he could not be persuaded to leave his bed. He was lying on a cot in his second-story bedroom when a shell came crashing through the wall. Terrified, the old man raced away, forgetting both his pain and his earlier resolve. Another shell exploded in a warehouse where animal hides were stored. Glancing upward, a Confederate soldier was amazed to see hides falling from the sky. Incredulous, he cried out, "My God, they're shooting goat skins at us!"

On the outskirts of Corpus Christi, the refugees waited apprehensively, listening to the distant noise of shells. Even for those beyond hearing distance, ground tremors indicated what was happening in the city. All passing couriers were hailed for information on the fight. Behind the earthworks, the men at the guns, now accustomed to their work, were laughing and cheering. In order to encourage them, Billy Mann had taken a position atop the works and was holding their flag. From this position, he directed the action, announced each hit, and warned of approaching shells. His own example of courage was the best proof his men needed to realize that "gunboats don't kill every time." Confederate riflemen fired their guns at Union sailors aboard the closest ships. One soldier, an ordnance sergeant, improvised an easel and sketched the battle in progress. When his easel was knocked down by a shell fragment, the soldier calmly put it back in place and resumed his work.

Four hours after the battle began, Kittredge broke off the action and sailed his ships out of range of the shore battery. After inspecting the damage and mending sails, he resumed the attack, but after both yacht and steamer were struck, he again withdrew out of range. The Federals had fired almost 300 shot and shell during the attack.

The next day, Sunday, Kittredge did not resume the action. Despite his official claim to have silenced the enemy battery "several times," he was furious at having been tricked and was determined to win the victory. An attempt to haul off a partially burned and grounded steamer at the entrance to the Nueces River resulted in failure. Meanwhile, the defenders of Corpus Christi made their own preparations. The number of defenders increased as volunteers arrived from neighboring communities, many attracted by the sound of cannon fire. Since the need for gunpowder was urgent, the defenders saw a ready supply in unexploded enemy shells. A number of these were located and their caps removed in order to extract the valuable powder. According to local tradition (it is unrecorded in official reports), several of the shells were found to contain whiskey. One source of the "whiskey-in-the-shells" story is Hobby, who related it to his family and friends many times before his death in 1881. Residents of Corpus Christi, including veterans of the action, also repeated the story over the years, but it was not actually recorded until 1892—thirty years after the battle. Hobby was then long dead, and Kittredge's whereabouts unknown. If the story is correct, then so is the conclusion that the shells "were a source of delight rather than death."

Early on the morning of August 18, Kittredge maneuvered his ships to about a mile south of the Confederate battery. He was prepared to outflank his enemy's works by a combined land and sea assault. A force of thirty men, led by Acting Master's Mate Alfred H. Reynolds and equipped with a 12-pounder rifled howitzer, was landed from the *Belle Italia*. The Federals advanced toward the battery, firing their howitzer rapidly and "with great precision." The danger to the Confederates was obvious. Hobby's three guns, facing the bay, could not be moved to new positions in time to meet the attack. Meanwhile, the Federal ships, only 400 yards from shore, fired continuous volleys of grape and shrapnel. Realizing that immediate action was imperative, Hobby called for volunteers as the enemy was only 600 yards from his position. Captain James A. Ware's company of cavalry was alerted to be ready to offer support. Hobby gave the order, and he and his men rushed forward, firing their guns and yelling. They were met by a barrage from the ships, but succeeded in halting the assault party. The Federals turned and fled, intent only on saving their lives and the howitzer. Their abandoned equipment included files which had been intended for spiking the Confederate guns. As the Federals fell back to their launch, Ware's cavalry joined the attack. The Confederates were under heavy fire from the ships. One Texan had already been killed and Hobby himself superficially wounded. Not wanting to risk any more lives, Hobby ordered his men to withdraw to their positions. Thus, although their capture had seemed certain, the Federals were able to reach the safety of the *Belle Italia*. The sole fatality, Private Henry Mote of Hobby's regiment, had been instantly killed by a grapeshot. On the Federal side, one sailor had been wounded in the thigh by a musket ball.

The Battle of Corpus Christi was no small victory for her defenders. A special edition of the Corpus Christi *Ranchero,* dated August 19, proclaimed Corpus Christi as "the Vicksburg of Texas," having "completely foiled and whipped" the enemy. An account of the battle in the Houston *Tri-Weekly News* proudly announced that "Vicksburg has not acted more nobly than our little city." Damage from Federal shelling was estimated as being so insignificant that a mere $600 would cover the cost of repairs.

After completing the shelling of buildings that he believed concealed enemy forces, Kittredge sailed his ships to the Shell Bank to make repairs and await the return of the *Arthur.* The Confederates were convinced that the *Sachem* was severely damaged, as "her steam-pumps were heard during the day and night she consumed in passing through the canal." Having expended about 450 shot and shell during the two days of fighting, Kittredge was short of ammunition. Writing his official report, he excused his inability to capture the enemy battery by claiming that Hobby's assault force had comprised 160 men instead of the 25 actually engaged. He also contended that 300 cavalrymen had charged his party. Instead of admitting a defeat, Kittredge claimed victory. He boasted of having silenced the battery and of having inflicted many casualties. His landing party had withdrawn, he stated, only because they had expended all their ammunition. In the most overblown statement of the entire affair, Kittredge wrote: "The moment we drew them from their cover they were made to bite the dust." Ware's cavalry were met with a "scathing storm of iron and were repulsed with evidently considerable loss, many being seen to fall. . . ." And so, despite or because of such distortions and lies, Kittredge's superiors would find no cause to censure him.

On August 20, General Hamilton P. Bee, commanding the Sub-Military District of the Rio Grande, arrived at Corpus Christi. Measures were taken to further strengthen the city's defenses, including building earthworks at water's edge on the south side and another on the bluff. On August 27 a company of well-trained artillerists arrived with six howitzers. Bee was profuse in his praise of the city's defenders. Among Corpus Christi's own "minute men" he singled out Blucher, Mann, and Gilpin for special commendation. All three were given field appointments: Blucher as major of engineers, Gilpin as quartermaster and commissary, and Mann as captain of artillery. Forced to decline the appointment because of ill health, Mann nevertheless agreed to command a battery until a replacement could be found.

Ironically, the Corpus Christi affair served to enhance Kittredge's reputation in the North, although events in far-off Texas were overshadowed by actions in other departments. Admiral David Farragut, writing officially, credited Kittredge with the capture of Corpus Christi, and the Admiral's congratulatory message praised his lieutenant's "energetic spirit and zeal." Three months after the action, the New York *Herald* headlined "The Capture of Corpus Christi, Texas" on its front page.

Kittredge continued to patrol the bay waters. On August 23 he captured the schooner *Water Witch* with a cargo that included 150 kegs of English gunpowder. This would be the energetic lieutenant's last good fortune while on his Texas station. Three weeks later he would be a prisoner of his enemies.

On September 12 Kittredge again landed at Corpus Christi under a flag of truce. He was met by Majors Hobby and Edward F. Gray, the city's new commander. Kittredge was under orders from Farragut to convey a message from a man regarded by the Texas secessionists as a dangerous "renegade." He was Edmund J. Davis, former United States district attorney and judge of the Rio Grande Valley. Davis was well known in Corpus Christi. He had once practiced law there and had married a daughter of Colonel Forbes Britton (1812–1861), a prominent citizen. Although he had been successful in escaping to New Orleans, Davis had been compelled to leave his wife behind in Corpus Christi. Now, Kittredge conveyed a letter from Davis requesting that she be allowed to join him in New Orleans. The Confederates did not know, however, that Davis was aboard the *Corypheus,* having arrived on the USS *Iroquois* five days earlier. Gray informed Kittredge that he lacked the authority to make a decision and that it would take at least ten days before he would have a reply from General Bee in San Antonio. Kittredge then boarded the yacht, but, because of unfavorable winds, he was unable to return to Aransas Bay. Instead, the *Corypheus* and *Breaker* sailed to Flour Bluff. Arriving there, they surprised several small vessels at anchor. The Federals, now joined by the *Belle Italia,* gave pursuit, but the vessels succeeded in escaping into the shallow waters of the Laguna de la Madre. Disappointed, but still determined to accomplish something, Kittredge came ashore. As a demonstration of the benefits that would be gained by loyalty to the United States, he had sugar, bacon, beans, and coffee brought from his ships' supplies and distributed to the civilians who remained on shore. But then he suddenly ordered three men seized and taken aboard the *Corypheus* as hostages until he completed his activities in the area.

Confederate authorities at Corpus Christi, informed of Kittredge's movements at Flour Bluff, hastily devised a plan for his capture. On the evening of September 13, sixty-five soldiers under the command of Captains Ware and Ireland left the city. They brought with them a light artillery piece. Arriving at Flour Bluff before sunup, they prepared their trap. Ware and twenty men stealthily gained entrance to a deserted house near the ocean, while the men with Ireland took the cannon and hid behind nearby sand dunes. They apparently succeeded in being undetected by Federals aboard the *Corypheus,* just offshore. However, Kittredge was wary, and, after daylight, seeing two men near the house, which was the home of one of his hostages, he had them shelled. But, when no further movement was observed, he prepared to land. With seven of his men, armed with cutlasses, revolvers, and rifles, he came ashore. As the party prepared to enter the home of their hostage, Ware and his men rushed out, capturing the Federals without firing a shot. The men aboard the *Corypheus* and the tenders, helpless to offer assistance to their companions, fired in frustration at the group on shore that now included their shipmates and commander. Ware and Ireland brought their prisoners to Corpus Christi, and once again

Hobby and Kittredge met face to face. But the delighted Confederates had no desire to further embarrass an enemy now incapable of doing them harm. To the Confederate officers, Kittredge was now an "honorable" enemy who had never "depreciated on private property, or allowed it to be done." All the prisoners were allowed to receive money, extra clothing, and other personal effects delivered under a truce.

During the two days that Kittredge was detained at Corpus Christi, he was shown the city he had shelled less than a month earlier. He was also shown the guns that had been used in the defense. Disdainfully, Kittredge dismissed them as obsolescent and inferior to his own. Northern forces, he insisted, had long since replaced their smooth bores with the new rifled cannon with which he was equipped. Their effectiveness had been demonstrated earlier in 1862 by the reduction of Confederate Fort Pulaski on the coast of Georgia. Kittredge was interested in other aspects of his own recent fight. According to Lee C. Harby, writing in 1892, Kittredge and Hobby began discussing the matter of unexploded shells that had been found about the city. A bemused Hobby expressed his bewilderment that whiskey had been found in a number of these shells. Finally understanding, Kittredge explained the reason. Sometime prior to the battle, he had missed a barrel of his own special bourbon whiskey and naturally suspected that it had been stolen by his men. But, although some sailors were occasionally found to be smelling of liquor while on night watch, none was ever discovered on them. Now, after listening to Hobby, Kittredge realized that the stolen whiskey had been hidden in his supply of shells, the men having first removed the powder.

After being kept prisoner at San Antonio a month, all eight prisoners were paroled and returned to Corpus Christi. They arrived there on October 2. Accompanied by Hobby, who had been assigned charge of him after his capture, Kittredge was brought aboard the *Corypheus*. He was moved to tears at the rousing welcome rendered by officers and crew. Transferred to the *Arthur*, Kittredge, still on parole, was a passenger aboard that vessel to Pensacola. He presented a personal report to Admiral Farragut at that station. He continued on to New York, where he was officially exchanged. In January of 1863, Kittredge was given command of the steamer *Wamsutta* and assigned to blockade duty on the Georgia coast. But the *Wamsutta*, less than half the size of the *Arthur*, was no promotion for the ambitious lieutenant, and blockade duty proved all too routine. Until June of 1863, Kittredge's superiors had no cause to be critical of his conduct despite his reputation as a strict disciplinarian. But, then, aboard the *Wamsutta,* an incident occurred during which Kittredge struck one of his men several times with his fist and a revolver. The regular navy officers who made up the court-martial board were unimpressed with Kittredge's defense that the man he struck was profane, disobedient, and had a reputation as a troublemaker. Nor were they impressed with the statement that he, as their "adopted brother," had "proudly sought to win glory for himself and reflect it upon the American Navy." To their verdict of guilty and sentence of dismissal, Secretary Welles added an admonition that "this example will have a proper effect on officers and seamen of the Navy." Welles regarded Kittredge's conduct as "a wanton and tyrannous abuse of authority."

On the Confederate side, Hobby, Ware, and Ireland received a special resolution of thanks from members of the Texas legislature, and Hobby's promotion to colonel was assured. But, for Corpus Christi, tragic days were ahead. Kittredge had succeeded in his major objective of halting the south Texas coastal traffic. Privation and ruin were the lot of those citizens who remained. And, with her defenders transferred to other stations, the few who remained in Corpus Christi were helpless against frequent Federal forays that occurred after a Federal force was established on Mustang Island in 1863. On April 10, 1864, Thomas Noakes, a veteran of Corpus Christi's earlier triumph, added another gloomy entry to his diary:

> There is nothing growing, and the country presents a sandy waste. There is nothing here that is fit for food. About half the people in Corpus have deserted to the Yankee and when you are talking to your most intimate acquaintance you cannot tell whether you are addressing a friend or foe politically.

Following the withdrawal of Federal military units from the area in 1864, the region remained bitterly divided and economically devastated. Indictments for treason were filed by Confederate authorities against Berry and other Corpus Christi "renegades" accused of aiding the Federals, but the war ended before their cases could be brought to trial. With war's end came still other setbacks—a yellow fever epidemic in 1867 and several disastrous hurricanes. Yet recovery and healing would eventually see the rise of a modern Corpus Christi, most of whose latter-day citizens are unaware that their "sparkling city by the sea" was once acclaimed as "the Vicksburg of Texas."

This chapter first appeared in the July 1977 issue of *Civil War Times Illustrated*.

13

Showdown off Cherbourg

JOHN M. TAYLOR

On June 10, 1864, in a gray morning drizzle, the world's most famous warship, the Confederate raider *Alabama*, stopped in the English Channel to pick up a pilot. The *Alabama*'s captain, 54-year-old Raphael Semmes, was suffering from a cold and fever; he felt a surge of relief at turning over his ship to the channel pilot who would take his cruiser into the French port of Cherbourg.

During her 22 months at sea, the *Alabama* had never dropped anchor at a Confederate port. Yet she had traveled some 75,000 miles and had overhauled 264 vessels, 64 of which had been Federal-owned merchantmen in international waters. Of the 64, 52 had been destroyed, and most of the remainder—which generally had been carrying neutral goods—had been released on bond. Along the way, Semmes and the *Alabama* had sunk the only Federal warship to engage him—the only defeat of a Federal warship in single combat during the war.

At the same time, the *Alabama* was about to demonstrate the weakness of all naval vessels: Eventually they must find a port for maintenance and refitting. For a dominant naval power, such port calls entail little more than an interruption in operations. For a weak naval power like the Confederacy, however, every anchorage was fraught with peril. The threat of being blockaded, perhaps far from home, was ever present. The weary *Alabama* now was obliged to find neutral repair facilities at a time when Confederate fortunes were waning and the U.S. Navy was at full strength.

At Cherbourg the port admiral received Semmes courteously, but with a suggestion that Confederate cruisers were perhaps showing too much partiality for French government facilities. Only the emperor could give the *Alabama* access to French navy docks, he advised, and Napoleon III was on holiday in Biarritz. The admiral would forward Semmes's request, but the implication was that there would be no decision for several days.

Semmes, still unwell, returned to his ship to await developments. Flag Officer Samuel Barron, in Paris, was the senior Confederate navy officer in Europe, and Semmes began reporting to him. He wrote on June 13 that he had funds enough to pay off his crew, but that he would require additional funds for repairs to his ship. As for himself, Semmes wrote, "My health has suffered so much from a constant and harassing service of three years, almost continuously at sea, that I shall have to ask for relief."[1]

On the same day, June 13, Semmes received word that changed all these plans: The USS *Kearsarge* was en route to Cherbourg and would be arriving imminently. Clearly, Semmes's tour as commander of the *Alabama* was not over. He suspended all plans for leave and exercised his crew at the guns. On the morning of June 14, Semmes and his executive officer, John Kell, watched through their glasses as the black-hulled *Kearsarge* made her way into Cherbourg harbor. Her captain, John Winslow, sent a boat ashore asking French authorities to turn over to him the *Alabama*'s recent prisoners. When this request was denied, the *Kearsarge* weighed anchor and took up a station outside the breakwater.

The 1,031-ton *Kearsarge*, commissioned in January 1862, was a few months older than the *Alabama*. Both Semmes and Kell had seen her before; she had been one of three Federal cruisers that had blockaded the *Sumter* at Gibraltar in 1862. Neither Confederate officer noticed the slight change in her lines. Winslow had followed an example set by Admiral David Farragut in draping chains around his hull amidships to protect his engines. To make the addition less unsightly, the chains were covered with boards, forming a box about 50 feet long.

The *Kearsarge* had spent two years in European waters, the past year under Winslow, looking for Confederate cruisers. Like Semmes, the 52-

Raphael Semmes, from a photograph taken in England following the loss of his ship. *(National Archives)*

year-old Winslow was not in the best of health. A disease that navy doctors diagnosed as malaria had nearly blinded his right eye. Unlike Semmes, the irascible Winslow was in disfavor with his superiors as a result of his undistinguished service early in the war. For Winslow to be commanding a single third-class steamer like the *Kearsarge* suggested that he had been given the lowliest posting consistent with his rank.

Meanwhile, Semmes made a crucial decision: He would fight the *Kearsarge*. His decision was based on both logic and his own combative temperament.

He could attempt to escape the *Kearsarge*. There were two channels for ships leaving Cherbourg, and although they were only two miles apart it would be difficult for a single ship to monitor them both, particularly at night. Any attempt would have to be made quickly, however, for the Yankees had doubtless put out a call for reinforcements. But what if the *Alabama* should succeed in breaking out? Her officers were weary, the crew homesick, and the ship herself desperately in need of drydocking. It would be difficult to keep the *Alabama* at sea in her present state, and in any case, to what purpose? Her very success as a commerce raider had made prizes scarce.

A second option was for Semmes to lay up the *Alabama* as he had the *Sumter* two years before when that vessel was blockaded at Gibraltar. The *Kearsarge* would doubtless be reinforced within days, and no one could expect the *Alabama* to take on two or three enemy cruisers. Semmes might well be offered another ship, but he would have to recruit and train a new crew. Meanwhile, the thought of the *Alabama* laid up—rotting away at some French wharf—was anathema to her captain. For the moment there was only one Yankee outside the breakwater, and that was the *Kearsarge*. Semmes had a mental list of Federal warships too powerful to be challenged, and the *Kearsarge* was not on it.

Semmes's decision reflected a number of other factors in addition to his reluctance to bid farewell to the ship that had made him famous. One, certainly, was the reduced utility of any Confederate cruiser in 1864. Because commerce raiding was no longer profitable, Semmes could justify putting his ship at risk in a way that he could not have done a year or two earlier. Another factor in Semmes's thinking was the indifferent level of professionalism he had observed in the U.S. Navy throughout the war. He remembered Winslow as a competent officer from their association during the Mexican War, but James Palmer of the *Iroquois* and Homer Blake of the *Hatteras* presumably had been competent as well. Palmer's ship Semmes had eluded, Blake's he had sunk in 13 minutes.

The critical factor, however, was Semmes's aggressive personality. He had cruised in South African waters almost within sight of the powerful *Vanderbilt*, convinced that if he encountered the Federal side-wheeler he could handle her. Two months later, spoiling for a fight, he had hoped to encounter a vessel of his own class, *Wyoming*, in the Sunda Strait. Now, with the war apparently lost, Semmes could at least strike a blow for the honor of the Confederate navy. He would defeat an enemy warship more powerful than his own, and he would do so in the great theater that was Europe!

Another psychological factor was at work as well, for Semmes was in search of personal vindication. Throughout his three years on the *Sumter* and then the *Alabama*, he had been called a pirate or a privateer. Another man might have shrugged off such canards, but Semmes was hypersensitive to any charge that touched on his honor. Facing an enemy warship that outgunned him, what better way to defy those who called him pirate than to fight and sink the *Kearsarge*? What pirate would deliberately seek combat with a warship more powerful than his own? In the words of one historian, Semmes fought "because he had to and because he wished to."[2]

On the afternoon of June 14, Semmes summoned Kell to his cabin. As his executive officer took a chair, Semmes said, "Kell, I am going out to fight the *Kearsarge*. What do you think of it?"[3] This statement says much of Semmes and his style of command. The critical decision had been made; Kell was now invited to comment on it. Semmes had rarely consulted Kell on matters of strategy during their three years together, and he was not now looking for a debate. Semmes went on:

> As you know, the arrival of the *Alabama* at this port has been telegraphed to all parts of Europe. Within a few days, Cherbourg will be effectively blockaded by Yankee cruisers. It is uncertain whether or not we shall be permitted to repair the *Alabama* here, and in the meantime the delay is to our advantage. I think we may whip the *Kearsarge*, the two vessels being of wood and carrying about the same number of men and guns. Besides, Mr. Kell, although the Confederate States government has ordered me to avoid engagements with the enemy's cruisers, I am tired of running from that flaunting rag![4]

Kell was not convinced that his captain's decision was wise, and reminded Semmes of some of the disparities between the two antagonists. The *Kearsarge* mounted two 11-inch pivot guns, which, while lacking the range of those on the *Alabama*, packed considerably more power at close range. And whereas the *Alabama* had been built for speed, her opponent had the sturdy construction of a man-of-war. Kell reminded Semmes that their powder had proved defective in the most recent target practice, with only one third of the fuses detonating properly. Semmes brushed off the warning, telling Kell, "I will take the chances of one in three."[5]

Kell set to work to prepare for battle. The raider took on 100 tons of coal, in part to keep her hull low in the water and in part to protect her engines. The yards were slung in chains, the deck holystoned, and the

One of the *Kearsarge's* destructive pivot guns in action against the *Alabama*. *(Library of Congress)*

brasswork polished. Guns, magazines, and shell rooms were carefully examined. To Kell's dismay, several barrels of powder were found to have been exposed to damp and had to be thrown overboard. He could only hope that other powder, packed in canisters, would prove sound.

Word that they would be fighting the *Kearsarge* spread like wildfire through the *Alabama*. No one seemed surprised at Semmes's decision to fight, and few wanted to miss the battle. The motley collection of wharf rats whom Semmes had browbeaten across the seven seas were eager to risk their lives for a country most had never seen. They worked to a song:

> We're homeward bound, we're homeward bound,
> And soon we'll stand on English ground
> But ere that English land we see,
> We first must fight the *Kearsargee*.[6]

On June 15 Semmes penned a letter to M. Bonfils, the Confederate agent in Cherbourg. Bonfils was to inform his U.S. counterpart that Captain Semmes hoped that the *Kearsarge* was not at Cherbourg solely to pick up the prisoners discharged by the *Alabama*. Semmes issued a formal challenge: "I desire you to say to the United States consul that my intention is to fight the *Kearsarge* as soon as I can make the necessary arrangements. . . . I beg she will not depart before I am ready to go out."[7] Ever prudent, he then entrusted to Bonfils's care the raider's operating funds—some 4,700 gold sovereigns—and the 60 or so chronometers that the *Alabama* had collected during her epic cruise.

For three days the *Alabama*'s crew coaled and drilled for battle. The emphasis on boarding drill, complete with pistols and cutlasses, convinced many on the raider that Semmes—secretive as always—planned to lay his ship along the enemy and board her. Although French authorities would not allow either warship to recruit new crewmen, two of the *Alabama*'s petty officers who had returned from Paris to be in on the fight were allowed to rejoin their ship.

By the afternoon of June 18, Confederate preparations were complete. Semmes advised the port admiral of his intention to engage the *Kearsarge* the following day, Sunday. Was there a touch of faith in the supernatural in Semmes's makeup? The crew thought Sunday his lucky day; the commissioning of the *Alabama*, the capture of the famous *Ariel*, and the defeat of the *Hatteras* had all taken place on Sundays.

Even on the day before the battle there was no shortage of visitors. Several friendly Frenchmen, including the loyal Bonfils, warned Semmes against fighting a "superior force." Bonfils was so apprehensive that he wired the Confederate minister in Paris, John Slidell, urging him to forbid Semmes from fighting. Slidell declined to interfere, stating that he had full confidence in Semmes's judgment.[8]

In Cherbourg there was talk of Winslow's having employed chains to protect his ship's hull. Among those who heard such rumors was Semmes's own secretary, Breedlove Smith. But Cherbourg was full of rumors—the *Alabama*, for instance, was alleged to have recruited sailors from a British man-of-war—and if Semmes heard anything about chains, he was undeterred. A last-minute visitor to the raider was Commander George T. Sinclair, a Confederate naval agent who had come from Paris to view the battle. He thought the *Alabama*'s officers "jaded and worn out," but wrote of Semmes, "He seems to have weighed the matter well in his own mind, and determination was marked in every line of his faded and worn countenance."[9]

Saturday night, many of the *Alabama's* officers attended a banquet in Cherbourg hosted by local Confederate partisans. Responding to toasts, the officers vowed that they would either sink the *Kearsarge* or "make another corsair out of her"—a hint that the result they most desired was to capture the enemy ship. While his officers exchanged toasts, Semmes slipped into one of the *Alabama's* boats and was rowed to the town. There, by special arrangement, he celebrated Mass in a small Catholic church. He was back on his ship by 10:00 p.m.[10]

Semmes's challenge had been relayed to John Winslow on Wednesday, June 15. Semmes's sarcasm in asking that Winslow not depart was wasted on the stolid Yankee; having pursued Rebel raiders for more than a year, Winslow had no intention of leaving station for any reason.

In contrast to Semmes, who asked no one's advice on how to fight the *Kearsarge*, Winslow called in his officers to discuss tactics. He speculated that the battle would be fought on parallel lines and that Semmes would seek sanctuary in French waters should the fighting go badly. Visitors from Cherbourg told of comings and goings on the *Alabama*; the loading of coal, the removal of specie, and the exercises with sword and cutlass. The initiative lay with Semmes, for he alone could determine the day and time of the engagement.

On the morning of June 19, at about 10 o'clock, the *Kearsarge's* crew had been inspected and dismissed to attend religious services. The morning was warm, with only a hint of haze. Winslow was about to read from the Scripture when the lookout cried, "She's coming out, and she's heading straight for us!" Winslow laid his Bible aside and picked up his spyglass. The drums beat to quarters.

Whatever was to happen that Sunday would take place before a great audience. Cherbourg was overflowing with visitors who had come to see the battle, and some 15,000 people crowded along the bluffs that afforded the best view of the Channel. There was plenty of betting. The two ships were screw steamers of about the same tonnage, each powered by two engines. The *Alabama*, with a crew of 149, boasted as its forward pivot the 110-pound Blakely rifle that was considered one of the most advanced weapons of its day. The *Kearsarge*, with a complement of 163, mounted seven guns—one fewer than her antagonist—but the word among naval profes-

Captain John Winslow poses with his officers after the *Kearsarge* has sunk the *Alabama*. *(National Archives)*

sionals was that her two 11-inch Dahlgrens were formidable weapons indeed.

One boat in the harbor would carry painter Edouard Manet, complete with pencils and sketchbook, to the scene of the action; he would convert his initial sketches into a famous painting of the battle. Among others who happened to be in Cherbourg that weekend was John Lancaster, a wealthy English businessman on holiday with his family in his sleek yacht, the *Deerhound*. His children had elected to watch the battle rather than go to church, and the *Deerhound* left the harbor early in the morning to find a good viewing point in the Channel.

On the *Alabama*, chief engineer Miles Freeman started his fires about 6:00 a.m. Shortly thereafter, the port admiral informed Semmes that the French ironclad *Couronne* would escort the *Alabama* to sea, to ensure that there was no violation of the three-mile limit. Semmes inspected his crew at muster, commenting on their smart appearance in white shirts and blue trousers. Commander Sinclair was one of the last visitors to the ship. He urged Semmes to keep away from the enemy's 11-inch guns, drawing from the Alabamian a rare hint as to his battle plan. In an apparent reference to his Blakely, Semmes replied, "I shall feel him first and it will all depend on that." When Sinclair asked to be allowed to join the *Alabama* for the battle, Semmes demurred. He was honor bound not to increase his complement.[11]

The *Alabama* got under way a few minutes before 10:00 a.m. She steamed past the *Couronne*, which fell in behind her. She approached the breakwater, moving, in Semmes's earlier description, "with the lightness and grace of a swan." As the raider passed a French liner, the *Napoleon*, her crew cheered the *Alabama* and the band struck up "Dixie."

As soon as the *Alabama* passed the breakwater, her officers could see the *Kearsarge* some five miles away. Semmes pointed directly toward her. Then, calling his crew aft, he mounted a gun carriage and gave a brief but rousing exhortation:

> Officers and Seamen of the *Alabama*!—You have, at length, another opportunity of meeting the enemy—the first that has been presented to you since you sank the *Hatteras*! In the meantime, you have been all over the world, and it is not too much to say, that you have destroyed and driven for protection under neutral flags one half of the enemy's commerce, which, at the beginning of the war, covered every sea. This is an achievement of which you may well be proud; and a grateful nation will not be unmindful of it. The name of your ship has become a household word wherever civilization extends. Shall that name be tarnished by defeat?

Semmes's words drew from more than a hundred voices a cry of "Never!" He went on:

> Remember that you are in the English Channel, the theatre of so much of the naval glory of our race, and that the eyes of all Europe are at this moment upon you. The flag that floats over you is that of a young Republic, who bids to her enemies, whenever and wherever found. Show the world that you know how to uphold it! Go to your quarters.[12]

As the *Alabama* steered toward her opponent, sailors opened the magazines and shell rooms, filled tubs of water with which to combat fires, and sanded the decks to prevent their becoming slippery with blood. Semmes planned to fight his starboard guns, and to strengthen his broadside he shifted one of his port 32-pounders to starboard. This caused the ship to list slightly, but it also reduced the amount of hull exposed to enemy fire.

Winslow spotted his opponent at about 10:20. He turned his ship away, in part to avoid any infringement of French waters but primarily to deny Semmes a sanctuary inside the marine league should things go badly for the Confederates. About seven miles from shore the *Kearsarge* reversed course and headed directly for the *Alabama*. Winslow's plan, according to his official report, was to run his antagonist down and thus at least cripple her. When the two ships were about 1,800 yards apart, however, Semmes turned to port. Were the gunners ready? he asked Kell. When Kell said they were, Semmes gave the order to open fire.

The *Alabama's* pivot guns opened the battle at 10:57. For several minutes only the Confederate vessel was in effective range, but her shots were high and had no effect except in the *Kearsarge's* rigging. When the range was down to about 900 yards, Winslow reconsidered his plan to close on the *Alabama* lest he receive "raking fire"—a full broadside from the enemy's starboard guns. Instead, the *Kearsarge* turned to port and opened fire with her own starboard battery, attempting at the same time to reach a position from which to rake the *Alabama*. It quickly became apparent that the *Kearsarge* was the faster of the two vessels, and that Semmes was unlikely to reach a position from which he might rake his opponent. With the range narrowed to less than 700 yards, the brief period when the *Alabama's* guns outranged those of her antagonist had passed.

Naval gunnery in 1864 had progressed somewhat since British admiral Horatio Nelson's day, with the development of rifled cannon; nevertheless, 10 percent accuracy under battle conditions was still considered good shooting. In the clash between the *Alabama* and the *Kearsarge*, at least 15 minutes passed before either ship inflicted significant damage. Then a shell from the *Alabama* passed through the *Kearsarge's* starboard bulwarks and exploded on the quarterdeck, wounding three members of a gun crew. A few minutes later the Federal vessel was struck again. A 110-pound projectile from the *Alabama's* forward pivot glanced off the *Kearsarge's* counter and lodged in her stern post. The stern post—a great, curved timber that anchored the planks of the upper hull—was a vulnerable point on any vessel, and the impact, according to the *Kearsarge's* surgeon, shook the ship from stem to stern.[13] Had the shell exploded it might have crippled the Federal warship, but it did not explode.

Almost immediately the battle began to turn. A shot from the *Kearsarge* destroyed the *Alabama's* steering apparatus; for the remainder of the engagement the Confederate cruiser could only be steered with tackles. Shells from the *Kearsarge's* Dahlgrens began to smash into the raider. Semmes was heard to say of his antagonists, "Confound them, they've been fighting 20 minutes and they're cool as posts!"[14]

Lieutenant Joseph Wilson —"Fighting Joe" to his messmates—commanded 22 men at the *Alabama's* aft pivot. He was about to fire a round when a shell from the *Kearsarge* exploded alongside the gun, killing or wounding all but a few of its crew. Coxswain Michael Mars, one of the uninjured, took in the devastation and shoveled the human fragments into the sea. While Mars cleared and resanded the deck, Kell ordered the crew of a 32-pounder to man the pivot. At one point in the action a shot from the *Kearsarge* cut down the *Alabama's* colors. They were quickly run up the mizzenmast.

Winslow commanded his ship from a chest on the *Kearsarge's* starboard quarter; Semmes commanded from the horse block, a similar raised section of the quarterdeck. One of Semmes's officers recalled him "leaning on the hammock-rail; at times watching earnestly the enemy, and then casting his eye about our ship. . . . Nothing seemed to escape his active mind or eye."[15] Midway in the action a shell fragment inflicted a painful wound to Semmes's right hand. He called on a petty officer to bandage it but did not leave the quarterdeck.

By now sailors on both ships had stripped to the waist to work the heavy guns. They were drenched with sweat and black from smoke and powder. From time to time there were pauses in the firing when one of the combatants was obscured by smoke. The two ships were fighting clockwise on a circular track, much of the time at a range of about 500 yards. Only steamers could have fought as they did, maintaining a circular course in light winds. The day of ramming and boarding a well-armed enemy was past.

William Alsdorf was a loader at one of the *Kearsarge*'s Dahlgrens, and his narrative catches some of the excitement on the Federal cruiser:

> Our 1st Lt. Thornton went along to each Gun telling the Gunners to take good aim. "Don't fire, boys, unless you have good aim, for one hit is worth 50 thrown away." Every man was doing his duty. There was no flinching. . . . Both of our ships were completely enveloped in smoke, but as we were fighting in a Circle we soon ran out of it and the shells flew thick & fast.[16]

Semmes was so preoccupied with keeping the *Kearsarge* from crossing his stern that he made no attempt to supervise his gunners, leaving that task to Kell. Unfortunately for the Confederates, the *Alabama* had few experienced gunners. Commander Sinclair, watching from the shore, noted that although the *Alabama* was firing at least three shots for every two of her opponent, she usually fired high. Sinclair noticed something else: The smoke from the *Alabama*'s guns was much heavier than that from the *Kearsarge*, at times resembling heavy steam. The raider's powder had deteriorated more than Semmes had realized.

After some 45 minutes of battle, an 11-inch shell passed through the *Alabama*'s starboard side and exploded inside, collapsing a coal bunker and raising a cloud of coal dust that brought cheers from the *Kearsarge*. Other rounds struck between the mainmast and the mizzenmast, near the waterline. With steam pressure falling and his ship down by the stern, Semmes attempted one final throw of the dice. He ordered Kell to hoist jibs and trysails, to shift guns to the port side in order to raise some shot holes above water, and to point for the French coast. As Winslow had predicted, Semmes was seeking refuge in French waters.

Semmes now ordered Kell to inspect below decks, and the executive officer was appalled at what he saw. Surgeon David Llewellyn was at his operating table, but the casualty he had been treating had just been swept away by a shell. Water was entering the hull through holes the size of a wheelbarrow, and over the creak of timbers Kell could hear the popping of air bubbles from drowned compartments. He returned to the quarterdeck and told Semmes that the ship could not float for more than 10 minutes. By this time Winslow had maneuvered his vessel between the *Alabama* and the French coast and was in position to rake his foe. A few minutes after noon Semmes made the most painful decision of his naval career, telling Kell to cease firing, shorten sail, and haul down the colors.

The *Alabama's* final, chaotic moments do not lend themselves to orderly narrative. Although the raider was now attempting to surrender, previous pauses in her firing had been followed by renewed fighting, and the Federals were wary. The Confederates would claim that the *Kearsarge* fired repeatedly on the *Alabama* after the latter had flown a white flag. The Federals, for their part, charged that the *Alabama* fired several rounds after her nominal surrender.

A few minutes after noon, with a white flag now visible on the *Alabama's* spanker boom, the *Kearsarge* ceased firing. The once-graceful raider was a woeful sight. There were great gaps in her bulwarks, and several spars were supported aloft only by their wire rigging. The funnel was riddled with holes. The deck had been torn up by the *Kearsarge's* fire and was littered with the *Alabama's* own shell boxes. The raider, still under sail, forged slowly ahead, leaving a trail of wreckage and a few bobbing heads astern.

Kell put two of the *Alabama's* officers, Fullam and Wilson, in charge of the raider's two seaworthy boats, filled them with wounded, and sent them to the *Kearsarge* with a request for assistance. Aboard the Federal cruiser, Fullam looked up and down the deck and asked about casualties. When told that only three men had been wounded, he was incredulous. "My God!" Fullam exclaimed. "It's a slaughterhouse over there."[17]

With the *Alabama's* bow now high in the air, Semmes and Kell were among the last to leave the ship. The sea was filled with bobbing heads, but Winslow—to Semmes's everlasting scorn—was slow in sending boats. John Lancaster, who had viewed the battle from the *Deerhound,* ordered his captain to save such survivors as he could, and Semmes proved to be among those rescued by the *Deerhound*. Kell estimated that he had been in the water for about 20 minutes when he was picked up by one of the *Deerhound's* boats and reunited with Semmes.

On the *Deerhound* Semmes was introduced to his benefactor, Lancaster. The Englishman told him that he believed all survivors had been picked up; where did Semmes want to go? Raphael Semmes was wounded, half drowned, and shattered by the loss of his ship, but he still had his wits about him. "I am now under English colors," he whispered, "and the sooner you put me with my officers and men on English soil, the better."[18]

While Semmes caught his breath, his ship was in her death throes. The mainmast, which had been damaged by gunfire, crashed into the sea as the *Alabama*'s bow rose higher in the air. Dr. Browne, the surgeon aboard the *Kearsarge*, was struck by the way the raider assumed a near-perpendicular position as her ordnance and engines collapsed into the stern. He thought it remarkable that her final plunge—shown in the victor's log as taking place at 12:24 p.m.—brought no cheering from the crew of the *Kearsarge*, only silence.

Casualties aboard the *Alabama* were heavy. Although only 9 men died in the action, 20 were wounded and 12 more drowned after the ship foundered. In contrast, there were no immediate fatalities aboard the *Kearsarge*, although one of her three wounded crewmen later died. The Federal vessel had been fortunate; two rounds from the *Alabama* had passed through gun ports but had inflicted no casualties. Winslow, in his official report, wrote that the *Alabama*'s gunnery had been rapid and wild at first, but had improved toward the close of the action. He estimated that the *Alabama* had fired some 370 shot and shell—more than twice the number fired by the *Kearsarge*—and that 13 or 14 had struck the *Kearsarge*'s hull and 16 or 17 others had damaged her rigging.[19] The most visible damage to the Federal cruiser was a great hole in her funnel where one of the Confederate shells had exploded.

For his victory John Winslow was promoted to commodore, notwithstanding displeasure in Washington at Semmes's escape to England. As for Semmes, he never discussed how he had expected to defeat the *Kearsarge*. He had known in May that a large number of his fuses were defective. He had discovered either in Cherbourg or earlier that much of his powder had deteriorated as well. Apart from these critical problems, the *Alabama* was short of experienced gunners, and those on board had been permitted little live practice. All things considered, the *Alabama* was in no condition to challenge such a staunch opponent as the *Kearsarge*.

For the rest of his life—most of it passed in Mobile, Alabama—Semmes would maintain that he knew nothing of the chains protecting the *Kearsarge*. His petulant reaction was somehow in character: the chains were a typically underhanded Yankee trick! But he would find little support for this view even from dedicated Confederates, for professional navy men recognized that Winslow had every right to protect his ship by whatever means he chose.

The last word on the engagement may have come from the influential London *Times*:

> Fathoms deep in Norman waters lies the good ship *Alabama*, the swift sea rover, just so many tons of broken-up iron and wood . . . wearing away in the huge depository of that genuine and original marine store-dealer, Father Neptune. . . .
>
> The *Alabama* could have found no more fitting grave, for she had lived on the waters, their child and playmate. She hailed from no Southern harbor, she was warned off from many a neutral port, and went away to her wild work amid the loneliness of the watery waste. . . .
>
> So end the log of the *Alabama*—a vessel of which it may be said that nothing in her whole career became her like its close! Although a legitimate and recognized form of hostilities, the capture and destruction of peaceful merchantmen is one barbarism of war which civilized society is beginning to deprecate.[20]

Notwithstanding that it had been a notably one-sided engagement, an aura of romance clung to the *Alabama*'s last battle. For Southern sympathizers—and there were many in Europe—the clash off Cherbourg was the Civil War in microcosm: the gallant but outgunned South, ignoring its deficiencies in matériel, fearlessly taking on a superior force. It did not matter that the result would have no effect whatever on the land war in North America. In the words of a Frenchman who observed the battle, "The Confederates have lost their ship, but not their honor."[21]

Notes

1. John M. Taylor, *Confederate Raider: Raphael Semmes of the* Alabama (Washington, D.C.: Brassey's, 1994), 196.
2. George W. Dalzell, *The Flight From the Flag* (Chapel Hill: University of North Carolina Press, 1940), 245.
3. John Kell, *Recollections of a Naval Life*, 244.
4. Taylor, *Confederate Raider*, 199.
5. Norman C. Delaney, *John McIntosh Kell of the Raider* Alabama (University of Alabama Press, 1973), 159.
6. Dalzell, *The Flight from the Flag*, 161.

7. Taylor, *Confederate Raider*, 200.
8. Ibid., 201.
9. Delaney, *John McIntosh Kell*, 160.
10. Roberts, *Semmes of the* Alabama, 228.
11. Frank J. Merli, ed., "Letters on the *Alabama*," *Mariner's Mirror*, May 1972.
12. Raphael Semmes, *Memoirs of Service Afloat During the War Between the States* (Louisiana State University Press, 1996), 756.
13. John M. Browne, "The Duel Between the *Alabama* and the *Kearsarge*." In Robert U. Johnson, ed., *Battles and Leaders of the Civil War*, 4, 623.
14. Taylor, *Confederate Raider*, 205.
15. Arthur Sinclair, *Two Years on the* Alabama (Boston: Lee and Shepard, 1896), 281.
16. John M. Taylor, "Showdown Off Cherbourg," *Yankee*, July 1984.
17. Taylor, *Confederate Raider*, 208.
18. Sinclair, *Two Years on the* Alabama, 613.
19. *Official Records (Navy)*, Series I, vol. 3, 79–80.
20. Taylor, *Confederate Raider*, 217.
21. Ibid., 213.

14

The Raider and the Rascal: P. D. Haywood's *Cruise of the* Alabama

Norman C. Delaney

In the historical nonfiction sections of many libraries is a book, *The Cruise of the* Alabama, *by One of the Crew, With Notes from Historical Authorities* by "Philip D. Haywood," published in 1886 by Houghton, Mifflin Company. It is high time for "Haywood" and his book of fiction to be exposed again—hopefully for the last time.

Published material on the *Alabama* is inadequate. First Officer John McIntosh Kell's autobiography, *Recollections of a Naval Life* (Washington, 1900) lacks many important details of the cruise; the recollections of Admiral Raphael Semmes, *Service Afloat* (Baltimore, 1869), are too bitterly partisan to be satisfactory; and the recollections of a junior lieutenant, Arthur Sinclair, *Two Years on the* Alabama (Boston, 1896)—written thirty years after the cruise—are overly romanticized. But these books, despite their shortcomings, were written by men who had sailed aboard the *Alabama,* and what they wrote about their ship and her cruise must be taken seriously; the Haywood story should not. Unfortunately, bibliographies of several secondary works on the *Alabama* and other Confederate raiders indicate that at least some authors have considered the Haywood book a reliable source, although a few admit to having reservations about it.

In 1967 Volume I of *Civil War Books: A Critical Bibliography,* edited by Allan Nevins, James I. Robertson, Jr., and Bell I. Wiley, appeared. The section on "The Navies," compiled and written by the late Thomas Wells, says of *The Cruise of the Alabama*: "An interesting account purportedly written by a sailor, but regarded as spurious by officers who served on the *Alabama*." This summation of the book is too inconclusive, and the inauthenticity of the book should be firmly established once and for all. Research into the career of John McIntosh Kell and the story of "Haywood" reveals how this bogus history originated.

The April 1886 issue of *Century Magazine* featured three articles on the *Alabama*. Two focus on her battle of June 19, 1864, with USS *Kearsarge* off Cherbourg, France. One was written by Kell, the senior surviving officer of the raider since the death of Raphael Semmes in 1877, and another was written by John M. Browne, former surgeon aboard the *Kearsarge*. The third article was by "P. D. Haywood," alleged to have been a member of the *Alabama*'s crew. Haywood's reminiscences of the cruise included illustrations by professional artists based on the author's sketches of sailor life aboard the raider. All three articles aroused special interest when they first appeared, as the *Alabama* story provided dramatic reading to a public anxious to learn about the mysterious raider and her already legendary cruise.

John Kell, engaged in farming at Sunnyside, Georgia, since the end of the war, was incensed at what he considered unfair and inaccurate reporting of the *Alabama*'s cruise and her battle with the *Kearsarge*. He insisted that Browne's account of the battle was hearsay, since the ship's surgeon could not have actually witnessed the action he was describing: "The surgeon's place at such a time is in the cockpit in the bottom of the ship to care for the sick and to be ready to receive the wounded. He knows nothing of what is transpiring on deck." But it was the Haywood article that most irritated Kell. For one thing, he had no recollection of any Haywood aboard the *Alabama*. There is no Haywood listed in the roster of officers and crew in Arthur Sinclair's *Two Years on the* Alabama, although he admitted that Haywood might have sailed under an assumed name. His doubts were supported by former officers William P. Brooks, Matt O'Brien, and Dr. Francis L. Galt. Brooks had a meeting with Michael Mars, one of the *Alabama*'s crew, and both men, after comparing notes, were convinced that Haywood was an impostor. When an expanded version of Haywood's article appeared as *The Cruise of the* Alabama later in 1886, Kell became even more

John McIntosh Kell as adjutant general of Georgia in 1886. *(From* The Life and Services of John Newland Maffit *by Emma Martin Maffit)*

determined to discredit both author and book. In an interview with a sympathetic news reporter, Kell charged that Haywood convicted himself as an impostor in a dozen different places. Kell observed that "in every instance where [Haywood] presents something new [about the *Alabama*] it is something false." He cited examples:

[Haywood] says . . . that the crew defied the authorities of Terceira and rode the policemen on their backs. Not a man of the crew was allowed to go on shore at Terceira. . . .

He speaks of Forrest, a man who gave us considerable trouble, as a deserter from the *Sumter*. Forrest was never on the *Sumter*. [Kell is incorrect: the crew list of the *Sumter* lists George Forrest as a sailor aboard that vessel.] Further, he says of [Forrest]: "He was tall, powerful and had considerable manly beauty." Now, Forrest was a short, thickset fellow with dingy yellowish hair. . . . He was positively ugly and one of the most vicious fellows I ever knew. . . . [Haywood] says on our cruise we usually set the English ensign "to deceive Uncle Sam" when the truth is, that we rarely used the English flag, for the simple reason that the U.S. flag was better suited to our purpose. . . . Haywood says "we coaled from lighters near Singapore." The manner of our coaling at Singapore was such as to especially impress the memory of all on board. We went to the wharf and lay there a whole day while three hundred Chinamen brought coal on board in their queer little pans. . . . He says that the crew almost mutinied near Singapore; that as they were "paid by the month," they would not have lost much money by such action. In no branch of naval service are the men paid by the month. Merchantmen and war vessels alike pay at the end of a voyage or cruise. In the case of the Alabama, the men never were paid off until after the ship was sunk, when Mr. Bulloch, our agent at Liverpool, made a full statement with all of the crew who escaped to that port. On "liberty days" we would give the men a little money, but never more than a pound apiece. That one false statement is enough to expose Haywood. . . .

Kell defended his crew against one of Haywood's most damning assertions. Haywood had written: "I had never been on a ship with such a bad lot. [They] were mostly of that class . . . that ship for the 'run' (from port to port), and not for the voyage, and are always a rough, mutinous set." Kell contended that the crew's accomplishments during the Alabama's twenty-two months' cruise belied such a characterization. He could not let such statements go unchallenged because they would also bring into question his own competence as ship's executive officer. In his Century article Kell described his role as an officer aboard the Alabama: "With our peculiar service, and with our ports locked against us, we were compelled to observe the strictest discipline with both officers and crew. As the executive officer who enforced this discipline I may say that a nobler set of young men filling the position of officers, and a braver and more willing crew, never floated." In his interview, Kell pointed out that the Alabama's crew had had only five liberty days during the entire cruise and that two of these had been on barren coasts where no whiskey was available. However, he admitted, "some [sailors] did get tipsy, and once we had considerable trouble with a party of them but these were the usual incidents of the service. . . . When we took a prize and found whiskey on board it was the first thing destroyed. . . ."

Kell found another opportunity to defend the "sobriety of the officers and crew of the Alabama" upon receipt of a letter of inquiry from Professor Henry A. Scomp of Emory College. Scomp was researching a history of the liquor traffic in Georgia and wanted information on the use of spirits in the

Confederate Navy. Kell replied promptly in order to "disabuse [Scomp's] mind of the iniquitous lies and most infamous slanders that the *Century Magazine* and other so-called 'respectable' publishing houses have placed before the public." His letter repeated his earlier contention that "sobriety, discipline, and thorough cleanliness prevailed aboard the *Alabama*" (although he now claimed that during the twenty-two months, the *Alabama's* crew were in only two places where they could have obtained liquor). He wrote: "I, in person, superintended the distribution of every prize, and never allowed my boat's crew to come on board of the prize until all the liquor was thrown overboard, or put where the crew could not get it."

In the meantime Haywood exposed himself as a liar and impostor. Because of the initially favorable public response to Haywood's article, the *Century* editors requested him to contribute a biographical sketch of himself, and his answering letter was published in their issue of July 1886. He gave his place of birth as Charleston, South Carolina, in 1836. At age 2 he was taken to England by his father, "a retired East India naval officer," and later he was schooled at a Catholic seminary in France. (This information may be partly correct, as it was later said of him—as "James Horton"—that he was an "accomplished scholar" who spoke and wrote French, German, Spanish, and English fluently.) Haywood's "adventurous" life included service as an officer in the British and Chinese navies from 1853 to 1860. During this time he claimed to have seen action in the Crimean War, the Sepoy Mutiny in India, and the Taiping Rebellion in China. The ships aboard which he served were identified as the *Swiftsure, Britannia,* and *Redoute.* In late 1861, Haywood wrote, he returned to England and the following year shipped aboard the *Alabama.* After she sank in 1864, he spent the remainder of the war engaged in blockade running.

Haywood's biographical sketch convinced the *Century* editors that the author was a continuing source of popular adventure stories, and they contracted him to write another book. But it should have been obvious by this time that Haywood was a fraud. A check with *Colburn's United Service Magazine, and Naval and Military Journal* of 1853 or 1854 would have shown that no Haywood was listed among the promoted and appointed British naval officers during the time he claimed to have served.

Further investigation would have revealed no vessel named *Swiftsure* listed in the British Navy until 1870, nor was a *Redoute* commissioned in the

British Navy during the period when Haywood claimed service. But it was not until their issue of March 1887 that the *Century* finally announced that P. D. Haywood, "from his own admission . . . was not a seaman on the Confederate raider though at the time the article was accepted he assured us he was." The editors had no choice but to admit that they had been duped. Their sole satisfaction was in being able to announce that the Haywood article was exposed in time for its exclusion from their four-volume series, *Battles and Leaders of the Civil War.*

Credit for the full exposure of both book and author goes to an enterprising, anonymous reporter for the Philadelphia *Weekly Times.* In its issue of December 11, 1886, the paper headlined the Haywood exposé:

A LITERARY CRIMINAL

The Romantic, Criminal and Literary Career of James Young.

A FORGER AND CONFIDENCE MAN

Turns Up as James H. Horton, F. A. Vaughan, Marcus T. Young and Philip D. Haywood.

HIS LITERARY IMPOSTURES

Houghton, Mifflin & Co. and the Century Magazine Among His Victims.

HIS THEFT IN PHILADELPHIA

He is Again in Philadelphia After a Long and Varied Criminal Career.

The *Weekly Times* took an obvious delight in showing that the *Century* and Houghton, Mifflin editors had been made fools of. In a six-column feature article the newspaper examined in detail the question of Haywood's identity and the authenticity of his book. Selected facts from the book were compared with those from his article, and the most glaring inconsistencies were exposed. Several of the dates in Haywood's book differed from those he had used in his article. Other discrepancies included the fact that the *Tycoon* had actually been captured by the *Alabama* off Brazil, near Bahia, whereas Haywood wrote in his book that the place of capture was "just outside of the harbor" off Cape Town, South Africa. (Ironically, the map used in Haywood's book shows the correct place of capture.)

The *Weekly Times* reporter investigating Haywood was apparently in contact with Kell, since he listed the same inaccuracies that had already been pointed out by the *Alabama*'s first officer. These included the conflicting descriptions of Seaman Forrest; the *Alabama*'s crew having been refused permission to land at Terceira; the unusual manner of taking on coal at Singapore; and the paying of the men at the end of the cruise rather than on a monthly basis.

The reporter did his work thoroughly. Not content to expose the book as a fraud, he had carefully investigated Haywood, whom he identified as James Young of Philadelphia. From police and newspaper reports, he pieced together the following story: Having completed his training as an engraver by 1863, James Young became an office assistant to Joshua Searle, a Philadelphia broker. Sometime during 1864 he stole $45,000 in government bonds from his employer and fled to Minneapolis. While in that city, boarding with the D. H. Horton family, Young swindled (by forging a mortgage) an elderly retired teacher he had known in Philadelphia. The old man refused to press charges against Young, however, because of their earlier friendship.

In 1867 Young went to Strasburg, Pennsylvania, where he assumed the name of James H. Horton. He married the daughter of the local hotel keeper, and the newlyweds moved to Lancaster soon afterward. In Lancaster he was joined by an elderly couple named Young, whom he identified as an uncle and aunt. (The woman, it was later discovered, was his mother.) During this time he was engaged in stock speculation and impressed the local people as being "a gentleman of culture and experience." It was later said of "James Horton" that he spoke of London, Paris, Berlin, and Calcutta as though he knew them well.

On June 11, 1873, Young was forced to leave abruptly and alone. For months he had been forging stock certificates and checks and in this way had stolen $75,000 from four Pennsylvania banks and from the Pennsylvania Reading Railroad. A $1,000 reward was offered through the Pinkerton Detective Agency for information leading to his arrest, and 60,000 circulars were sent to chiefs of police and postmasters throughout the country. "Horton" was described as being a corpulent 180 pounds, 5'7" or 8" tall, with small black eyes, heavy black eyebrows, short black hair (thinning in front), short side whiskers and a mustache sprinkled with gray, a prominent nose, high bridge, good teeth, generally good features, and a short, thick

Frank Leslie's Illustrated Newspaper, August 9, 1873

$1,000 REWARD.

PINKERTON'S NATIONAL DETECTIVE AGENCY.

ONE THOUSAND DOLLARS REWARD will be paid for the arrest, and detention for a requisition, of J. H. Horton, who, on May 26th, 1873, passed upon Reed. McGrann & Co., Bankers, of Lancaster, Pa., a forged Certificate of Stock of the Philadelphia and Reading Railroad Company, purporting to represent a value of $10,000. The amount realized by Horton from this and other similar transactions is about $75,000, and includes United States Treasury Gold Certificates, as follows, viz.: Letter A, Nos. 7,965 and 9,155 for $5,000 each; and Nos. 21,379, 24,519, 23,521, 25,206, 23,507, 25,199, 24,504, 24,794, 20,969 and 21,839 for $1,000 each, which he may endeavor to exchange, and for the recovery of which a liberal per centage will be paid.

Horton is about 40 years old, 5 feet 7 to 8 inches high, weighs 180 pounds, erect, broad-shouldered, pretty full chested, rather corpulent, sallow complexion, possibly flushed from heavy drinking, rather small black eyes, heavy black eyebrows, short black hair, short side whiskers and mustache, very slightly sprinkled with gray; hair thin on the forehead; rather prominent nose, high bridge; good teeth; generally good features; short thick neck; will probably be dressed in new clothes; wore on little finger a cameo ring, black oval ground, about ¾ by ½ inch, with white female head, mounting moderately heavy, and rather plain. Is short step, rapid walker, and proficient in pencil and pen sketching.

Pinkerton reward offer for apprehension of "J.H. Horton" for forgery of railroad stock certificates.

A reward offer for the arrest of J. H. Horton. *(Frank Leslie's Illustrated Newspaper)* neck. A pen-and-ink portrait of "Horton," sketched from memory by a Strasburg artist, was published as part of the reward circular. The vice president of the Pennsylvania Reading Railroad directed the Pinkertons to spare no expense in finding Horton in order to "make an example" of the man who had forged his company's stocks. It was publication of the wanted circular in *Frank Leslie's Illustrated Magazine,* August 9, 1873, that led to recognition of the forger soon afterward. "Horton" had made only a slight change in his appearance by shaving off his side whiskers. He was still wearing the cameo ring described in the circular.

Young was arrested in Providence, Rhode Island, where he was living under the alias F. A. Vaughan. He had made a good impression on the family with whom he boarded in a "quiet, peaceful, but aristocratic neighborhood" because of his "social qualifications" and his skill as an artist. When taken to the police station by the Pinkerton detective who had been tracking him, Young at first acted indignant. However, on learning that the detective would receive the $1,000 reward, he held up four fingers, asking, "How would that do?" He said he would write to New York City and have the money in hand by the next evening. When his attempt at bribery failed, Young admitted his identity and confessed that he had been preparing to commit the same fraud upon the Providence banks that he had perpetrated in Lancaster. He at first claimed to have lost most of his loot in speculation, but later admitted that some of it was invested in railroad bonds. In order to gain a commutation of his prison sentence, Young—after being returned to Lancaster for arraignment—agreed to restore $19,000 to the banks he had defrauded. This he did, and in return for immunity from prosecution on more than a single charge, he pleaded guilty and was fined and sentenced to two years' imprisonment.

After his release from prison, Young again took up residence in Lancaster, living a life of leisure and resuming his speculation in the stock market. He later moved to Philadelphia, where he suffered some business setbacks and became addicted to opium. A suicide attempt failed, and he recovered sufficiently to take an occasional job illustrating school books, a task for which he showed some talent.

In December 1886, the *Weekly Times* reporter found Young at his residence on Franklin Street in Philadelphia. The man who now claimed to be Philip Haywood appeared to be in his mid-forties. He was broad shouldered, weighed about 250 pounds, had a large head, small, fat hands, a massive forehead, silvery hair, white moustache, and imperial-style whiskers. A pair of eyeglasses dangled from his neck on a black cord. The reporter also noted Haywood's "very bright" eyes, "well-shaped" nose, and "beautiful, well-kept" teeth. However, his general appearance struck the reporter as being untidy and "seedy." Upon being questioned, Haywood told the reporter that he had written his *Alabama* book hurriedly in only ten days. He had first sent the manuscript to J. B. Lippincott's publishing house in Philadelphia, but when they offered only $50 for it, he turned to Houghton, Mifflin and accepted their offer of $600. (He had earlier been paid $200 by the *Century* Company for his article.) Haywood had already completed the second book he had agreed to write for the *Century* Company. Unaware that he was about to be exposed by his interviewer, Young told him:

> I'm not particularly proud of my connection with the Alabama, and don't care for any notoriety of that part of my record.
>
> There is a big field for sea stories. . . . The great secret of a sea story is to use the language of a sailor. . . . At present I am out of literature, although I may write a sea story or two in the future. I know I could make money at it, because the men who write these stories don't know anything about seamen or ships. . . . I'm engaged now in a brass enterprise. I'm of an inventive turn, somewhat of an artist, too. I have a thorough knowledge of machinery and I have invented several novelties lately in buttons, which are now being manufactured. Unless a man can find a publisher who will create a steady demand for his writings, storytelling is mere drudgery. There's nothing in it but bread. If the brass button business is not a success then I shall probably return to literature, a field that is so crowded today that men jostle each other every time their pens touch paper.
>
> . . . I'm out of literature for the present. I don't care to have anything said about what I have done, at least I'm not anxious. What I did write about myself was the outcome of my story and at the solicitation of the publishers, whose liberality has been remarkable.

His interview with "Haywood" confirmed the reporter's conviction that the man was unquestionably James Young, alias "F. A. Vaughan," alias "James H. Horton," and the exposé that appeared in the *Weekly Times* at last destroyed the credibility of the bogus *Alabama* sailor. The surviving officers of that vessel were delighted at Haywood's unmasking, believing it to be a vindication for them and for the *Alabama*. They would have been far from pleased, however, had they known that the mischief had already been done. Hundreds of copies of *The Cruise of the* Alabama were already in circulation and could not be recalled. Of these, many remain today in countless college and public libraries and in private collections—purportedly an authentic firsthand account of a seaman's cruise on the Confederate raider *Alabama*.

Copyright© 1973 Historical Times Inc.
This chapter first appeared in the May 1973 issue of *Civil War Times Illustrated*.

15

Reluctant Raider

JOHN M. TAYLOR

On a gray March day in 1863, nine Confederate naval officers living under false names at London boardinghouses received their orders. They were to gather their gear and proceed to an agreed rendezvous on Little St. James Street. From there, traveling in small groups, they would make their way by rail to Glasgow on Scotland's west coast to board a brand new ship. The vessel was called the *Japan,* but that would change as soon as she was well at sea. Then she would become the Confederate States Ship *Georgia,* a world-ranging commerce raider with orders to seize and burn every Union merchant ship she could find.

The *Georgia* was the project of two men who shared a venerable Virginia name. Matthew Fontaine Maury, author of scientific treatises such as *The Physical Geography of the Sea,* was the first. Matthew Maury was perhaps the most respected oceanographer of his day and, for many, his adherence to the Southern cause brought the Confederacy a measure of scientific respectability. Maury was outspoken, however, and by October 1862, his criticism of the Confederate Navy Department—headed by his Old Navy foe Stephen R. Mallory—soon landed him across the Atlantic, where his international reputation would make him an ideal agent in England. His dual mission there was to report on British attitudes toward the South's new government and to purchase ships for the Confederate Navy.

In February 1863, Navy Secretary Mallory directed Maury to locate and buy a ship suitable for service as a commerce destroyer. To do so, Maury would need to overcome some serious obstacles. Few available vessels had the speed and endurance necessary for a naval cruiser. And finding one that did would be difficult because of Britain's official neutrality; ever since the summer of 1862, when the famous C.S.S. *Alabama* had slipped away to avoid seizure by British authorities, Britain had been more careful to block the sale of war goods to the North American belligerents. Secrecy was essential, yet Matthew Maury was the most visible Confederate in Britain. He would have to conduct his search with great discretion to avoid detection by British officials and by the spies of U.S. Minister Charles Francis Adams.

Maury was not deterred. He had a number of friends who were sympathetic to the Southern cause, and he put them to good use. One was Captain Marin H. Jansen of the Royal Netherlands Navy, posted in London, with whom he had corresponded on scientific matters for a decade. Jansen was visiting British shipyards on behalf of the Dutch navy, and Maury asked him to keep Confederate requirements in mind—in blatant violation of Dutch neutrality. He asked Jansen to "note every vessel that they have in progress—from frames to completion—her size and draft and fitness for armaments. She should not be over 15 ft. draft—good under canvas, fast under steam—with the ability to keep the sea for a year, using steam only when necessary for the chase."

By early 1863, Maury had identified several possibilities, the most promising of which was the *Japan*. His main problem was that he had no money with which to make a purchase. On February 1, that problem was solved. Matthew's cousin and fellow Confederate naval officer, William Lewis Maury, arrived in London with $1.5 million in cotton warrants for ship purchases. This was the first money of any consequence Matthew Maury had seen since leaving home. Using the cotton warrants as collateral, he soon had the wherewithal to purchase the *Japan*.

He also had orders from the Navy Department naming the commander of the new raider: Lieutenant William Lewis Maury. Like Matthew, Lewis was an alumnus of the Old Navy. Born in Virginia in 1813 and appointed a midshipman in 1835, he had worked his way slowly through the ranks to command one of the vessels in Commodore Matthew Perry's expedition to Japan in 1852. Maury charted the Japanese coast and led

Commander William L. Maury of the CSS *Georgia*. *(U.S. Navy Imaging Center)*

one of the first American parties to enter Edo, the city we know today as Tokyo.

Returning to Virginia from his adventure in Japan, Lewis courted his English-born cousin Anne Fontaine, and the two were married in 1856. The wedding followed a difficult year. Only months before, Lewis had been required to serve on a controversial navy retirement board (chaired by Stephen Mallory). One of the board's actions had been to place Matthew Maury on indefinite leave of absence, ostensibly because of an old hip injury. Lewis so regretted his participation in this "plucking board" that it may have contributed to an illness; Matthew wrote later that year that "the odious business of that Board helped to make [Lewis] sick. . . . No man can love right and hate wrong more than he does." In 1858, after considerable lobbying by Matthew Maury and his friends, President James Buchanan restored the oceanographer to active duty.

Lewis was seven years younger than his famous cousin, and quite different in appearance. In contrast to the stocky Matthew, Lewis was slim and nearly six feet tall. He entered the Confederate Navy at age 49, with a touch of gray in his close-cropped beard. His health less than robust, he may have been a bit too frail for rigorous sea duty. Neither of the Maurys was an avid secessionist, but Lewis in particular—despite his devotion to his family, his church, and his home state—may have been a reluctant Confederate. Whereas Matthew Maury left the U.S. Navy three days after Virginia seceded, Lewis waited another three weeks before resigning.

In Richmond, Virginia, the Confederacy's capital, Lewis Maury was appointed a lieutenant in the Navy, the same rank he had held in Federal service. A lack of naval vessels made sea commands scarce in the Confederacy, and for much of 1861 he was land-bound, engaged in erecting defenses on Sewell's Point near Norfolk. When Matthew was ordered to Britain in the fall of 1862, he probably made a strong appeal to Secretary Mallory on Lewis's behalf, for within weeks of Matthew's departure, Lewis was ordered to follow. In sending Lewis with the cotton warrants, Mallory informed him that he would command the vessel to be purchased and act as a commerce raider:

> At this distance the department will not undertake to rigidly prescribe your cruising ground. . . . You will not hesitate to assume responsibility whenever the interest of your country may seem to demand it, and should your judgment ever hesitate in seeking the solution of any difficulty . . . you are to do the enemy's commerce the greatest injury in the shortest time.

On January 2, 1863, Lewis Maury and two other officers reached Havana, Cuba, aboard an unidentified blockade runner. While they waited for a fast ship to England, Lewis wrote his wife that Spanish officialdom in Cuba was sympathetic toward the Confederacy, but that "most of the Creoles who are inimical to the Spaniards are with the Federals." Within days of his arrival in Havana, Maury and two fellow travelers were aboard the speedy packet *Tasmanian,* and by the end of January he was sharing accommodations with Matthew at No. 10 Sackville Street, London.

Matthew briefed his cousin about the purchase of the *Japan,* doubtless noting that he had not been able to inspect the vessel personally. Rather than risk detection at this late date, he sent Lewis to a small village near the Clyde River where the *Japan* was near completion. There Lewis lived under an assumed name, receiving occasional visitors who followed the work at the yards. His principal contact was the Dutch officer, Jansen, whose official position allowed him to supervise the finishing and fitting-out of the new vessel. On March 6, the *Japan* was launched, and Jansen expressed his belief that she would be ready to sail any time after March 18. "Say what small arms and big guns you want," Matthew wrote Lewis, "and you shall have them."

Later that month, Lewis returned to London to discuss the arming and manning of his command. Confederate naval officers were waiting in London to take command of another ship intended for the Confederacy, the *Alexandra*. That vessel was on the verge of being seized by the British government, so Matthew Maury appropriated the officers for the *Japan*. All that remained was to find a crew. At London's Sailors' Home, Lewis managed to sign on about 50 men, ostensibly for a two-year voyage to Singapore.

On April 1, 1863, the *Japan* weighed anchor for the first time and headed down the Firth of Clyde for the Irish Sea. The fact that the departure took place with minimal ceremony, and that *Japan*'s officers were strangers to the Glasgow waterfront, seems not to have aroused any suspicion about the ship's intended use. Meanwhile, at the channel port of Newhaven, near Brighton, three other Confederate officers departed in a small steamer, the *Alar*. While British authorities concentrated their scrutiny on shipbuilding centers such as Glasgow and Liverpool, Confederate agents had quietly chartered the *Alar* and loaded her with ordnance and supplies for the *Japan*.

The *Japan* and the *Alar* rendezvoused off the French port of Ushant on April 4, where over a period of five days Lewis Maury supervised the transfer of a 32-pounder Blakely rifle, two 24-pounders, and two 10-pounder Whitworth guns from the *Alar* to his new command. The *Alar* returned to England bearing a small group of crewmen who had chosen not to sail aboard the *Japan* when they learned her nationality and true mission. In a short speech, Maury commissioned the newly armed vessel the C.S.S. *Georgia*.

He was exhilarated as he navigated his new command through the English Channel toward the south Atlantic. That the *Georgia* was in service at all represented a significant accomplishment. For the first time, the Confederacy had three commerce raiders at sea: the dreaded *Alabama* and *Florida*, and now the *Georgia*. In the Bay of Biscay, *Georgia* picked up the northeast trade winds; her bulwarks rose, trembled, and fell to the rhythm of the gray waters. Undermanned or not, thought Maury, the *Georgia* must prove herself a worthy consort to the *Alabama* and the *Florida*. Operating under sail, Maury worked his way south toward the Canary Islands.

Not a great deal is known about the 600-ton *Georgia*, which one observer described as "clipper-built, fiddle head, full poop, brig rigged with a short, thick funnel." The work required to prepare the vessel for military use was immense, for the *Georgia* had not been designed as a cruiser, and most of her crew consisted of merchant sailors. Not until he was 10 days out of Ushant was Maury able to get up steam for his 200 horsepower engine. Mounting the two Whitworth rifles required an additional three days. The *Georgia* carried considerably less armament than the *Alabama* or *Florida*, and even with all guns working she would be heavily outgunned by any Federal warship she might meet.

At daybreak on April 25 the lookout made his first sighting, which proved to be a Dutch bark. Later that day, however, the *Georgia* made out another sail in the distance. Maury set out in pursuit and, after deciding that she was probably an American vessel, hauled in his British colors and hoisted the Stars and Bars of the Confederacy. After an hour's chase and a warning shot, the quarry hove to, and Maury sent a boat to her under First Officer Bill Evans. Their prize was the *Dictator* out of New York, 1,293 tons, laden with coal oil and bound for Hong Kong. The raider's crew spent four hours transferring the *Dictator*'s crew to the *Georgia*, then halted work for the evening. The next morning the *Georgia* took on board as much of her victim's provisions as she could accommodate. Maury then put his first prize to the torch.

Confederate commerce raiders operated under a unique handicap. Because of the Federal blockade of Southern harbors, they had no home ports to which they could send their prizes for valuation and sale. Vessels such as the *Dictator* had to be burned, or, in exceptional circumstances, "bonded," a procedure by which a prize's master agreed to make a stipulated payment to the Confederate government at the close of hostilities. Bonding would, of course, prove meaningless if the South lost the war.

Maury returned the *Dictator*'s instruments to her skipper, Captain George Phillips, and advised him that he and his crew would be set ashore at Cape Verde. Phillips later reported that he thought the *Georgia*'s reported top speed of 14 miles per hour to be optimistic. He characterized most of her crew as "mere boys," but added, "They all treated us kindly while on board." Boys or not, their number was increased by 14 seamen and coal heavers recruited from the *Dictator*.

En route to the sea lanes off Brazil, the *Georgia* made for the island of St. Vincent in the Cape Verde chain only to spot a U.S. warship in the harbor. Maury turned away immediately, and there was no pursuit, but he still had his prisoners to land. Now he had no choice but to continue on to Brazil. Shortly after midnight on May 13, the *Georgia* anchored off Bahia (present-day Salvador), Brazil.

An armed vessel lay waiting in this harbor, too. Lookouts aboard the unfamiliar ship watched the *Georgia* with apprehension, and with the first light of morning, the stranger made a point of showing her colors. Remarkably, they were Confederate colors—the ship was none other than the *Alabama*! The relieved officers and crew of the two vessels mingled cheerfully for several days. Maury had known *Alabama* skipper Captain Raphael Semmes in the Old Navy, and two of Maury's officers, William Evans and Robert Chapman, had served under Semmes aboard CSS *Sumter*.

After putting her prisoners ashore at Bahia, the *Georgia* provided the *Alabama* with 528 pounds of powder, doubtless at Semmes's request. The *Alabama* had been involved in only one brief engagement by then, so it seems unlikely that her magazines had run empty. Perhaps the *Alabama* was already experiencing problems with her powder—problems that would be her undoing in her famous meeting with the USS *Kearsarge* a year later.

Semmes, as the senior officer, told Maury he planned to depart on the 21st and that, because both ships would be headed east, Maury should allow him a day's lead in order to increase their range of search. On the evening of May 22, after carefully planting rumors that the *Georgia* was headed for China, Maury again turned his ship seaward. He was at last operating along one of the world's major sea lanes and would find no shortage of prey. After stopping several neutral vessels, *Georgia* captured the *George Griswold*, with a cargo of Cardiff coal, off Rio. Because the cargo was British, Maury released the American ship on $100,000 bond. Veering further into the Atlantic, the *Georgia* made June her busiest month, capturing the *Good Hope, J.W. Seaver, Constitution,* and *City of Bath*. The *Good Hope* was a 436-ton bark out of Boston. When a party from the *Georgia* boarded her, they found that her master, a Captain Gordon, had died on the voyage and was being returned home pickled in brine. Maury ordered the remains brought aboard the *Georgia*, and while the bark went up in flames, the body of her late master was prepared for burial. The Confederate skipper was reading the service of burial at sea from his prayer book ("... Our dear brother here departed, we therefore commit his body to the deep ...") when the lookout reported a sail approaching. Maury completed the reading, closed his book, and nodded toward the rail. Two sailors slid the weighted shroud into the water from under a U.S. flag, and Maury ordered "Beat to quarters."

The approaching sail was the small American bark *J. W. Seaver*, which had spotted the burning *Good Hope*. Her master, puzzled at the sight of a burning ship, asked the *Georgia* whether he could be of assistance; he then watched with horror as the raider ran up Confederate colors. But Maury did not burn the *Seaver*. He later wrote that he would "stand court-martial" before he would "burn the ship of a man who had come ... to help fellow seamen in distress." Maury bonded the *Seaver* for $30,000 and required her master to accommodate his prisoners from earlier captures.

For five days in June the *Georgia* lay at anchor off the barren island of Trinidad. Her repeated chases off the Brazilian coast had exposed her shortcomings as a raider, for, unlike the *Alabama,* she was not fast enough to give chase under sail. At the same time, her fuel consumption under steam was so heavy that Maury was constantly in search of coal. The anchorage at Trinidad gave Maury a base from which he could watch for suspicious sail without expending fuel, and on the morning of June 25 his patience was rewarded. The *Georgia* chased and boarded the *Constitution* of New York, bound for Shanghai with a cargo of coal. Maury put a prize crew under Bill Evans on board and Evans brought the prize to Trinidad so the *Georgia* could take her coal. The next day Maury learned from the master of a Dutch bark that Confederate Lieutenant General Thomas J. "Stonewall" Jackson had died on May 10 in faraway Virginia. He ordered his ship's colors flown at half mast.

On July 8, after 10 days of operating out of Trinidad, Maury decided to try his luck elsewhere. He accompanied the *Constitution* to sea and used her for target practice before setting her afire. The *Georgia* then sailed east for more than a month, sighting few sails and those mostly British. On the morning of August 26 the *Georgia* arrived at the Cape of Good Hope, dropping anchor in St. Simon's Bay. She had missed the *Alabama*—on her way to the Far East—by only a few hours. As he had done at Bahia, Maury seized on the opportunity to write home, telling Anne of the hospitality being shown the *Georgia* in the Cape Colony, while revealing his homesickness: "Oh, how I long for this horrid war to cease, when we may all be again together under our roof. My thoughts are seldom away from you all & my constant prayer is for your comfort & protection & for peace to our distressed country."

By the time the *Georgia* reached South Africa she was showing the classic symptoms of a long stay in tropical waters. Her bottom was so fouled with marine growth that her speed was sharply reduced. There was no drydock at St. Simon's Bay, so Maury could do nothing to improve the situation. The *Georgia* was in real peril. The powerful Union warship *Vanderbilt* was known to be operating off the cape, meaning that at any moment the Confederate ship could be required to pour on all her speed—speed she did not have. The *Georgia* made a quiet escape by joining a British tea convoy returning from the Far East.

En route to the Canary Islands, Maury captured and bonded the *John Watts*. On October 9, he successfully chased another American merchantman, *Bold Hunter*. By late afternoon he had transferred her crew but not her provisions, and, with light failing, he left her in the hands of a prize crew. The next day, a falling barometer signaled a storm's approach, so Maury quickly took off all the food the *Georgia* could handle. But by the time he had fired *Bold Hunter*, the weather was blowing a full gale. Suddenly, the wind changed direction and the blazing ship bore down on the *Georgia*. At that moment *Georgia's* engine failed.

A Confederate midshipman recalled, "In an instant *Bold Hunter* was upon us. She recoiled and rushed at us again like a mad bull. . . . Plunging from the top of a huge wave, she came down upon our taff-rail doing much damage." The blazing prize then sheared off, "the fires seething in her vitals and leaping up her beautiful white sails to her mastheads and then running down her tarry rigging. . . . Never had a ship without a crew made a more desperate and damaging attack upon her pitiless tormentor."

Shaken, Maury resumed his northerly course, noting in his log that one boat davit and part of the poop rail had been damaged in the collision. In addition to his vessel's fouled bottom, he now had to contend with a balky engine. The *Georgia*—skimpily rigged and requiring the regular maintenance accorded merchantmen—was not equal to the demands of a raider with no home port. Maury was feeling the strain, and his health began to suffer.

At Tenerife, Maury landed his prisoners, took on coal and provisions, and gave his crew a liberty. Continuing his voyage north, Maury hailed several neutral vessels but none flying the Stars and Stripes. The *Georgia* had taken her last prize. On October 18 the raider dropped anchor at Cherbourg, France. Although the French port had the drydock facilities that *Georgia* desperately required, permission to dock her was initially denied. On October 29, Lewis Maury wrote to Matthew, "We require docking but there are none here but those of the government, & the admiral said he had no authority to let us have use of one." By the time permission was granted, four months later, Confederate authorities were losing interest in the *Georgia*. Maury was relieved as skipper, and First Officer Evans placed in command.

In February 1864, the *Georgia* left Cherbourg for a secret rendezvous off the coast of Morocco. There she was to transfer her guns, supplies, and part of her crew to a new cruiser, the *Rappahannock,* for which the Confederates had high hopes. But the *Rappahannock* never reached Morocco; at the last minute, French authorities refused to let her leave Calais.

The *Georgia* waited several weeks for the *Rappahannock* at their appointed rendezvous. When some of her crew were allowed shore leave, they were greeted by several hundred angry Moroccan tribesman armed with spears and ancient rifles. There appear to have been no casualties in the ensuing melee, but the outnumbered Confederate seamen beat a hasty retreat to their boats. When they returned to the *Georgia,* the raider ran out her guns and let loose a broadside, firing her guns in anger for the only time in the war. The surprised Moors quickly scattered, bringing to an end an incident that became known on the *Georgia* as "the Confederacy's only foreign war."

In May 1864, under Evans's command, the *Georgia* crossed to Liverpool, where her crew was discharged, her equipment removed, and her sale to a British buyer arranged. The transfer of a warship to neutral ownership during wartime was unusual, and Charles Francis Adams, the American minister in London, was not prepared to recognize the transaction. He directed that a U.S. warship follow the erstwhile raider when she left Britain. The upshot was that the USS *Niagara* intercepted the *Georgia* off Lisbon, seized her, and sent her to Boston, where she was condemned by a prize court and sold. So it was that the *Georgia* became the only Confederate cruiser to become a prize herself.

In statistical terms, the *Georgia* had an undistinguished career as a raider. Her nine captures pale in comparison to the 64 achieved by the *Alabama* under Semmes, or the 24 prizes captured by the *Florida* under Commander John Maffitt. In part, however, the *Georgia*'s small bag stemmed from the fact that a flight from the American flag was well under way before the *Georgia's* cruise began. Nearly 350 American ships were sold to British owners during 1863, and even the *Alabama* took only 10 prizes in her last 11 months of service.

Because the *Georgia* gave the Confederacy a third commerce raider in the decisive year of the war, her commissioning might have had strategic significance. But the North was fighting a land war and turning a blind eye to the disaster that had overtaken its merchant marine. Raphael Semmes noted after the war that the North at first could not comprehend the potential threat of Confederate commerce destroyers. And when the threat materialized, the North was "too deeply engaged in the contest to heed it."

Lewis Maury returned to Virginia in January 1864, bearing technical data from Matthew relating to the improvement of mine defenses in the rivers of the Confederacy. Later in the year, at Wilmington, North Carolina, he commanded a guard ship, the CSS *North Carolina,* which was so decrepit that she sank in the Cape Fear River as a result of accumulated leaks.

The postwar years were hard on Confederate Navy veterans, whose only line of work was denied them. Lewis Maury had returned to find his family well but in reduced circumstances. He spent years searching for employment as an engineer before he heard of a project to improve the James River—ironically, the very river Lewis had helped to mine in 1861. Matthew Maury recommended his cousin for the appointment, characterizing him as "without reproach ... altogether true & reliable." Remarkably, yet another testimonial came from a Union veteran, Admiral David D. Porter, whom Maury had known before the war. Maury got the job, and in the same year—1871—his political rights were restored to him.

What is to be made of Maury's record with the *Georgia*? The Virginian appears to have accomplished all that could have been expected, given the defects of his vessel. Yet he took no pleasure in his role as a raider, and statistics suggest he preferred to bond his prizes rather than destroy them. Of the *Georgia's* nine catches he burned only four; the others were bonded. In contrast, the *Alabama* burned 80 percent of her prizes, and the *Florida* under Maffitt destroyed 89 percent of hers. In the end, Lewis Maury may have been too softhearted to succeed as a commerce destroyer.

This chapter first appeared in the August 1995 issue of *Civil War Times Illustrated.*

16

Confederate Behemoth: The CSS *Louisiana*

WILLIAM N. STILL, JR.

Union strategy, formulated in the months after the fall of Fort Sumter, called for blockading the Southern coast and capturing the main transportation arteries from Ohio to the Gulf. Control of the Mississippi and its tributaries would provide communication between the interior cities of the North and the Gulf and simultaneously restrict the movement of important supplies from the trans-Mississippi to the heart of the Confederacy.

It was the recognition of this threat that persuaded the Confederate Government to build naval vessels in the West. The ironclad *Louisiana,* the largest warship laid down in the Confederate States, was among those constructed.

On September 18, 1861, the Confederate Navy Department contracted with E. C. Murray to build an ironclad warship. Murray, a steamboat builder from Kentucky with over twenty years of experience, had journeyed to Montgomery, Alabama, the Confederate capital, in April to submit a proposal to the department. Five months elapsed before he received a contract, partly because of difficulties in acquiring a suitable site for a shipyard and workmen, and partly because the money was not appropriated until August. A site was finally obtained late in the summer when the Navy Department leased four acres of land in Jefferson City, just above the New Orleans, Louisiana, city limits. Murray was permitted to use part of the land while the remainder was turned over to the builders of the *Mississippi,* another ironclad contracted for by the department.

Murray agreed to build a vessel 264 feet in length with a 64-foot beam for $196,000. The contract stated that the *Louisiana,* as the ironclad was to be named, was to be operational by January 25, 1862. Murray, who apparently had no experience in warship construction, was provided with explicit instructions and specifications. She was to be armored by two layers of railroad T-rails from the top of her casemate to two feet below the waterline. This casemate or shield which would house the guns was to be slanted forty-five degrees on its sides and ends and covered approximately two-thirds of the hull. Although she was supposed to carry twenty-two guns, her battery would actually consist of sixteen guns (two 7-inch rifles, seven 6-inch rifles, three 9-inch smoothbores and four 8-inch smoothbores). The builder was also instructed to erect small platforms 4 feet below the top of the casemate "so that men can use small arms in the upper opening and also for the men to have their hammocks." The platforms were to be located on the beams with "cross bridges" to connect them. These platforms were not mentioned in contemporary descriptions of the vessel; however, a four-foot bulkhead armored with sheet iron constructed on top of the casemate for sharpshooters is mentioned.

The vessel's machinery was to consist of two 9-foot stroke engines, two smaller engines, six 30-foot-long boilers, two paddle wheels 27 feet in diameter, and two 4-foot propellers, one on each side of the stern. These two propellers, along with twin rudders, were supposed to provide the ship with a unique steering system. The twin wheels were to be centerline, one abaft the other in a well extending 114 feet from the stern.

When completed and ready for sea with 325 officers and men on board, battery coal, stores, and provisions, she was calculated to weigh approximately 2,118 tons and draw six feet of water. The specifications and instructions were drawn up by Joseph Pierce, one of three experienced naval constructors in the Confederacy. However, Pierce had no experience with ironclad vessels and when the *Louisiana* was launched, her weight and draft were considerably more than expected. There were other mechanical and structural defects. Her propulsion system did not work, anchors could not

DIMENSIONS
4000 Tons,
4 Engines,
2 Wheels,
2 Propellers.

ARMAMENT.
16 Guns.

An artist's representation of the CSS *Louisiana.* *(U.S. Naval Historical Center)*

be weighed, the paddle-wheel well leaked badly, and the interior arrangement of the gun deck was such that it was impossible to work all the guns at the same time.

Yet, initially Murray had no doubts that he could build a powerful warship, capable of efficient service in the shoal waters of the South. He had rushed to New Orleans after receiving the contract and worked feverishly to get construction under way. He ordered some 1,700,000 feet of lumber, negotiated for the transfer and modification of a steamboat's shafts, engines, and wheels, persuaded a local machine shop to manufacture the propellers and smaller engines, and secured five hundred tons of railroad iron from the Vicksburg Shreveport Railroad.

He had hired enough skilled labor including ship carpenters by the middle of October to lay the keel. Nevertheless, from the beginning there were unfortunate delays. The timber had to be cut and transported from the other side of Lake Pontchartrain; bolt iron was not available locally and was finally obtained in Tennessee. On one occasion the New Orleans *Picayune* appealed for iron and said, "charge as much as your patriotism will admit." Although the river steamer *Ingomar* was purchased in order to transfer her enormous paddle-wheels and engines to the ironclad, new shafts had to be forged. These were ultimately completed and installed only a few days before the *Louisiana*'s destruction. Even the propellers were not delivered until the middle of February 1862—three weeks after she was to have been turned over to the Navy.

Early in November 1861 Murray was also confronted by a serious labor problem. Ship carpenters in New Orleans, including those working in his yard, went out on strike. Six crucial days were lost before the builders agreed to a wage hike. The labor situation was never stable. All of the workers were enrolled in militia units and work was frequently interrupted while they were called out for drill. In January, 1862—the month the vessel was due to be completed—some fifty carpenters were sent from New Orleans to Memphis to work on warships, apparently under orders from the Confederate Government. In order to launch the *Louisiana* carpenters had to be borrowed from the nearby shipyard.

Confederate Secretary of the Navy Stephen R. Mallory was extremely concerned about the vessel's progress. In late January (after the contract date for completion had passed) he sent Lieutenant Robert Minor to New Orleans to investigate the delay. Minor reported to Mallory that:

> the *Louisiana* will be launched on Monday or Wednesday the third or fifth of February—no machinery in—but all ready to be put on board . . . no iron on the roof but the two layers of T rails are ready and will be put on after [she is] launched. Men are working on the launching ways to take advantage of the rise in the river. Roof work is progressing and will be complete (24 inches thick) in 8 or 9 days . . . pilot houses forward and aft [to be built]. . . . In three weeks she will be ready for her armament. The vessel . . . has great capacity for fuel, water, and provisions. . . .

On February 6 a large crowd witnessed the *Louisiana*'s launching. According to the newspaper *True Delta,* as the vessel slid broadside into the river, thousands cheered. Yet she was far from being completed. Murray was still frantically searching for iron for armor and trying to install the remainder of the machinery. In the middle of March the first heavy guns were taken on board, but the carriages were not ready. The guns were not mounted until a month later when Union mortar boats opened a heavy bombardment upon Forts Jackson and Saint Philip located some seventy miles below New Orleans.

Early in January 1862 Flag Officer David G. Farragut received command of the West Gulf Blockading Squadron for the expressed purpose of capturing New Orleans. He assumed command of the squadron in February, and by the beginning of April, Union warships were over the bar and in the Mississippi River.

The presence of a powerful Union naval force in the lower Mississippi spurred Confederate officials to complete the two ironclads as quickly as possible. On April 5, Secretary Mallory telegraphed the naval commander in New Orleans to "work day and night to get [the ironclads] . . . ready for action. . . . Not an hour should be lost. . . . Spare neither men nor money."

The *Louisiana* was moored alongside the levee while workers toiled around the clock completing the vessel. The bombardment of the forts on April 19 by Union vessels persuaded General Mansfield Lovell, Confederate military commander in New Orleans, to order the unfinished ironclad to the forts' defense. Although only the paddle wheels were working on Easter Sunday, April 20, the lines holding the vessel to the levee were cast off. Commander Charles F. McIntosh, the *Louisiana*'s captain, ordered the vessel to steam up river a few hundred yards before making a circle and heading downstream. Lieutenant James Wilkinson, the ironclad's executive officer, later wrote, "as our big wheels were set in motion in the rapid current of the Mississippi, torrents of water rushed through the crevices in the bulkheads and deluged the gundeck, while the *Louisiana* drifted helpless down the river." She was unable to stem the current with her paddle wheels. "We accomplished our object of getting down to the forts," he wrote, "thanks to the current and to [two steamboats]."

The ironclad left the city without a full crew. A detachment from a Confederate army artillery unit volunteered to man the guns. Living quarters were incomplete, so these men along with the officers and crew, as well as workers who accompanied the vessel downstream, were quartered on the two steamboats.

Commander John K. Mitchell, in command of Confederate naval forces on the lower Mississippi, considered the *Louisiana* a failure. Nevertheless, during the interval from April 21 to 24, while the mortars continued

Commodore John K. Mitchell, who found the *Louisiana* badly under-powered. *(U.S. Naval Historical Center)*

their destructive fire on the forts, the workmen and ship's crew mounted six of the guns, installed the machinery for the propellers, and made her as serviceable as possible. The army commander of Fort Jackson urged Mitchell to place the ironclad below the fort and attempt to dislodge the mortar boats. Mitchell refused, pointing out that this would delay finishing her, and also that the guns could only be elevated some five degrees because of small gunports, thus limiting their range. On April 23 he informed the fort's commander that the ironclad was advanced enough to move her the following day. The following day was too late.

At 2:00 on the morning of April 24 two red lanterns were hoisted to the mizzen peak of the *Hartford,* the flagship of the Union naval squadron under Flag Officer Farragut. This was the signal for the force to get under way in an attempt to pass the forts. An hour and a half later the leading vessel was quietly gliding through a gap in the boom of hulks chained together between the forts. Within minutes the warships were discovered and the battle commenced as heavy guns in the forts hurled salvos at the ship's dark images.

The *Louisiana,* moored to the bank above Fort St. Philip, quickly entered the fray. "Objects were so obscured by the darkness and the dense smoke, that we could only fire, with effect, at the flashes of the ship's guns," Lieutenant Wilkinson recalled. The ironclad's three bow guns and three starboard broadside guns were the only ones that could be brought to bear.

The Confederate armorclad was hit by the fire from a number of the Union warships as they passed on up the river, but she was not seriously damaged. One large vessel (possibly the *Hartford*) swung in close to the *Louisiana* and fired two 11-inch shells at point blank range. The armor plate was dented but not penetrated. The only casualties occurred among some sharpshooters stationed on the spar deck (top of the casemate), where the thin iron plate was perforated by grape and canister. Captain McIntosh was mortally wounded here.

Farragut's warships continued up the river, destroying, immobilizing, or putting to flight the various Confederate vessels that tried to challenge them. On the morning of April 25, the incomplete ironclad *Mississippi* was put to the torch as the Union vessels were observed approaching New Orleans. Although the city surrendered, Forts St. Philip and Jackson were still in Confederate hands—and so was the *Louisiana*.

After the Federal vessels had passed, the workers and ship's crew, reinforced by survivors from other Confederate vessels, labored to complete the *Louisiana*'s machinery. With the wounding of McIntosh and the destruction of the Confederate naval force on the river, Mitchell assumed direct control of the ironclad. What he hoped to do is not clear. Lieutenant Wilkinson wrote that they expected to sortie up the river and attack the Union vessels off New Orleans. However, Mitchell in his official report said that "little confidence was felt [in the machinery] . . . to enable the *Louisiana* to stem the current." Years after the war another officer speculated that the naval commander planned to descend the river and make for Mobile, an unlikely move because of an inadequate fuel supply. The military commander in Fort Jackson believed that the ironclad was going to attack the mortar boats below the forts.

During the night of the 27th the machinery was finally ready, but early the following morning when Mitchell conferred with General J. K. Duncan, in command of Fort Jackson, he was informed that the forts were to be surrendered. The naval commander hurried back to the *Louisiana*, and after a conference with his officers, he decided to destroy the armorclad. He later defended this action on the grounds that sufficient coal was not available to take the vessel elsewhere. She was set afire, and when the securing hawsers burned away, the *Louisiana* drifted out into the stream and blew up only a few hundred yards away from the Union gunboats awaiting the forts' surrender.

Mitchell, after surrendering with a large number of the *Louisiana*'s officers and men (some escaped through the swamp), was later accused by Commander David D. Porter, in command of the mortar flotilla, of deliberately trying to blow up the Union vessels. Upon his orders Mitchell was kept in close confinement for several weeks, until finally being released and ultimately exchanged after the Confederate naval officer wrote a personal letter to Union Secretary of the Navy Gideon Welles.

The story of the *Louisiana* illustrates the problems encountered by the Confederate Navy in trying to challenge Union naval superiority. With virtually no experience in naval shipbuilding, the South had to rely on steamboat builders and ship carpenters more familiar with shaping the knees of coastal sloops and schooners than with building an armored man-of-war. The results were in many cases inferior warships or failures. The *Louisiana* was one of the latter. The ironclad's officers almost unanimously considered her a failure. Chief Engineer Wilson Youngblood wrote to Mitchell while a prisoner that "I do not think [the machinery] would have been able to handle the vessel, the wheels being put in the middle of the vessel, one right abaft the other, so that the after wheel could do no good whatever . . . when the wheels were working, they would force the water out under the stern so that it would form an eddy around the rudder so that she would not steer, and if we tried [to] steer her with the propellers, she could not stem the current. Consequently she was unmanageable. . . ."

The *Louisiana* illustrates the lack of expertise in the Confederacy to build warships. There were shipbuilders familiar with the construction of coastal sailing vessels and river steamboats, but no warship of any size had been built in the South since the War of 1812. The *Louisiana*'s designer made a fatal mistake—one made on a number of Confederate armorclads—in badly underestimating the power needed to move the heavy iron-covered vessels. The *Louisiana* was virtually powerless against the Mississippi's current, and nearly all of the Confederate ironclads were far too slow.

Secretary of the Navy Mallory's grandiose scheme of building powerful armored vessels such as the *Virginia, Mississippi,* and *Louisiana* failed because of the lack of building experience. Large ironclads would have to be built abroad, and smaller, less sophisticated warships would be built within the Confederacy to defend its waters.

The end of the *Louisiana* also typifies what happened to so many of the Confederate armorclads. A traveler in the Confederacy recounts the story of a group of women in Richmond who visited one of the ironclads with the naval secretary serving as guide. At the tour's end, he commented that they had seen everything worth seeing. One lady replied, "Everything but one . . . the place where you blow them up."

This chapter first appeared in the November 1977 issue of *Civil War Times Illustrated*.

17

Potomac Flotilla:
A Gunboat Captain's Diary

JOHN M. TAYLOR

On New Year's Day, 1862, Union Secretary of the Navy Gideon Welles took stock of the forces at his disposal as the Civil War neared the end of its first year. Six months earlier, Welles had been able to count no more than 100 vessels. Now the Federal navy totaled some 300 warships, the majority attempting to firm up the blockade of Confederate seaports. They came in all sizes and strengths, for the Navy sought not only to blockade Confederate ports but also to gain control of the country's important navigable riverways.

One of the lesser entries in Welles's order of battle was the fourth-class steamer *Reliance* of the Potomac flotilla. The *Reliance* represented a class of vessel that was not counted on for blockade duty; rather, the function of such vessels was to monitor the rivers and inlets of the Virginia and North Carolina coasts from Chesapeake Bay to Cape Fear. The *Reliance* was small—only 90 tons—and mounted only two guns. Its complement totaled only 20 men. But the gunboat was steam powered, screw propelled, and well suited to patrolling streams such as the Piankatank River, Matawomac Creek, and Coan River.

Acting master of the *Reliance* was 30-year-old Francis Josselyn, a man from Maine who had joined the Potomac Flotilla in September 1861. Slender and blue-eyed, Josselyn had left a wife and child in Maine when he had volunteered for the navy. Little is known of his prewar activities, but the fact that he joined the navy as a master's mate—a senior warrant officer—suggests that he had a seagoing background.

The Potomac flotilla, commanded by Lieutenant R. H. Wyman, faced formidable challenges. Whereas a Federal blockader offshore was rarely exposed to hostile fire, gunboats on inland waters were tempting targets for any Confederate artillery crew with time on its hands. Snipers, too, were fond of shooting at enemy gunboats. Yet, while a blockader offshore might go for months without sighting quarry, the Potomac flotilla attempted to stifle a flourishing coastal trade between Virginia and southern Maryland. The master of the *Resolute* reported in June 1862 that more provisions had been landed in Maryland's St. Mary's County in the previous month than could be consumed by its inhabitants in three years.[1]

The gunboats of the Potomac flotilla operated primarily between the mouths of the Potomac and Rappahannock rivers. They patrolled day and night, swatting mosquitoes and watching for sandbars. They varied their routes, but normally returned every 24 or 48 hours to supply depots at locations such as Piney Point and Blackstone's Island. Francis Josselyn chose to keep a personal diary, as well as his ship's log, and his diary provides a unique look at the brown-water war off the East Coast. The *Reliance*'s patrols were sometimes routine, but they were rarely uneventful. A sample entry:

April 14—Weather pleasant with light breeze from SE. At 6:30 *Jacob Bell* sent a boat ashore; were fired upon by soldiers on shore. Opened fire on them and shelled them out and proceeded up the river. At Carter's Wharf saw a flag of truce flying. Sent boat ashore; boat returned and we kept up the river. At Point Lowry saw a battery; got within range and hove a few shells into the works but received no reply. Boats went ashore and burned the barracks. Boats came off and we proceeded up to Tappahannock. Hoisted a flag of truce and went ashore. Found only three men in the town. Hoisted the flag on the courthouse. . . .

April 15—At 7 a.m. *Island Belle* went in pursuit of a sloop; succeeded in overhauling her which proved to be the *Rundors* of Tappahannock, from Fredericksburg with stores for the Rebel Army. Took her as a prize. At 10 a.m. got underweigh and proceeded down river. In time at a small creek saw two schrs. The *Island Belle* went after them, took them in tow, and brought them out. They proved to be *Japan* and *Sidney S. Jones*. Took

215

the *Japan* in tow and proceeded on down. At Carter's Wharf found two soldiers; took them prisoner with a valuable horse. Went on down to Tolis Island and anchored for the night.[2]

Though most of the Federal gunboats were equipped for sail as well as steam, they appear to have relied heavily on steam on their patrols, for Josselyn's diary alludes to coaling almost every two days. Occasionally, free blacks could be hired for this disagreeable task; more often, however, it appears to have fallen to the ordinary seamen of the *Reliance.* Considering that the steam engines of that day were notably unreliable, Josselyn's command appears to have experienced comparatively few mechanical difficulties. When a breakdown occurred, however, it could entail considerable down time:

> May 27th—Weather cloudy, winds SE. At night blowed off steam to repair the boiler, but getting the salt off found it so far gone could not get up steam again. Reported it to Lt. Badger, who ordered us to ly here for the present. . . .
>
> June 5—Weather cloudy; wind NW. At 9 a.m. *Wyantank* went alongside of *Anacostia* and put stores on board. From thence came alongside and took us in tow . . . to Washington.[3]

After repairs, *Reliance* returned to duty just in time for what would prove to be a busy August. Interestingly, Potomac flotilla patrols were aimed increasingly at the salt trade. Salt was a vital commodity in the Confederacy, providing as it did a sure means of preserving the meat on which armies relied in the field. Salt was already in short supply; in Richmond, one pound would shortly bring the astonishing price of 70 cents.[4] Southern Virginia was a major source of salt, and salt figured increasingly in supplies intercepted by the *Reliance* in the Potomac estuary:

> Aug. 7th—At 2 a.m. left Piney Point to cruise in the river of Machudar Creek. Took a boat loaded with salt. At 8 a.m. took three boats loaded with grain.
>
> Aug. 8th—Left Piney Point to cruise up the river. At ll p.m. took a boat loaded with grain bound for Maryland. Took another at 12 midnight loaded with groceries.
>
> Aug. 9th—At 1 a.m. took a boat loaded with salt and dry goods bound for Virginia. Took them to Piney Point and delivered them up to

the commander. At 9 p.m. got underweigh from Piney Point with Launch in tow. At 10 p.m. saw a boat crossing from Maryland to Virginia. Gave chase; in turning round filled the Launch and capsized her. Had to give up the chase. Succeeded after a while in righting the Launch.[5]

Far from imitating the florid prose of many a Civil War communiqué, Josselyn the diarist is painfully matter-of-fact, even when recounting what must have been harrowing experiences. On August 13, 1862, two troop transports, the *West Point* and the *George Peabody*, collided in the Potomac estuary with heavy loss of life. Fortunately for many on board, *Reliance* happened to be close by. Josselyn wrote in his diary, "At 8 p.m. got underweigh for a cruise in the river. At 9 fell in with the wreck of steamer *West Point*. Remained alongside throughout the night and rescued about 100 soldiers."[6]

The next day *Reliance* resumed her search for illegal traders. The prospect of destroying some smuggling craft may have led Josselyn into an attempted Rebel ambush:

Aug. 21st—At 9 a.m. got underweigh in company with the *Resolute* and went to Sturgeon Creek. Came to anchor outside and manned the Launch with the crew from the *Resolute* and proceeded up the creek to burn some schooners. Succeeded in burning them and on our way down was fired upon by about thirty men from the bushes. Killed one man from the *Resolute* and wounded acting MM Newton and two men, A. Springer and Chas. Miller, belonging to this vessel. We returned the fire with grape and shell and Sharp's rifles and succeeded in beating them up with what effect is not known. Not thinking it prudent to land with our small force returned to our respective vessels, and the *Resolute* proceeded to the Potomac and this vessel to Fredericksburg to get the men's wounds dressed. . . .

Aug. 22—Got underweigh and proceeded to Fredericksburg. Arrived there at 3 p.m. Took two wounded men to the hospital; left one there.[7]

The autumn of 1862 brought an unwelcome break in Josselyn's naval responsibilities. The records indicate that his wife became seriously ill, and that Josselyn was allowed leave to attend her in what proved to be a fatal illness. His diary is blank for this period, but by the end of October he had returned to duty, this time as acting master of a larger vessel, the 376-ton sidewheeler *Commodore Hull*. The *Commodore Hull* mounted six guns, carried a complement of 68 men, and represented a great step up from the little *Reliance*. Although Josselyn was still only "acting master," his new command constituted a vote of confidence in his performance.

Josselyn neglected his diary until the spring of 1863, when he took the *Hull* into what he viewed as his most important action in the war—relief of the Confederate siege of the port town of Washington, North Carolina. Washington, at the western end of the Pamlico River, had been captured by the Federals in March 1862. They had no plans for the port beyond denying it to the enemy, but one of Robert E. Lee's senior lieutenants, General James Longstreet, saw its continued occupation by the Yankees as an obstacle to foraging operations in the area. To immobilize the Union garrison, and to evict it if possible, Longstreet ordered General D. H. Hill's division to lay siege to the town. By April 1863, Hill had some 9,000 troops in the vicinity. When the Union commander, General John G. Foster, refused to surrender, Hill ordered all noncombatants out of the town and began to shell it.[8]

When the siege began, two Federal gunboats, Josselyn's *Commodore Hull* and the *Louisiana*, were close by on the river. They were separated from the remainder of their flotilla by a sandbar that was navigable only at high water, and by strong Confederate batteries at Hill's Point, seven miles downriver from the town. For the first days of the siege, the two gunboats exchanged fire with Hill's field artillery as best they could. At one point, however, the *Commodore Hull* found herself aground:

> On April 1st, two batteries opened on us, one from Rodman's Point and one above, within 500 yards of us, which placed us under a cross fire. We soon succeeded in silencing the battery near us in the corn field. We found the tide falling very fast, and if we remained where we were would soon be hard and fast aground, so we concluded to move up in deeper water. In doing so got hopelessly aground, which gave the enemy a raking fire, and they improved their time[?]. We replied shot for shot while our ammunition lasted, which was not long, with what guns we could bring to bear.
>
> Most every shot from the enemy's guns struck us; fortunately we had but few wounded and none killed. (We counted 78 holes after this day's fight.) We fired the last shot at them as the sun went down, which we

Action between the Potomac flotilla and Confederate batteries at Aquia Creek. *(U.S. Naval Historical Center)*

had reserved for that purpose. The *Louisiana*, with an 8 inch and 32 pdr never offered us any assistance through the day, but the *Eagle*, commanded by Mr. Lay, 2nd Assistant Engr. and Paymaster of the *Louisiana*, done all in their power to help us.[9]

Had the Confederates been more venturesome they might have captured the *Commodore Hull*, but they were not. Josselyn's vessel refloated with the high tide and maintained her position on the river east of Washington. The *Commodore Hull*'s position remained precarious, however, for Yankee commanders do not appear to have recognized the vulnerability of gunboats to shore batteries. Few supplies reached the two forward gunboats, obliging them to conserve ammunition and to shift positions repeatedly. In Josselyn's somewhat confused account,

> The 3d of April, after lying in our position that we took the day before, and getting well pepered and having no ammunition for the Pivot gun, we concluded to haul up farther. So all hands were turned out at 4 a.m.

to haul ship and had just succeeded in making fast when we were opened on from a battery abreast of us within 300 yards, which was what we wanted them to do, for they were within range of our 24 pdr. They fired about a dozen shell at us; half of them exploded on board, but they did not [three words unintelligible] for we knocked their battery into a cocked hat and they left on the double quick. . . .

I was sent down to the lower fleet with the 1st Cutter and a picked crew with dispatches and for ammunition. (In the mean time some small boats had been sent up with a small quantity.) In passing Rodman's Point they opened on me with artillery and musketry and kept it up to Hill's Point, a distance of 5 miles, and there I found three boats loaded with men who commanded me to halt when twenty feet of them. But I could not see it and told the men to dodge the flash and give way strong while they were [re]loading. By this means we got by without accident, one man having his cap shot off his head and several striking the boat. I found the *Hunchback* and went on board for the remainder of the night.[10]

It appeared at the end of a week's siege that the Confederates might take Washington. There were Federal vessels on the Pamlico, but they were unable to pass Hill's Point—to the great disgust of Francis Josselyn, for he believed that Federal ground forces could have seized this strategic point weeks earlier. General Foster belatedly attempted to march a 6,000-man relief column from New Bern to Washington, but the force was badly led, and it returned to New Bern.

The siege of Washington might have continued to a successful conclusion had Robert E. Lee not required every Confederate unit to deal with General Joe Hooker and the Army of the Potomac. On April 15 Longstreet told Hill that Lee could not keep Hill's division at Washington, and that if he could not maintain his siege with reduced numbers he should give it up.[11] The Federal gunboats helped make up Hill's mind, for that same day two supply ships successfully ran the batteries and delivered supplies to Washington. Reluctantly, Hill withdrew his troops.

The lifting of the siege could not be credited entirely to the gunboats, but their opening of the river had made it impossible for Hill to capture the town in the time allowed him. Josselyn wrote gratefully that although his ship had been struck by as many as 20 shells, there had been no fatalities. In

A *Harper's Weekly* illustration of the Federal steamer *Sassacus* attempting to ram the Confederate ironclad *Albemarle*. *(U.S. Naval Historical Center)*

the round of congratulations that followed the lifting of the siege, Admiral Samuel P. Lee, who commanded the North Atlantic Blockading Squadron, commended Josselyn, among others, "to special notice for their good conduct and bravery in battle."[12]

With the lifting of the siege of Washington, Josselyn's diary comes to a close. Why this is so is unclear, for he continued to command the *Commodore Hull* in coastal operations. In May 1864, the *Commodore Hull* was one of several Federal gunboats at the mouth of the Roanoke River charged with keeping an eye on a formidable Confederate ironclad, the *Albemarle*. Despite the vast expansion of the U.S. Navy since the onset of war, the *Albemarle* appeared to be as feared in Washington in 1864 as the *Merrimack* had been feared two years earlier. When the Confederate ram made a trial run on May 5, it was Josselyn in the *Commodore Hull* who first spotted her:

> I first sighted the ram at half past 1 o'clock p.m., coming out of the river in company with two steamers, distance about 2 miles. In accordance with my previous instructions I retreated slowly down the sound, keeping out of range of her guns until the flagship came up, when I fell into line astern of the *Miami*. About 5 o'clock I fired several shots from my pivot guns at the ram, striking it once or twice.

> At half past 6 I engaged the ram at close quarters, firing shell from my pivot and broadside guns, many of which struck the vessel, effectively preventing the opening of her ports. As I steamed ahead, in padding the ram's bow, I paid out a large seine for the purpose of fouling his propeller, but though encompassing the ram it did not have the desired effect.
>
> I ceased firing when it became too dark to distinguish the enemy.[13]

The *Albemarle* continued to pose the threat of a breakout, and the U.S. Navy sought the means to control or destroy her. The Navy would achieve its objective in October, when a special raiding party led by the enterprising Lieutenant William Cushing succeeded in reaching the *Albemarle* and detonating a primitive torpedo against her hull.

Josselyn, meanwhile, continued his patrols off the Carolina coast. While Cushing planned his daring raid, Josselyn was prostrated by a fever that was eventually diagnosed as malaria. Nevertheless, he recovered in time to command the *Commodore Hull* in an assault on the town of Plymouth, North Carolina, by seven Federal gunboats. The navy force succeeded in capturing the town, but only after a spirited duel against four Confederate shore batteries. The *Commodore Hull* alone suffered four dead and several wounded, more casualties than in any previous engagement.

Shortly after the action at Plymouth, Josselyn had occasion to report an incident that, although of little long-term consequence, must have caused a stir in the town of Edenton, North Carolina:

> U.S.S. *Commodore Hull*
> November 8, 1864
>
> Sir: I have the honor to report that, agreeably to your instructions, I landed with a detachment of men this afternoon at Edenton and adjourned *sine die* a county court which was in session in the courthouse at that place under so-called Confederate authority. This court was the first that has been held at Edenton since the breaking out of the war, the authorities had the impertinence to hold under my very guns.[14]

With the close of the war, Francis Josselyn, like most other volunteer officers, faced an uncertain future. The navy was cutting back, and the depletion of the Federal merchant marine during the war had sharply reduced the number of berths available to men like Josselyn. He was able to stay in the navy until 1868, however, when he landed a job as inspector in the Boston Customs House. He remarried, and became the father of three more children.

Josselyn continued to suffer from the malaria he contracted during the war, and in 1891 was granted a partial disability pension. The deposition by one physician in connection with his pension claim offers a rare glimpse of the man behind the gunboat skipper. "Mr. Josselyn was a man of strict integrity," wrote Dr. J. M. Keniston. He was "of excellent habits, of strong will, devoted to home and family, rarely out evenings, and usually retiring early."[15]

Many a man has had a worse obituary!

Notes

1. Virgil C. Jones, *The Civil War at Sea*, 1, 130.
2. Francis Josselyn, diary. Josselyn's unpublished diary, covering 70 pages, deals with the period December 1861–April 1863.
3. Ibid., May 27 and June 5, 1862.
4. John B. Jones, *A Rebel War Clerk's Diary*, 116.
5. Josselyn Diary, August 7–9, 1862.
6. Ibid., August 13, 1862.
7. Ibid., August 21–22, 1862.
8. Hal Bridges, *Lee's Maverick General*, 175.
9. Josselyn Diary, April 1863.
10. Ibid.
11. Bridges, *Lee's Maverick General*, 177.
12. *Official Records (Navy)*, Series I, vol. 8, 679.
13. Ibid., vol. 9, 453.
14. *Official Records (Navy)*, vol. 11, 58.
15. Josselyn Pension File (WO 22160), National Archives.

18

Franklin Buchanan and the Mobile Squadron

WILLIAM N. STILL, JR.

During the early months of the Civil War Mobile was generally ignored by the Confederate Navy Department. Naval affairs were left in the hands of Lieutenant James D. Johnston, CSN, with the title of "Keeper of the Light House," and Colin J. McRae, who acted as civilian agent for the department. Fortunately, both were men of ability and realized the urgency of creating a naval force for the defense of the bay. By the fall of 1861 two vessels, the *Alert* and *Florida*,[1] had been converted into gunboats, and contracts were signed for the construction of two light-draft warships. Johnston and McRae were also instrumental in persuading the Navy Department to negotiate for two more ironclads to be built at Selma, and the state of Alabama to build another.

The Alabama General Assembly on November 8, 1861, passed an act appropriating $150,000 for the "construction of an iron clad gunboat and ram for the defense of the bay and harbor of Mobile," and appointed a committee to superintend construction of the vessel. In December this group purchased the *Baltic*, a lighter used to transport cotton from Mobile to ships in the lower bay. By January 1862, the work of converting the *Baltic* into an ironclad was well under way. Conversion was completed in May and the vessel was turned over to the Confederate government on the twenty-seventh of that month.[2]

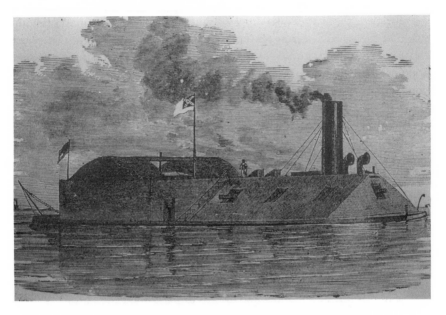

The CSS *Baltic. (National Archives)*

In February 1862, Captain Victor Randolph, CSN, assumed command of the Mobile Station with Johnston as his executive officer. Randolph was described by one of his officers as "a charming old gentleman in the parlor, very amiable and very kind and polite in his manners and you cannot help liking him, but he is sixty-five years old and hasn't all the fire of youth . . . and at best [is] never remarkable for energy or decision. . . . We are without a head, there is no controlling spirit."[3] Although he was the first naval officer of flag rank to resign his commission in the United States Navy to join the South, his Confederate career was jeopardized from the beginning because of animosity between him and the secretary of the navy Stephen R. Mallory. He tried, in fact, to block Mallory's appointment through correspondence with members of the provisional Congress, and later attempted to pressure the naval committee of the first regular Congress into investigating Mallory. He refused to divulge his reasons, although later he confided to a fellow officer: "I have made no statement of the Hon. Secretary's disloyalty which I did not hold myself prepared to prove."

Nevertheless, the matter was dropped when Mallory gave Randolph command of the naval batteries on the York River.[4] Strained relations between the two continued, and later when Franklin Buchanan, his junior, was appointed admiral, the embittered captain wrote to several congressmen complaining of this "slight." "Mr. Mallory would never employ me, or allow me to be placed in a position by which I might be brought honorably before the country, or where I would distinguish myself in my profession," he lamented to one congressman.[5] But as commander of the Mobile Station and Squadron from February until September 1862, Randolph certainly had every opportunity to "distinguish" himself.

Randolph was ordered to open communications and to convoy ships between Mobile and New Orleans by way of Grant's Pass and Mississippi Sound. Flag Officer George N. Hollins was to cooperate with his Lake Pontchartrain flotilla. The plan was never carried out because the army refused to remove the obstructions placed in Grant's Pass by the Confederates, and Hollins had all that he could handle in the Mississippi River.[6]

The Mobile commander was also to disperse the Federal forces blockading the main entrance to the bay as soon as the gunboats under construction were completed. By the beginning of April the *Morgan* and *Gaines* were ready, and on the night of the third these vessels, along with the *Florida* and *Alert*, made a half-hearted attack against the blockaders. After firing for several hours in their general direction, the Mobile Squadron withdrew. Scharf called this affair a "reconnaissance," but the executive officer of the flagship *Morgan* wrote that it was a planned attack and called Randolph an "old coward" for not pushing it.[7] This was the only attempt to strike at the Union blockading force off Mobile in 1862, in spite of the weakness of the Union force there. The flag officer contented himself with guarding the passes while urging the department to provide ironclads. He called his wooden gunboats "cockle shells," almost worthless as fighting ships because "one well directed shot would cripple [any of them]."[8]

In August 1862, Mallory relieved Randolph of his command and ordered him to Jackson, Mississippi, to stand trial by court-martial. What the charges were and whether or not he was actually tried have not been ascertained, but he never held an active command in the Confederate navy again.

Admiral Buchanan, the new flag officer, was at that time the most respected officer in Confederate naval service. When the crusty old warrior,

Adm. Franklin Buchanan, the senior officer of the Confederate Navy. *(U.S. Naval Historical Center)*

limping from wounds received while commanding the *Virginia*, arrived in Mobile, one officer admiringly wrote, "Buchanan is a man and a Commander." Another one noted, "warm work is expected in a few days."

Though aggressive and anxious to challenge his adversary beyond the bay, Buchanan was not imprudent. Shortly after reaching Mobile, the new flag officer reported that he found the squadron "in a state of efficiency, highly creditable to their officers and the service." But he also cautioned the navy secretary that the squadron would be no match in an engagement with Union ironclads.[9] All that he could hope for was that the expected attack would be delayed long enough to allow completion of the two ironclads under construction.

On May 1, 1862, Henry D. Bassett, a Mobile shipbuilder, signed a contract to construct two ironclad floating batteries for $100,000 each. The first of these, the *Tuscaloosa*, was to be completed by July 1, 1862, and the second, the *Huntsville*, thirty days later. Selma, a small city about 150 miles up the Alabama River from Mobile, was chosen as the construction site, probably because of the influence of Colin McRae. An iron foundry and arsenal were being developed at Selma by McRae, and he promised to provide the guns, boilers, and armor plate for the vessels.

In August, Commander Ebenezer Farrand, who was engaged in selecting defensive sites on the Alabama and Tombigbee Rivers, was ordered to obtain suitable locations for shipyards and to initiate the building of additional ironclads. On August 19, he contracted for one large side-wheel ironclad and two 150-foot propeller ironclads to be built at Ovens Bluff on the Tombigbee River. Early in September he negotiated for another side-wheel vessel to be built at Montgomery, and a powerful ram at Selma. By the time Buchanan arrived in Alabama, seven ironclads either were under construction or were on the verge of being laid down. When these vessels were completed and commissioned, he would have eight armored warships, counting the *Baltic*, to defend the bay and to challenge Union control of the Gulf and the Mississippi River. For the next eighteen months the task of finishing and manning them absorbed most of his time.[10]

The two ironclads building at Selma were behind schedule—three-fifths completed at the end of the stipulated time—but Farrand reported to Buchanan at the end of September that the first one would be ready in about six weeks. Within two weeks, however, his optimism had decreased considerably. "I cannot write with the least encouragement with regard to the completion of the floating batteries here. They are at almost a dead stand still waiting for iron plating and machinery . . . . not a particle of machinery for either and only the boiler for one has been received." In passing on this information to the navy secretary, Buchanan wrote, "this deprives me of the use of these boats for at least two months, which I regret, as I relied principally upon them to prevent the passage of the enemy through the obstructions in the Bay."[11]

The power plants for the several Alabama ironclads were originally to have been built at the naval iron works in Columbus, Georgia, but the Columbus establishment lacked the facilities to equip all the ships. In October 1862, McRae wrote to the Shelby Iron Company to forward twenty-five tons of pig iron to Columbus. When two-thirds of this order was held up at Selma by inadequate transportation facilities, McRae sent an urgent message to the army quartermaster to ship the iron immediately, as "this iron is required to complete the engines and machinery for the floating batteries at this place [Selma]. . . . "[12] By January 1863 the machinery for the *Tuscaloosa* was installed, but the *Huntsville's* boilers and engine failed to arrive before the vessel was towed to Mobile. The Tombigbee vessels received their power plants in the latter part of 1863 and early 1864. Machinery for the *Tennessee,* the large ram building at Selma, and the *Nashville,* the side-wheel ironclad on the stocks at Montgomery, was obtained from Mississippi riverboats stranded up the Yazoo River.[13]

The inadequate supply of iron also retarded armoring the vessels. When Selma was selected as suitable for a navy yard, one of its supposed advantages was the availability of iron and of the facilities to manufacture it into plate. McRae was under contract with the Navy Department to erect a rolling mill and foundry, while the Shelby Iron Company was rapidly converting its facilities in order to roll plate. By the fall of 1862 this situation had changed considerably. McRae's rolling mill was delayed indefinitely, and although Shelby had begun to turn out armor plate, pig iron was becoming increasingly scarce. A sufficient quantity of plate arrived in December 1862 and January 1863 from the Scofield and Markham works in Atlanta to cover the *Tuscaloosa.* Both the Atlanta and Shelby works supplied armor for the *Huntsville* and *Tennessee,* but the three Tombigbee vessels were never finished because of lack of plate, and the *Nashville* was only partly clad with armor taken from the *Baltic.*[14]

On February 7, 1863, Farrand wired Governor John Gill Shorter of Alabama that the *Tuscaloosa* and *Huntsville* had been successfully launched, "amid enthusiastic cheering." Three weeks later the hull of the much larger *Tennessee* slid into the muddy waters of the Alabama River. Lieutenant Johnston in Selma, who was to take the vessel to Mobile for completion, gave this account of her launching:

> About midday there was heard the sound of a gun, and immediately afterwards the *Tennessee* was shot into the swift current like an arrow, and the water had risen to such a height that she struck in her course the corner of a brick warehouse, situated on an adjoining bluff and demolished it. This was her first and only experience as a ram.[15]

The *Tennessee* and *Huntsville* were launched before completion in order to take advantage of the prevailing high water. Buchanan ordered the vessels to Mobile immediately, by tow if necessary, because of the "danger of the river falling so much that [they] . . . cannot cross the shoals. . . . " The

Tuscaloosa steamed to the port city under her own power, but the other two had to be towed by the pride of the Alabama River, the magnificent steamboat *Southern Republic*. The trip down the twisting river with its steep banks took over a week. Because of snags and the difficulty of towing, the boat and her charge tied up at a landing during the night. The appearance of the *Southern Republic* with her calliope shrilling "Dixie" always drew a crowd of curious people, and the presence of the strange-looking craft under tow added to the interest.[16]

Once the vessels reached Mobile, Buchanan, with his driving energy, tackled the job of getting them fitted out and ready for action. "I have neither flag-captain nor flag-lieutenant, nor midshipman for aides; consequently, I have all the various duties to attend to from the grade of midshipman up. My office duties increase daily, which keeps me in the office until 3 o'clock, and then in the afternoon I visit the navy yard, navy store, ordnance, etc. . . . ," he confided to Catesby Jones. Fearful of being attacked before his squadron was ready, Buchanan was reluctant to delegate responsibility and hypercritical of everything and everyone connected with the ships under construction. On June 13 he wrote: "The idleness of the workmen has caused remarks by citizens and others and I have been obliged [*sic*] to make a short speech but a *strong one* to the men, and have also stirred up Mr. [Joseph] Pierce and Engineer [George W.] Fisher. . . . I spare no one if he is delinquent." On July 5: "Old Pierce the constructor can plan work, perhaps, but he cannot control men. He is a perfect old woman. I have gone on much further since he left here. . . . Pierce delayed the work [on the *Tennessee*] by putting on the wrong iron."

"Old Buck" was just as hard on the civilians, both workers and contractors. When a number of carpenters struck at Selma and traveled to Mobile looking for work, marines met their boat, arrested them, and hauled them off to the guard house. When the admiral threatened to turn them over to the conscription officer, they agreed to return to work. Pep talks and threats apparently did not motivate the workers enough, at least as far as Buchanan was concerned, for in August he had all of them conscripted and detailed to work under his orders.[17] The contractors, too, came in for their share of his criticism. After the *Nashville* reached Mobile in June, Buchanan complained frequently of their absence. In August, two months after the side-wheel ironclad reached the city, he reported to Mallory:

"Great delay on the *Nashville* is caused for want of material, which could be procured without difficulty if either of the contractors were here to attend to it, only one of them, Mr. Montgomery has been here, and then only one day. . . . "

Buchanan was also displeased with the builders at the Tombigbee River yard. The site had been ill-chosen; its location near a swamp resulted in a great deal of sickness and dissension among the workmen. On October 1, 1863, Buchanan informed the naval secretary that one of the contractors was unpopular with the workmen and the other "a hard drinker [who] . . . spends much of his time in Mobile." With the department's approval, the flag officer took the vessels out of the contractors' hands, appointed a naval officer to supervise the shipyard, and commissioned Sidney Porter as a naval constructor. Porter was the former contractor who drank and was absent much of the time, and Buchanan hoped to control his negligence by subjecting him to naval discipline. Considering these problems, and remembering that Buchanan, like many professional military officers, found working with civilians disagreeable, it is not surprising that he wrote in January 1864, "I have lost all confidence in *all* contractors."[18]

Under the flag officer's constant surveillance, the vessels as they arrived in Mobile received their armor, guns, and crews; after a shakedown cruise they were commissioned. The *Tuscaloosa* made her trial run early in April 1863, followed two weeks later by the *Huntsville*. By summer both of these floating batteries were operational, although Buchanan decided not to send them into the bay because of their slowness. With 125 pounds of steam pressure, the *Tuscaloosa* made only two and a half knots.

On June 18, 1863, the hull of the *Nashville* arrived from Montgomery and was towed to the navy yard for completion. Her 270-foot length and 62-foot beam gave her an impressive appearance—one officer after visiting the vessel wrote that he was "perfectly delighted with her. Never was so much pleased in my life. She is a tremendous monster. . . . The *Tennessee* is insignificant along side of her. . . ."[19]

Buchanan hoped that the *Nashville* and *Tennessee* would be ready by the end of the summer, but the *Tennessee* would not be commissioned until February of 1864 and the *Nashville* more than six months afterwards. Because of the problem of acquiring sufficient plate for armor, the flag officer determined to complete one vessel at a time. The *Nashville*, naked

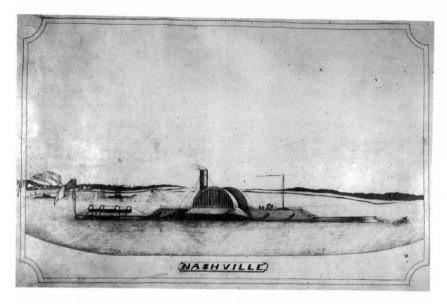

The CSS *Nashville. (National Archives)*

without her covering of iron armor, lay moored to a wharf, while the *Tennessee* was completed. In September Buchanan reported,

> The work on the *Tennessee* has progressed for some weeks past. . . . There is much delay for want of plate and bolt iron; it was impossible to iron both sponsons at the same time, as the vessel had to be careened several feet to enable them to put the iron on; even then several of the workmen were waist deep in the water to accomplish it. . . . The work has been carried on night and day when it could be done advantageously. The first course of iron and part of the second are on one side of the *Tennessee* and nearly all the first course on the opposite side.

By December 1863 she was ready, and Buchanan wrote wishfully, "if I only had her guns and crews, and had her across the short water on the bar, I would be satisfied it would not be long before she should try her strength."[20] But guns were not available and would not be for some time.

Originally, the ordnance for the Mobile vessels was to have been supplied by the iron works Colin McRae had acquired in Selma. The contract for the casting of cannon signed between representatives of the War and Navy Departments with McRae in February 1862 stipulated that the first guns were to be delivered by September 1 of that year. It was, however, January 1864 before the first piece was forwarded to Mobile. In June 1863, the foundry had come under exclusive naval control with the former executive officer of the *Virginia*, Catesby R. Jones, as its commanding officer. From the casting of the first experimental gun a month after he took charge, until the spring of 1865, nearly two hundred guns were manufactured.

Because the Selma foundry was unable to provide the *Huntsville* and *Tuscaloosa* with guns, other means had to be found. Six, including two 42-pounders, two 32-pounder smooth-bores, and two 32-pounder rifles, were obtained from the army as temporary batteries, and later two 7-inch Brooke guns were sent from Tredegar and two more from Charleston.[21]

The origin of the *Tennessee's* battery of six guns is uncertain. Presumably, part of it came from the Selma foundry, which shipped its first two 7-inch Brooke rifles to Mobile early in January 1864. But it is highly unlikely—as some historians state—that her entire battery came from the Selma works, at least not at first. On January 26 Buchanan wrote that her battery was complete; and records of the naval iron works do not indicate that additional guns were shipped to Mobile during January. More than likely the other four guns (6.4-inch Brooke rifles) came from two stationary floating batteries in the harbor, for that is what Buchanan proposed to the Navy Department.[22]

The *Nashville's* armament was unusual for a Confederate ironclad. Because her builders increased the forward inclination of the shield to twenty-nine degrees, more than the specifications called for, the 7-inch bow gun had to be lengthened several inches. The *Nashville* was also one of the first Confederate ironclads to use 7-inch guns in her broadside. The standard broadside was the 6.4-inch Brooke, but the introduction of a new type of carriage enabled the side-wheel armored ship to carry 7-inch guns.[23]

Finding seamen to man the ships was probably the most irksome problem Buchanan encountered. He wrote dozens of letters to Mallory and to the various officers who headed the Office of Orders and Detail requesting men. He complained frequently of his inability to obtain men from the army. For example, on April 6, 1863, he wrote: "I am much in want of men and unless the Secretary of War and the Generals are more liberal toward the Navy in permitting transfers from the Army to the Navy we cannot man either the Gun boats or floating batteries." He told Augusta J. Evans, a well-known writer in Mobile, that of 650 applications to the War Department for seamen in the army to be detailed for naval service, only 20 had been approved.[24] He did receive a sufficient number of men from the army to fill his ship complements, and contrary to his complaints, most military commanders, particularly General D. H. Maury at Mobile, were cooperative. Perhaps they were impressed by the admiral's rank and reputation or by his pugnacious stubbornness, for military commanders elsewhere were notoriously uncooperative in detailing men to the navy. On December 12, 1863, Maury asked the Adjutant General: "Please call the attention of the Secretary of War to the importance of affording every aid to the naval commander here in procuring the transfer of men from the Army to the Navy."[25] In March 1864 he offered Buchanan artillery details to man the guns in the naval vessels if the flag officer decided on an attack before his crews were completed. Eventually, about 150 men were detailed from a Tennessee unit to serve on the *Tennessee*.

Although these Tennesseans were praised during and after the war by Buchanan as well as Johnston, the admiral was not entirely pleased with the personnel of the squadron. "There are on board . . . these vessels some of the greatest vagabonds you will ever read of," he related to Mitchell. "One or two such hung during this time would have a wonderful effect." Buchanan's opinion was probably inevitable considering the fact that a large percentage of men who manned his ships, as well as those throughout the Confederate navy, were not seamen; they had never been to sea or experienced the life of a jack tar in a ship-of-war in the old navy. Only a well-disciplined ship was a good ship to a naval officer steeped in the tradition of Stephen Decatur and Oliver Hazard Perry. Buchanan was a disciplinarian. "If we could use the lash we should have no trials for desertion or thefts—I never knew solitary confinement to have any effect upon a crew."[26] Buchanan strongly disapproved of the regulations against corporal punishment in the Confederate navy and so informed Secretary Mallory.

The flag officer was not alone in his censorious opinion of the enlisted personnel in the Mobile Squadron. An officer reporting on board the *Morgan* for the first time was shocked at her crew. "To call the *Morgan*'s crew sailors would be disgracing the name," he wrote with a touch of xenophobia. "Out of a hundred and fifty not one is even *American*, much less a Southerner. We have Irish, Dutch, Norwegian, Danes, French, Spanish, Italian, Mexicans, Indians, and Mutezos [*sic*]—a set of desperate cut throats. But worst of all their loyalty is doubtful. . . . I could go into the country and get *ten Southerners* and teach them more in one week about seamanship and gunnery than these fellows will learn in twelve months."[27] A similar description was given of the *Selma's* crew by one of her officers. By June 1864, there were more than 800 enlisted men and 133 officers in the squadron, enough to man the vessels and station.

Buchanan appealed almost as frequently for officers as for enlisted men, and, characteristically, he was constantly deriding the officers' competence. Many officers, he wrote, "appear to think that the Navy was made for their *pleasure and accommodation*, and I take good care to assure to them that such is not the case." He could be intemperate and vituperative in his remarks about individual officers, and rank, age, or experience meant little to him. "_____ is a very nice gentleman, but he is not enough of a *navy officer* for me. He has never felt much interest in the life." "Why did you send me old _____? I don't think I ever had an officer of so little force. *He is of no earthly use to me.*" "I am obliged to ask a court of Inquiry on _____. You are aware that he never was worth anything in the old Navy." "_____'s Lieutenants and officers are dissatisfied with him . . . he makes enemies of nearly all [of them]." "_____ is nothing—not worth his salt." "_____ is here on board the *Huntsville*—wish he was anywhere else."

Although to his officers he was much more free with his criticisms, he could give compliments. Farrand was "respected," Lieutenant George W. Gift a "fine officer," Lieutenant John R. Eggleston "a clever man." "I cannot get along here without [Johnston] . . . he is never idle; he is constantly employed with matters connected with the vessels of the Squadron . . . a thousand things which I cannot enumerate." He was so impressed with the abilities of Johnston that he persuaded the department to advance him over a number of senior officers to the rank of commander in command of the *Tennessee*.[28]

Any attempt to generalize about the attitude of the personnel in the Mobile Squadron toward Buchanan would be at best haphazard; there are no known records or diaries of enlisted men who served in the squadron, and personal papers from officers are scanty. Buchanan, however, was the type of personality that a young officer would write home about and we can gain some impressions from these letters. He was universally admired and respected for his courage and aggressiveness. In contrast to officers at other stations in the Confederacy, the officers in Mobile were apparently quite confident about what Buchanan would be able to do—right up to the battle of Mobile Bay. Most complaints concerned his strict observance of regulations, particularly about the wearing of uniforms. Shortly after taking command of the station, Buchanan issued an order requiring all officers to wear "at all times when on duty" the prescribed uniform. Elsewhere in the Confederacy, even in Richmond, wearing the gray uniform, although required by regulations, was not strictly enforced. Many officers who had been in the old navy simply changed the buttons on their blue coats. Buchanan, however, was indignant when, as he wrote to Mitchell, one officer "reported to me for duty in a *black coat,* said he had no uniform and had never had one since he received his appointment." Lieutenant Gift's admiration for the admiral dimmed somewhat over the uniform incident. "A week or more since the remnant of the crew of the *Arkansas* arrived here," he wrote, "Admiral Buchanan . . . [informed] the officers that he had no use for them, as they had no uniforms! I have heard it said that with some ladies a sleek coat . . . with brass buttons has a wonderful effect, but I was not prepared to believe that with a man who claimed to be a warrior of age (there is no doubt of that). . . . From this, I deduct that a fashionable tailor can do more to make a good officer in the estimation of old Buchanan than the great creating Prince of Heaven."[29] Gift was not altogether fair, for some of the *Arkansas's* crew were retained; but most of them were transferred to Charleston.

In spite of Old Buck's penchant for regulations and discipline; in spite of the discomforts and ill-health that were always present while serving on ironclads in a semi-tropical area, life was generally pleasant for the officers of the Mobile Squadron. Mobile, with a population of approximately 25,000 inhabitants, was one of the most cosmopolitan cities in the Confederacy. William Howard Russell, the famous correspondent of the London *Times,* noted in his diary: "The city . . . abounds in oyster saloons, drinking houses, lager-beer and wine-shops, and gambling and dancing places . . . the most foreign-looking city I have yet seen in the States."[30] Naval duty was such that officers and men could take advantage of the many diversions in the city. The wooden vessels of the squadron rotated at guarding the passes to the bay—a tour down the bay lasting for two weeks to a month. When in harbor they usually anchored near the center of the city—opposite the post office and Battle House hotel. Gift described a typical day at anchor in the harbor: "We are in four watches, which gives me two days on duty and two days off. On my liberty days I go on shore at half past nine and find some friends and acquaintances with whom I consume the time until 2:00 P.M. I then return on board to dinner (and by the way we live very well) and remain until after quarters at 4 and then go ashore until tea time. It seems precisely like living a very short distance from the city."

The war had little effect on social activities in the city. The genteel custom of calling upon certain prominent families in the city was still customary and naval officers frequented the homes of Augusta Evans, Madame Le Vert, and others. The navy reciprocated by holding shipboard balls and dinners, and by taking moonlight cruises down the bay. The old admiral himself did not disdain such affairs; a journalist describing a river boat excursion which included the governor of Alabama, General Maury, and Buchanan, wrote: "A very good band of music from one of the regiments of the garrison played, and dancing was soon got up in the splendid saloon. . . . Admiral Buchanan, who was looking on, joined in this, and naturally by doing so created a great deal of confusion and merriment, at which he was in high glee."[31]

Social duties were a tonic for the monotonous but normal wartime duty of waiting. Occasionally, some excitement would be generated when a blockade runner would slip into the bay. The Confederate steamers would then fire a few shells to discourage the blockaders from venturing too close. This respite was only temporary, however, and by 1864 blockade running had slowed down to a trickle.

On February 16, 1864, the *Tennessee* was placed in commission. Considered by many, including Alfred T. Mahan, to be the most powerful ironclad built from the keel up within the Confederacy, she was slightly over two hundred feet in overall length with a rather broad beam of forty-eight feet.

Mallory originally had sent his most aggressive senior officer to Mobile not only to raise the blockade off that city, but also to cooperate in a combined effort to regain New Orleans and the lower Mississippi River. Several plans were suggested which included, at one time or another, the cooperation of armorclads building in Europe, as well as the armies of first

Beauregard, later Joseph E. Johnston, and finally Kirby Smith. Any plan to attack New Orleans hinged upon the availability of a powerful force of ironclads, and by the late spring of 1864, it was crystal clear that such a force would not be ready in the near future. The three vessels under construction on the Tombigbee were without armor, and no armor was available; the *Tuscaloosa* and *Huntsville* were unseaworthy; the *Nashville* was nearly ready, but she was weak because of her exposed wheels, slow speed, and inadequate armor. In order to provide her with a limited amount of armor (bow and forward part of the shield), plate had to be taken from the decrepit *Baltic*. The old converted cotton lighter and first ironclad in the bay was so worm-eaten that she was no longer seaworthy; "rotten as punk, about as fit to go into action as a mud scow," her commanding officer described her. In brief, Buchanan's ironclad squadron for offensive operations consisted of one ship—the *Tennessee*. Unfortunately, this vessel was the only ironclad that the flag officer had to defend the bay against Farragut's attack early in August. The *Nashville* was too vulnerable, and the *Huntsville*'s and *Tuscaloosa*'s power plants were so weak that they would not have been able to escape back up the river in case of disaster. Buchanan was forced to face the powerful Union fleet with one ironclad and three small wooden gunboats.

Notes

Reprinted with permission of the Alabama Department of Archives and History, Montgomery, Alabama

1. The *Florida*'s name was changed to *Selma* in September 1862.
2. *Acts of the Second Called Session, 1861, and of The First Regular Annual Session General Assembly of Alabama Held in The City of Montgomery* (Montgomery: Montgomery Advertiser Book and Job Office, 1862), 211–213; *Baltic* Construction Papers, Military Records Division, Navy Records, File 34 (Department of Archives and History, Montgomery, Alabama); Mallory to Baker, March 5, 1863, construction at Mobile file, Confederate Subject and Area File, National Archives Record Group 45 (National Archives, Washington, D.C.). For Johnston's role in building naval vessels in Alabama see Johnston to Wright, February 11, 1861, in James D. Johnston folder (Naval History Division, Department of the Navy, National Archives Building, Washington, D.C.); Governor Shorter to Mallory, October 15, 1862, Shorter Executive Papers, Letterbook, 1861–63 (Alabama Department of Archives and History,

Montgomery); Johnston to Mitchell, May 22, 1863, John K. Mitchell Papers (Virginia Historical Society, Richmond). For McRae see various letters from September 1861 to June 1862 in the Colin J. McRae Collection (Alabama Department of Archives and History, Montgomery); Edwin Layton, "Colin J. McRae and the Selma Arsenal," *Alabama Review*, XVIII (1966), 129–130; Charles S. Davis, *Colin J. McRae: Confederate Financial Agent* (Tuscaloosa, 1961). Johnston actually superintended the construction of the *Baltic, Morgan*, and *Gaines*, and commanded the *Baltic* before receiving command of the *Tennessee*.

3. Charles Graves to cousin, May 1, 1862, Charles Graves Papers (Southern Historical Collection, University of North Carolina Library, Chapel Hill).

4. The appointment was made eight months after he first entered the Confederate naval service.

5. Randolph to Drepe (?), August 19, 1862, construction at Mobile file, National Archives Record Group 45; see also to Yancy, August 18, 1862, construction at Mobile file, National Archives Record Group 45.

6. Graves to Maggie, April 21, 1862, Graves Papers; Randolph to Buchanan, February 15, 1862, construction at Mobile file, National Archives Record Group 45.

7. Graves to cousin, April 6, 1862, Graves Papers; Scharf, *Confederate States Navy*, 536; see also Johnston to Mitchell, June 19, 1863, Mitchell Papers.

8. The *Morgan*'s first commanding officer agreed as to her weakness: "Her steam pipes are entirely above the water line, and her boilers and magazines partly above it, so we have the comfortable appearance of being blown up or scalded by any chance shot that may not take off our heads." C. H. Kennedy to Charles Ellis, n.d., Charles Ellis Papers (Duke University Library, Durham, North Carolina). The blockade off Mobile was practically ineffective during most of 1863. Most of the blockaders were sailing vessels unable to stop steamers. *Official Records, Navies*, Ser. I, XIX, 102–03; Charles L. Lewis, *David Glasgow Farragut* (2 vols., Annapolis, 1941–43), II, 136.

9. Buchanan to Forrest, September 12, 1862, Franklin Buchanan Letterbook, (Southern Historical Collection, University of North Carolina.)

10. Farrand was placed in charge of all shipbuilding in the state, but he was evidently subordinated to Buchanan. Mallory to Farrand, August 1, 1862, Ebenezer Farrand folder, BZ File; Mallory to Farrand, September 2, 1862, Area file, National Archives Record Group 45.

11. October 15, 1862, Buchanan Letterbook.

12. McRae to Harris, October 31, 1862, McRae Collection.

13. The detailed survey of the *Tennessee* made by a board of Union naval officers after she was captured indicated that her machinery came from the riverboat

Alonzo Child. This is apparently a mistake for the machinery from this boat was not removed until December 1863 to be transported to Selma; probably to be installed in a fourth ironclad under construction there. The *Tennessee's* machinery was being installed in the summer and fall of 1863—at the time the *Alonzo Child* was being stripped of her power plant. On December 15, 1863, Buchanan wrote, "will try the machinery tomorrow or the next day." *Official Records, Navies,* Ser. I, XX, 856; see also Farrand to Engineer G. W. Fisher, March 6, April 13, and June 1, 1863, construction at Selma file, National Archives Record Group 45; Farrand to DeHaven, December 30, 1863, in *Alonzo Child* folder, Vessel File, National Archives Record Group 109; Farrand to Whitesides, December 30, 1863, Confederate Navy Brigade Personal Papers, National Archives Record Group 109; Savannah *Morning News,* December 23, 1863.

14. *Official Records, Navies,* Ser. I, XXI, 600; Simms to Jones, July 5, 1864. Area file, National Archives Record Group 45; Farrand to Myers, December 1862, construction at Selma file, National Archives Record Group 45; Farrand to Jones, December 23, 1862; McCarrick to Kennan, January 12, 1863; Farrand to Hunt, January 25, 1863 (copy), Shelby Iron Company Papers (University of Alabama Library, Tuscaloosa).

15. From an address delivered by James D. Johnston before the Georgia Historical Society, copy in National Archives Record Group 45.

16. Montgomery *Daily Advertiser,* March 9, 1863; Ware to Pierce, May 7, 1863, Ware Letterbooks, National Archives Record Group 45; Buchanan to Comstock, February 12, 1863, Area file, National Archives Record Group 45; Memorandum from deserter February 24, 1863, Gustavus Fox Papers (New York Historical Society, New York City). For a description of the *Southern Republic* see Thomas C. DeLeon, *Four Years in Rebel Capitals* (New York, 1962), 57–63; and William H. Russell, *My Diary North and South*, ed, Fletcher Pratt (New York, 1954), 103–07.

17. Buchanan to Mallory, September 20, 1863, Buchanan Letterbook; Buchanan to Mitchell, June 13, 1863, Mitchell Papers.

18. Buchanan to Mitchell, January 26, 1864, Mitchell Papers; see also Buchanan to Mallory, October 1, 1863, Buchanan Letterbook; Buchanan to Farrand, December 1, 1863, Area file, National Archives Record Group 45; Farrand to Buchanan, April 5, 1864, Ebenezer Farrand folder, Citizens File, National Archives Record Group 109; Voucher, November 19, 1863, construction at Selma file, National Archives Record Group 45.

19. Gift to Ellen Shackleford, June 19, 1868, Gift Papers (Southern Historical Collection, University of North Carolina).

20. Buchanan to Mitchell, December 11, 1863, Mitchell Papers.

21. The latter two brought on a controversy between the Navy Department and Beauregard that went all the way to the President before being decided in favor of the navy. Tredegar Foundry Sale Book, December 3, 1862, Tredegar Rolling Mill and Foundry Collection (Virginia State Library, Richmond); Buchanan to Minor, October 9, 1862, Buchanan Letterbook.

22. Buchanan to Mitchell, October 7, 1863, Mitchell Papers; Buchanan to Mallory, October 1, 1863, Buchanan Letterbook; Walter Stephens, "The Brooke Guns from Selma," *Alabama Historical Quarterly*, XX (1958), 465. Johnston states that her battery came from Selma, James D. Johnston, "The Ram *Tennessee* at Mobile Bay," *Battles and Leaders*, IV, 401.

23. Brooke to Catesby Jones, January 15, 1864; Jones to McCorkle, January 28, 1864; McCorkle to Jones, February 1, 27, 1864; Brooke to Buchanan, January 21, 1864, Selma Foundry Papers, National Archives Record Group 45.

24. Quoted in Clement Eaton, *A History of the Southern Confederacy* (New York, 1954), 325.

25. War Department Papers, National Archives Record Group 109.

26. to Mitchell, June 22, 1863, Mitchell Papers.

27. Graves to cousin, March 2, 1862, Graves Papers.

28. For remarks about various officers see Buchanan to Mitchell, April 5, June 3, October 17, December 1, 3, 1863, and March 1, 1864, in the Mitchell Papers. See also letters and documents concerning a Court of Inquiry for two officers in the Mobile squadron, Wirt Family Papers (Southern Historical Collection, University of North Carolina, Chapel Hill).

29. Gift to Ellen, August 2, 1863, Gift Papers; see also Simms to Jones, March 4, 20, 1864, Area file, National Archives Record Group 45.

30. Russell, *My Diary, North and South*, 108. Other wartime descriptions of Mobile can be found in DeLeon, *Four Years in Rebel Capitals*, 71–73; FitzGerald Ross, *Cities and Camps of the Confederate States*, ed., Richard Harwell (Urbana, 1958), 193–94; Arthur Freemantle, *The Freemantle Diary*, ed., Walter Lord (Boston, 1954), 103–04.

31. Ross, *Cities and Camps of the Confederate States*, 196. For social activities in Mobile see Gift to Ellen, June 13, August 2, 1863, Gift Papers; Grimball to mother, October 10, 25, 1862, John Grimball Collection (Duke University Library, Durham); George C. Waterman, "Notable Naval Events of the War," *Confederate Veteran*, VII (1899), 450; Mary Waring, *Miss Waring's Journal, 1863 and 1865*, ed., Thad Holt, Jr. (Mobile, 1964), 4.

19

John Taylor Wood: Confederate Commando

JOHN M. TAYLOR

No family exemplified the divisions imposed by the Civil War more than did the descendants of the 12th president of the United States, Zachary Taylor. When secession and war came to the nation a decade after Taylor's death, his descendants would be found on both sides. The late president's son-in-law, Jefferson Davis, became president of the Confederacy. Conversely, one of his brothers, Joseph, became a Union general, and a son-in-law, Robert Crooke Wood, was a senior officer in the Union medical corps. A younger generation of Taylors, however, tended to side with the Confederacy. Richard Taylor, one of Zachary's sons, developed into one of the Confederacy's ablest commanders. And a grandson, John Taylor Wood, became one of the heroes of the South's fledgling navy.

Wood was born in 1830 at Fort Snelling, Minnesota, then part of Iowa Territory. His mother, Anne Mackall Taylor, was one of Zachary Taylor's daughters. Brought up far from the sea, Wood never explained his reasons for choosing the navy as a career. Nevertheless, he entered the newly opened naval academy at Annapolis in 1848, and, after a course of study interspersed with long periods of sea duty, graduated second in his class in June 1853.

Wood's first tours at sea, on vessels such as the frigate *Brandywine* and the sloop-of-war *Cumberland*, were exciting. But he fell in love with a Maryland girl, Lola Mackubin, and the two were married in 1856. Wood knew that a navy career would entail extended separations, but rather than resign he negotiated an appointment as instructor at the Naval Academy. At the time of the bombardment of Fort Sumter, the 30-year-old Wood had a hand in two professions. At Annapolis he was an instructor in seamanship, tactics, and gunnery; but he also worked a small farm, Woodland, in nearby Maryland.

Although his heart was with the South, Wood took no satisfaction in the disintegration of the Union, in whose navy he served. Following the bombardment of Fort Sumter he wrote in his diary, "War, that terrible calamity, is upon us. . . . The news has made me sick at heart."[1] The young officer's sentiment was genuine, for the war was tearing his immediate family apart. John Taylor Wood's father was a staunch Union man, and when John indicated his intention to go South, his father broke off all contact.

John Taylor Wood sold his farm and headed for Richmond, where he received a commission as a lieutenant in the Confederate navy, the same rank he had held in the Old Navy. Considering that his uncle was Jefferson Davis, Wood could have passed the war in relative comfort as a naval aide to the president. Indeed, Wood was not above making use of his political connections, but he appears to have done so most often to find billets that promised action.

In the fall of 1861 Wood learned of the work in progress to convert the steam frigate *Merrimack* into an ironclad. He was curious about the new technology, and in January 1862 wrangled an assignment as a gunnery officer on the ironclad, renamed the *Virginia*. Her most immediate need was for a crew, and Wood's first assignment from Captain Franklin Buchanan was to recruit soldiers to serve on the ironclad with promises of prize money and adventure.

When the *Virginia* steamed for Hampton Roads on her first wartime mission, Wood commanded her aft pivot gun, a 7-inch Brooke rifle. On March 8, 1862, the Confederate ironclad wreaked havoc among the wooden ships of the Federal fleet, ramming and sinking the sloop *Cumberland*, on which Wood had served before the war, setting afire the 50-gun frigate *Congress*, and causing another frigate, the *Minnesota*, to run aground. "After making preparations for the next day's fight," Wood later recalled, "we slept at our guns, dreaming of other victories in the morning."[2]

The following day, when the *Virginia* met her match in John Ericsson's *Monitor*, Wood was in the thick of the fighting. At one point in the battle he called for volunteers to board the *Monitor* and immobilize her turret with wedges and hammers. He had assembled a boarding party when the *Monitor* sheared off, making boarding impossible. Shortly thereafter, a shell from Wood's pivot gun struck the *Monitor*'s pilot house at pointblank range, spraying its interior with fragments and putting her captain, John Worden, out of action for the rest of the drawn battle.[3]

Wood spent much of the remainder of 1862 on staff duty, including a tour inspecting naval construction throughout the Confederacy. On January 26, 1863, President Davis appointed him an aide with the rank of colonel of cavalry, making Wood one of a handful of officers to hold commissions in two services.

But the restless Marylander was again in search of action, and because the James River flotilla was relatively inactive he proposed to Secretary of the Navy Mallory a series of raids on the Yankee-controlled rivers that empty into Chesapeake Bay. In October 1862 he had led a small expedition to the mouth of the Potomac, where he had burned two Federal schooners. Now he was authorized to launch a larger expedition. On August 12 he began moving four cutters and 70 men by wagon from the James to the Piankatank River, where Federal gunboats were known to be patrolling. On the night of August 22, Wood's raiders surprised first the 217-ton USS *Satellite* and then the 90-ton USS *Reliance*, capturing both after fierce hand-to-hand fighting.

This action was the first of Wood's "midnight raids," which, while having little effect on the land war, caused acute embarrassment to the enemy. Wood, for his part, was emerging as an exceptional leader of men—careful in his preparations, resolute in battle. He was a brown-water "Jeb" Stuart, striking by water behind Federal lines when the enemy least expected him.

In July 1863 Wood gained Robert E. Lee's support for what would have been his most daring exploit of the war, an expedition across the mouth of the Potomac to free some 20,000 Confederate prisoners confined at Point Lookout, Maryland. The camp was one of the Federals' largest, yet it was vulnerable to attack from the sea. Security in planning for the raid appears to have been poor, however; the Federals, hearing that something was up, moved most of the Point Lookout prisoners to upstate New York. On July 9, President Davis himself directed that the rescue mission be aborted.

....

Later that year Wood convinced Davis that Federal control of the waterways around Wilmington, North Carolina, threatened access to that key port and must be challenged if the port was to be kept open. Davis concurred, and authorized Wood to conduct a joint operation with the army aimed at reclaiming North Carolina waters for the Confederacy.

In the end the operation failed, in part because of poor coordination between Wood's force and Confederate army units commanded by General George E. Pickett. Nevertheless, Wood led a party that seized and burned the *Underwriter*, one of the largest Federal gunboats on North Carolina waters. Wood's role in the enterprise was viewed as a success, however; General Robert E. Lee reported, "Commander Wood, who had the hardest part to perform, did his part well."[4] The enemy was also impressed. The Federals' assistant secretary of the navy, Gustavus Fox, in a letter to Admiral Samuel P. Lee, had some backhanded praise for Wood:

> You may be very sure the Department will not find any fault with any dashing expeditions that give reasonable hope of a result injurious to the enemy, even though they fail occasionally. See how much they make out of John Taylor Wood's exploits, a solemn vote of thanks and everybody cheerful over the capture of three tugs [sic].[5]

Meanwhile, Wood was looking for new worlds to conquer, and his entrée to Jefferson Davis in effect gave him first refusal on any promising mission. Davis and Mallory had long been unhappy with the Confederacy's dependence on privately owned blockade-runners, whose owners often crammed them with high-profit luxury goods rather than military supplies. Davis and Mallory wanted a fleet of government-owned blockade runners, responsible to orders from Richmond. Early in 1863 Mallory had told his purchasing agent in Britain, James Bulloch, to try to purchase one or more of the shallow-draft steamers that he understood to be under construction there. Secrecy was essential, lest Bulloch run afoul of Britain's neutrality laws.

In March 1864, the firm of J. and W. Dudgeon launched the first of the new ships sought by Mallory. The *Atlanta* was, according to her builders, destined for cross-channel service. In that role she would certainly have set a new standard, because the 700-ton vessel boasted not only the newest iron construction but also twin screws that gave her a top speed of about 17

John Taylor Wood, in a sketch probably made after the war. *(Author's collection)*

knots. Without cargo, she drew only 9 feet of water. Because her propellers could be operated separately and even in opposite directions, the new ship had a remarkably small turning radius and could sail rings around almost any vessel of her day.[6]

Atlanta was just the type of vessel that Mallory was looking for, and the navy appropriated the speedy blockade runner for its own use, paying its owners half again their original purchase price. On July 23, 1864, Wood was named to command the ship, renamed the CSS *Tallahassee*. The erstwhile blockade runner was now a Confederate cruiser.

Wood's command was unlike any of the Confederate commerce destroyers that had preceded her. In contrast to heavily armed vessels such as the *Alabama* and the *Florida*, *Tallahassee* mounted only three guns: a rifled 3-pounder forward, a rifled 100-pounder amidships, and a Parrott gun aft. She was not expected to engage enemy warships, but to outrun them. At the same time, the *Tallahassee* had one significant weakness—a limited range. She carried coal enough for only 1,000 miles under steam, and her fore-and-aft schooner rig provided little power under sail.

Wood's first task was to escape the Federal blockaders outside Wilmington, who were stationed in a formidable series of concentric rings outside the port. His main ally was the enemy's ennui. Blockade duty in the summer heat off the Carolina coast was a trial to Yankees of all ranks. Even the prospect of prize money for a captured blockader could not assuage the boredom.

Despite the *Tallahassee*'s speed and maneuverability, attempting a breakout required considerable daring. The Confederate vessel was heavily outgunned by virtually all of the 50 or so Federal vessels blockading Wilmington. Coal had been loaded in every vacant space on the *Tallahassee*, which reduced her speed and increased her draft from 9 to nearly 14 feet. Wood's first two attempts at a breakout ended with his ship's being towed off a sandbar. For Wood, the most nervewracking part of the cruise would be passing out of the Old Inlet:

> As the moon went down on the night of August 6, at ten, we approached the bar. . . . As the leadsman called out the water in a low tone, our hearts rose in our mouths as it shoaled: "By the mark three,—and a quarter less three,—and a half two,—and a quarter two." She touched but did not bring up. Then came the joyful words: "And a half two."[7]

The black-bearded Wood turned to his chief engineer, John Tynan, ordering, "Let her go for all she is worth!"[8]

Tynan did so, but in the course of priming his fires with pine knots he produced a streak of flame that betrayed the *Tallahassee*'s location. Almost immediately the raider was challenged by a Federal warship, whose flare in turn alerted the *Montgomery*. That vessel beat to quarters and soon spied a ship on her port bow, moving south at a high speed. The *Montgomery* challenged the stranger but received no answer, and the *Tallahassee* disappeared into the night.

The next few days were uneventful. The *Tallahassee* cruised northward, helped along by the Gulf Stream, occasionally encountering sail but no Yankee shipping. Then, off the New Jersey coast, the raider took her first prize, the schooner *Sarah A. Boyce*, on August 11. After the crew had been taken aboard, the prize was scuttled. Wood was now in a lucrative hunting ground. It was customary in that day for pilot boats—often sleek schooners—to loiter off New York harbor, seeking incoming merchantmen to guide into the harbor. One such vessel was the *James Funk*, also captured on August 11. Wood relieved her of her crew and a portion of her provisions; he then placed a prize crew aboard the pilot boat and sent the *James Funk* in search of other small craft. Between them, the raider and her consort burned or bonded a total of seven vessels in one day—the largest single-day total for any Confederate cruiser.

Wood was determined to offload his prisoners as rapidly as possible, for space on the raider was at a premium. One of his officers wrote to his sweetheart:

> We are overcrowded with men, and officers have very small quarters and plenty of dirt. It is impossible to keep clean. The coal dust on deck and from the firerooms fills the air with a fine powder which settles in and upon everything in a most provoking and disgusting manner.[9]

Wood's plans went far beyond destroying a handful of pilot boats. Two years before, Secretary Mallory had hoped that the clumsy *Virginia* might be employed to attack that citadel of Yankeedom, New York City. Much later, he may have held out the same prospect to the captains of other commerce destroyers. Wood, for his part, claimed to have looked for a competent pilot who could be either paid or coerced to lead the *Tallahassee* into Long Island Sound:

> It was my intention to run up the harbor just after dark, as I knew the way in by Sandy Hook, then go on up the East River, setting fire to the shipping on both sides, and when abreast of the navy-yard to open fire, hoping some of our shells might set fire to the buildings and any vessels that might be at the docks, and finally to steam through Hell Gate into the Sound. I knew from the daily papers, which we received only a day or two old, what vessels were in port, and there was nothing then ready that could oppose us.[10]

Coming from some skippers, such a statement of intent would smack of bravado. Coming from John Taylor Wood, it was no more than a statement of fact. Alas, he found no pilot equal to the task on that first day, and once his presence became known, such a daring raid became impracticable. Nevertheless, the *Tallahassee* passed three days between New York harbor and Montauk Point, burning 20 more ships, mostly small barks and schooners engaged in the coastal trade, but including a large and valuable packet, the *Adriatic*. In Washington, Secretary of the Navy Welles was moved to self-pity. He wrote in his diary, "Depredations by the piratical Rebel *Tallahassee* continue. We have sixteen vessels in pursuit, and yet I have no confidence in their capturing her."[11]

After burning the *Adriatic* at night—Wood thought the blazing ship "a picture of rare beauty"—he turned his ship north toward Boston. By then he had his enemy's full attention, and Wood decided to burn his tender, the *James Funk*, in the interest of speed. For the moment, however, *Tallahassee's* most pressing need was for fuel. This problem appeared to have been solved with the capture, on August 14, of the ship *James Littlefield*, laden with anthracite coal. But a persistent fog off the Maine coast precluded the transfer of fuel, and Wood reluctantly ordered the prize scuttled. Much of the time the *Tallahassee* operated in patchy fog, which required a sharp lookout, regular sounding of the ship's bell, and careful attention to water depth. Wood wrote later of the cruise, "I slept and lived on the bridge or in the chart-room, hardly taking off my clothes for weeks."[12]

On August 13 the *Tallahassee* captured and later scuttled a large bark, the 790-ton *Glenavon*, carrying a cargo of iron from Glasgow. In the case of many ships destroyed by Confederate cruisers, the principal loss was borne by some faceless Yankee insurance company. This was not so with the *Glenavon*. In Wood's recollection, he and the prize's skipper watched as the bark slowly settled, "as quietly as if human hands were lowering her into the depths."

> Captain Watt and his wife never took their eyes off their floating home, but side by side, with tears in their eyes, watched her disappear. "Poor fellow," she said afterward; "he has been going to sea for thirty years, and all our savings were in that ship. We were saving for our dear children at home—five of them."[13]

In her week-long rampage up the Atlantic coast, the *Tallahassee* had, by August 18, destroyed 25 vessels and released five others on ransom bond—an arrangement under which a prize's captain executed a bond promising to pay Confederate authorities a stated amount at the close of hostilities. Wood's biographer concludes that these numbers placed Wood "in the elite company of such resourceful captains as James Waddell [of the *Shenandoah*] and Raphael Semmes [of the *Alabama*]."[14] Such a comparison is simplistic.

Although Wood was bold almost to a fault in operating as he did off the enemy's coast, most of his prizes were of little consequence. The average size of the 14 vessels he captured off the New England coast between August 15 and 17 was 104 tons. Indeed, in destroying fishing craft that did little more than provide subsistence for their owners, Wood was pressing the bounds of acceptable behavior. International law, as interpreted in 1864, made enemy property at sea subject to capture and confiscation. But did this mean *all* property? Voices were being raised against commerce raiders, even when their prizes were tall ships. The London *Times* editorialized with respect to the *Alabama*, "Although a legitimate and recognized form of hostilities, the capture and destruction of peaceful merchantmen is one barbarism of war which civilized society is beginning to deprecate."[15]

On August 18, with only 40 tons of coal in his bunkers, Wood ran into Halifax, Nova Scotia. For most of the war Confederate cruisers had found a warm welcome in the ports of the British Empire. Now, London had belatedly concluded that the South was not going to win the war, and had taken steps to improve its relations with the probable victors. Thus, when Wood dropped anchor in Halifax, his reception was decidedly chilly—even though the skipper borrowed wearing apparel from his officers in order to make his formal calls in proper uniform. When Wood himself called on the ranking naval officer, Rear Admiral Sir James Hope, the Britisher was actively rude, declining even to shake hands or to offer his visitor a seat.

The lieutenant governor advised Wood that he could remain in port for 24 hours, or for whatever time might be required to take on coal in an amount to be determined by Admiral Hope. Wood located a good supply of Welsh coal, and in order to fill his bunkers contrived a story of damage to his mainmast. By sunset on August 19, he had taken on enough coal to get the *Tallahassee* back to Wilmington. But escape from Halifax would prove almost as challenging as the initial breakout from Wilmington.

Gideon Welles had ordered every available Federal ship to pursue the *Tallahassee*, and, by the time Wood was ready to raise anchor on the evening of August 19, five Federal warships were waiting offshore. Such odds appeared overwhelming, but Wood was a hard man to intimidate. He asked the local Confederate agent to find him the best harbor pilot in Halifax, who turned out to be a seagoing giant named Jock Fleming. "Don't be 'feared," the Nova Scotian told Wood, "I'll get you out all right." As Wood told the story, Fleming brought his hand down on Wood's shoulder "with a thud that I felt in my boots."[16] Fleming showed the raider captain a little-used inlet leading to the Atlantic, and at 1:00 a.m. on August 20, the *Tallahassee* proceeded through a passage that could accommodate only a vessel as nimble as the Rebel raider. Within an hour Wood could detect the change in his ship's motion as she moved into deep water. He set course for Wilmington.

The *Tallahassee's* return voyage was uneventful. Wood could not venture far off course because of the shortage of coal, and coastal waters were by then largely barren of prey. Only a single ship, the brig *Roan*, was captured on the cruise south. Off Wilmington, the raider again faced the daunting prospect of passing through the Federal blockade. But the *Tallahassee* made her dash at a time of Wood's choosing, and at a speed no blockader could match.

There was lavish praise for Wood and his band on their return to Wilmington. Secretary Mallory, in a report, contended that "the immediate losses inflicted upon the enemy by [Wood's] captures were greatly enhanced by the delay and detention of his commercial ships in port from a feeling of insecurity, and by the augmentation of the rates of marine insurance."[17] The *Richmond Examiner* called Wood "as enterprising and intrepid an officer who ever trod a quarter-deck."[18]

Others were not so sure. Governor Zeb Vance of North Carolina complained that Wood's exploits would only cause the Federals to further reinforce the blockade, to the detriment of his state. A Wilmington newspaper acknowledged that the *Tallahassee* "had certainly kicked up a fuss," but doubted whether she had done much to weaken the enemy. The Confederate military commander in Wilmington, Major General W. H. C. Whiting, was even more critical, complaining that the raider had taken all the available hard coal, leaving only soft coal for blockade runners, which now trailed black smoke while trying to evade the ubiquitous Yankee cruisers.[19]

Meanwhile, what was to be done with the *Tallahassee*? Wood persuaded President Davis to retain her as a cruiser, rather than decommissioning her and sending her to sea once again as a blockade runner. The raider undertook one more cruise, this time under the command of Wood's erstwhile first officer, Lieutenant William Ward. Renamed the CSS *Olustee*, she slipped out of Wilmington in November and in the course of a short cruise destroyed six Yankee vessels. By the time of her return, however, the Confederacy was desperately short of manpower. *Olustee*'s complement was transferred to shore billets and her guns were removed; the ship herself was sold to a blockade runner in Wilmington. Under the command of John Wilkinson, one of the most resourceful of the Confederate blockade runners, the *Tallahassee*—now, appropriately, named *Chameleon*—made several successful runs in the closing months of the war.

Wood, meanwhile, continued as part of Jefferson Davis's official family. He accompanied the presidential party on its flight south following the evacuation of Richmond, and on May 10 was captured by Federal cavalry along with Davis near Irwinville, Georgia.[20] He escaped by bribing a guard, and in June became one of a small number of Confederates who made the perilous crossing from Florida to Cuba in a small sloop. From there, Wood made his way to Halifax, Nova Scotia, where he had spent 40 busy hours the previous August with the *Tallahassee*.

Wood might be excused for taking refuge in Canada; not only was he excluded from amnesty by virtue of his rank and Naval Academy training, but he soon received word of the arrest of Raphael Semmes, the erstwhile skipper of the *Alabama*. Semmes's subsequent release in March 1866 was a signal that Wood could safely return without fearing trial as a "pirate." By that time, however, he was a prominent resident of Halifax, the head of a trading house in partnership with John Wilkinson.

Wood became the only one of the Confederate cruiser captains to live out his life in exile. There was a reconciliation of sorts with his father, but Wood refused to take advantage of various amnesties in the postwar years. His brief visits to the United States came many years after the war had ended and were usually to attend some Confederate reunion. In May 1890, at the request of the Lee family, he attended the unveiling of the statue of Robert E. Lee at the capitol in Richmond.

Two years later, Wood participated in ceremonies commemorating the 30th anniversary of the battle between the *Virginia* and the *Monitor*—his first major engagement in the late war. But John Taylor Wood was never "reconstructed." He lived until 1904, and to the day of his death his company's premises in Halifax were readily identified by a Confederate flag flying overhead.[21]

Notes

Copyright © 1997, *America's Civil War*. This chapter first appeared in the March 1997 issue of *America's Civil War*.

1. Royce G. Shingleton, *John Taylor Wood* (University of Georgia Press, 1979), 14.
2. A. A. Hoehling, *Thunder at Hampton Roads* (Englewood Cliffs, N.J.: Prentice-Hall, 1976), 150.
3. William C. Davis, *Duel Between the First Ironclads* (Baton Rouge: Louisiana State University Press, 1975), 130–32.
4. Shingleton, *John Taylor Wood*, 110.
5. Gustavus V. Fox to S. P. Lee, April 8, 1864, *Official Records (Navy)* Series I, vol. 9, 589.
6. Chester G. Hearn, *Gray Raiders of the Sea* (Camden, Maine: International Marine, 1992), 129.
7. John Taylor Wood, "The *Tallahassee's* Dash into New York Waters," *Century*, July 1898.
8. Shingleton, *John Taylor Wood*, 125.
9. Jones, *The Civil War at Sea*, vol. 3, 265.
10. Wood, "The *Tallahassee's* Dash," July 1898.
11. Howard K. Beale, editor, *Diary of Gideon Welles* (New York: W. W. Norton, 1960), vol. 2, 105.
12. Wood, "The *Tallahassee's* Dash," July 1898.
13. Ibid.
14. Shingleton, *John Taylor Wood*, 132.
15. John M. Taylor, *Confederate Raider: Raphael Semmes of the* Alabama (Washington, D.C.: Brassey's, 1994), 217.
16. Shingleton, *John Taylor Wood*, 138.
17. Jones, *The Civil War at Sea*, vol. 3, 268.
18. Shingleton, *John Taylor Wood*, 141.
19. Ibid., 142.
20. Ironically, considering Wood's devotion to Davis and the Confederacy, the

diary that Wood maintained during the retreat lends substance to allegations that Davis attempted to escape disguised as a woman. Wood wrote:

> The President came out of the tent with a gown and hood on, a bucket on his arm, with Helen the mulatto nurse. They advanced some distance toward the stream. . . . [A] Yankee rode up, ordering them to halt . . . recognizing a man but not the President. . . . Others rode up and the President was obliged to make his identity known. This attempted escape in disguise I regret exceedingly. Only Mrs. Davis's distress could ever have induced him to adopt it.

Shingleton, *John Taylor Wood*, 161–62.
21. Ibid.

Index

Adams, Charles Francis, 4, 15, 101, 106, 195, 203
Adams, Ephraim Douglas, 15
Adriatic, 249
Alcohol
  rationing of, 72–73, 93
  Union sailors use of, 71–74
Alert, 224
Alexandra, 9, 198
Alligator, 50
Altar, 198
Anderson, Bern, 44, 132, 133, 135
Ariel, 172
Arkansas, 45
Arthur, 151, 152, 155, 160, 163

Baker, James, 97
Baltic, 224, 228
Banks, Nathaniel P., 29, 117, 121
Barney, J. N., 81
Barron, Samuel, 10
Bassett, Henry D., 227
Bauer, K. Jack, 38
Baxter, James P., 16, 18, 20, 35
Bee, Hamilton P., 161
Bell, Henry H., 125
Belle Italia, 153, 155, 157, 159, 162
Benjamin, Judah P., 2, 106

Bernard, James, 158
Berry, Henry, 155, 164
Bessemer, Sir Henry, 13
Bienville, 2
Bigelow, John, 15
Black Warrior, 2
Blackhawk, 121
Blacks
  dramatic performances derogatory to, 69
  in Union Navy, 56–57
Blair, Postmaster General, 107
Blake, Homer C., 123–130
Blakely rifle, 173
Blockade
  as Civil War strategy, 131–135
  function of, 131
  technology in implementation of, 38–40
  Union navy and, 52, 53, 135–139
Blucher, Felix, 156, 161
Bold Hunter, 202
Bonfils, M., 171, 172
Borie, Adolph, 122
Boyer, Sergeon, 78
Brandywine, 242
Breach-loading guns, 37
Breaker, 154
Britton, Forbes, 161
Brodie, Bernard, 14, 17, 38, 39

Brodie, Fawn, 17

Brooke, John M., 47

Brooke guns, 47, 233, 243

Brooklyn, 126

Brooks, William P., 184

Brown, Isaac N., 82, 83

Browne, John M., 180, 184

Browning, Robert, 138

Buchanan, Franklin, 82, 83, 86, 226–238, 243

Buchanan, James, 106

Bulloch, James Dunwoody, 245

   background of, 1–2

   CSS *Alabama* and, 8–9

   end of war and, 11–12

   French operations of, 10–11

   navy vessel assignment of, 1–12

   return to England by, 5–8

   Terceira Island and, 4–5

Burnside, Ambrose E., 142

Bushnell, David, 38

Butler, Benjamin F., 115, 119, 121

Butman, John, 126–127

Cairo, 68

Card playing, aboard Union ships, 69

Catton, Bruce, 16

Chameleon, 252

Charleston Squadron, 87

Chestnut, Mary, 101

Cheyenne, 18

Chicora, 40

Churchill, Winston, 16

City of Bath, 200

Civil War

   shortage of naval material on, vii–ix

   technology and, 35–51. *See also*
      Technological advances

Civil War Books: A Critical Bibliography
   (Nevins, Robertson, & Wiley),
   183–184

Clifton, 126

Cloutier, Paul, 123

Coles, Cowper P., 19, 42

Comanche, 18

Commodore Hull, 218, 219, 221, 222

Confederate navy

   overview of, 80–81

   Union blockade and, 135–139

   vessels in, 84–85

Confederate sailors

   alcohol use by, 9394

   in battle, 98

   blacks as, 87

   description of, 85–88

   desertion by, 94–95

   discipline of, 95–96

   drills of, 89–90

   food for, 92–93, 95

   illness among, 97–98

   liberty for, 94

   pay for, 85, 88

   recruitment of, 81–84

   shipboard entertainment for, 91–92

   shipboard life for, 88–89

   shipboard responsibilities of, 90–91

   uniforms for, 96–97

Conkling, Henry, 127, 129

Conscription acts, Confederate, 82

Constitution, 200, 201

Cooper, Samuel, 83–84

Corpus Christi, 153–165

Corypheus, 153–155, 157, 162, 163

Coulter, E. Merton, 132

Couronne, 174

Covert, Abraham, 127

Crimean War, 37–38

The Cruise of the Alabama, *by One of the*
   Crew With Notes from Historical
   Authorities (Haywood), 183–193

Crystal Palace Exposition, 17

CSS *Alabama,* vii, viii, 7–11, 28–34, 40,
   44, 195, 250

   crew of, 84–85

Index

Kearsarge and, 57, 90, 98, 123, 166–181, 184
life on, 90–91
prizes of, 204
published material on, 183–193
smuggled liquor and, 93
USS *Hatteras* and, 126–130
CSS *Albemarle,* 40, 50, 89, 92, 98, 221, 222
CSS *Arkansas,* 82, 98
CSS *Atlanta,* 60, 90, 245, 246
CSS *Beauford,* 87
CSS *Chattahoochee,* 89
CSS *Chicora,* 87
CSS *Florida,* 86, 135, 203
CSS *Fredericksburg,* 87
CSS *Georgia,* 2, 87, 112, 194, 198–204
CSS *Huntsville,* 97, 98, 227, 229, 231, 238
CSS *Louisiana,* 45, 118, 205–213, 218
CSS *Missouri,* 98
CSS *Morgan,* 86, 226, 234
CSS *North Carolina,* 88, 90, 204
CSS *Olustee,* 252
CSS *Palmetto State,* 90
CSS *Rappahannock,* 85, 94, 147, 148, 203
CSS *Savannah,* 87, 93, 98
CSS *Shenandoah,* 11, 44, 85, 91–93, 147, 148
CSS *Stonewall,* 10–11, 147
CSS *Sumter,* 7, 27–28, 33, 34, 84, 114, 167, 169
CSS *Tallahassee,* 84, 94, 147, 148, 246–252
CSS *Tennessee,* 45, 83, 98, 229, 231, 234, 235, 237
CSS *Tuscaloosa,* 98, 227, 229–231, 238
CSS *Virginia,* 14, 18, 40, 98, 142, 143, 243, 248
crew of, 83
Monitor battle with, 14, 42, 43, 144, 145, 243–244, 253
Cumberland, 40, 242
Cushing, William, 52, 222

Dahlgren, John A., 37, 47, 73
David, 50
Davids, 49
Davis, Charles, 115, 116
Davis, Edmund J., 161–162
Davis, Jefferson, 26, 80, 242
foreign policy and, 101
naval affairs and, 136, 244–245
Davis, William C., 16, 19
Debray, Xavier B., 153
Decatur, Stephen, 234
Deerhound, 174, 179
Delaney, Norman, vii
Deserters, Confederate, 94–95
Desertion, by Union sailors, 79
Dictator, 199
Disciplinary problems, Union sailors and, 79
Dix, John, 157–158
Douglas, Stephen A., 25
Drama, aboard Union ships, 68–69
Dreyer, Maximilian, 158
Du Pont, Samuel F., 39, 40, 44, 56, 68, 146–147, 149
Duncan, J. K., 211
Dunderberg, 41

Eads, James B., 19
Early, Jubal, 147
Eastport, 118
Eggleston, John R., 235
Ely, Robert B., 77, 78
Emmons, George F., 124
Enrica, 7
Entertainment
aboard Confederate ships, 91–92
aboard Union ships, 68–69
Ericsson, John, 14, 17, 42, 243
European Squadron, 147–148
Evans, Augusta J., 234, 237
Evans, Bill, 199
Evans, Robert D., 71

Fairfax, Donald, 103, 104

"Farewell to Grog," 73

Farragut, David G., 40, 52, 56, 79, 114, 115, 118, 120, 146, 161, 163, 167, 209–211

Farrand, Ebenezer, 228

Fawcett, Preston, & Company, 4

Fingal, 4, 5

Fisher, George W., 230

Fishing, aboard Union ships, 69

Fleming, Jock, 251

Food, for Union blue jackets, 74–75

Foote, Andrew Hull, 55

Foote, Shelby, ix, vii

Foreign Enlistment Act, 4

Forest Rose, 76

Forrest, Douglas, 86

Forshey, Caleb G., 152

Fort Caswell, 120

Fort Fisher, 118–120

Fort Pickens, 113

Foster, John G., 218

Fox, Gustavus V., 42, 114, 115, 143, 245

Fraser, Trenholm & Company, 3, 9, 11–12

Fredericksburg, 95, 97

Freeman, Miles, 174

Gaines, 226

Galt, Francis L., 184

George Griswold, 200

George Peabody, 217

Gift, George W., 235

Gilpin, Henry A., 154, 161

Glenavon, 249

Gloire, 38

Golden Age, 112

Golden Rocket, 27

Goldsborough, Charles W., 141

Goldsborough, Louis M., viii, 40, 42
    background of, 141–142
    career of, 149–150

European Squadron and, 147–148
    North Atlantic Blockading Squadron and, 142–147

Good Hope, 200, 201

Gorgas, Josiah, 136

Grant, Ulysses S., 55, 116, 119, 120

Gray, Edward F., 161

Great Britain
    Confederacy and, 100, 101, 194
    ship purchases in, 194–195
    Trent affair and, 103, 106–110

Greenhorns, 58

Guerrero, 112

Guerrillas, harassment of Union ships by, 77

Gunboats, 54–55

Harby, Lee C., 163

Hatteras, Jr., 124

Hayes, John D., 40

Haywood, Philip D., 183

Hill, D. H., 218, 220

Hobby, Alfred M., 154–157, 159, 160, 162–164

Hollins, George N., 226

Holmes, Oliver Wendell, 14

Hope, Sir James, 250

Hopeman, Lieut., 55

Horton, James H., 189–191

Housatonic, 49

Howe, Elias, 17

Hunley, 49

Hunter, William, 87, 152

Huse, Major, 4

Huson, Hobart, 155

Hydrography, 39

Illness, among Union sailors, 72, 78

Ingomar, 207–208

The Introduction of the Ironclad Warship (Baxter), 35

Ironclad warships
American Civil War vs. European, 46–47
background of, 35
commissioning of, 38
Confederate construction of, 45–46
design of, 50
employment of, 40–41
offensive operations and, 43–44
types of, 41–43
Union policy concerning, 4

Jackson, Thomas J. "Stonewall," 201
James Funk, 248
James Littlefield, 249
James River Squadron, 84, 87, 92, 94, 95
Jansen, Marin H., 195, 197–198
Japan, 194, 195, 198. *See also* CSS *Georgia*
J.J.McNeil, 151–152
John Watts, 202
Johnson, Andrew, 32–33, 148–149
Johnston, James D., 224, 225, 229, 238
Johnston, Joseph E., 32
Jones, Catesby R., 230, 233
Josselyn, Francis, 214–223
J.W. Seaver, 200, 201

Kate, 73
Keeler, William, 57, 58, 61, 64, 69, 70, 73, 77
Kell, John McIntosh, 30, 32, 93, 129, 167, 170, 171, 177–179
Haywood and, 183–187
Keniston, J. M., 223
Keokuk, 43
Kittredge, John W., 151–164

Laird Brothers, 4, 10
Lancaster, John, 174, 179
Landsmen, 58
Larder, James, 71
Le Vert, Madame, 237

Lealtad, 112
Lee, Robert E., 39, 220, 221, 244, 252
Lee, Samuel P., 118, 138
Liberty, for Union sailors, 70–72
Libraries, aboard Union ships, 69
Lincoln, Abraham, 25, 52, 53, 93, 107, 131, 144
Llewellyn, David, 178
Longstreet, James, 218
Lonn, Ella, 57
Lovell, Mansfield, 209
Lovenskiold, Charles G., 154
Low, John, 7
Luraghi, Raimondo, 136
Lynch, William F., 82
Lyons, Lord, 106–108

Mackubin. Lola, 243
Maffitt, Eugene, 1, 12
Maffitt, James Newland, 7, 86
Maffitt, John, 203
Magruder, John B., 82, 83
Mahan, Alfred T., 237
Malaria, 78
Mallory, Stephen R.
building of navy by, 80–81, 83, 194, 195, 197, 212–213, 246
Bullock and, 1–3, 5–8, 10
guns and, 47
ironclads and, 44–46
Louisiana and, 208, 209, 212–213
Mobile and, 237
Randolph and, 225–226
Semmes and, 26
Manassas, 7
Manet, Edouard, 174
Mann, Billy, 156–158, 161
Mann, Esther, 156
Mars, Michael, 177, 184
Mason, James, 101, 104, 107, 110
Matthews, Edward, 126, 129
Maury, D. H., 234

Maury, Matthew Fontaine, vii–viii, 194–204
Maury, William Lewis, 195–198, 204
McClellan, George B., 142
McClernand, John A., 116
McCormick, Cyrus, 17
McIntosh, Charles F., 209
McRae, Colin J., 224, 228, 232, 233
Meigs, Montgomery C., 113
Memoirs of Service Afloat During the War Between the States (Semmes), 33
Merrill, James M., 76
Michigan, 38
Milligan, John, 121
Millis, Walter, 39
Mines, Union-planted undersea, 49–50
Minor, Robert, 208
Mississippi, 45, 211
Mississippi Squadron, 111, 116
Mitchell, John K., 97, 209, 210, 212
Mobile Squadron, 224–238
Moir, James, 104
Monitors, life on, 77–78
Montgomery, 247
Murray, E. C., 205–208
Music, aboard Union ships, 68

Napoleon, 175
Napoleon III, 4, 10, 15, 167
Napoleonic Wars, 36
Nashville, 44, 230–233, 238
Naval guns, 36–37
Navy. *See* Confederate navy; Union navy
Navy Medal of Honor, 57
Navy sherry, 73
Neal, Benjamin F., 156
Nevins, Allan, 105
New Ironsides, 41, 43, 49
New London, 126
Newton, Isaac, 18
Noakes, Thomas, 164
North, Lieutenant, 5–8

North Atlantic Blockading Squadron, 138, 141, 142–147, 221

O'Brien, Matt, 184
Ocmulgee, 28
Oliver, John W., 17
Ordnance developments, 36–38, 47–51
Oreto, 4–6. *See also Manassas*
Owsley, Frank L., 133–134

Page, Thomas J., 11
Paixhans, Henri-Joseph, 36
Paixhans gun, 36–37
Palmer, James, 169
Palmetto State, 40
Panama, 112
Parker, William H., 87
Parrott, Robert P., 37
Parrott gun, 37–38
Patterson, Daniel, 112
Pennell, Richard, Lord Lyons, 106, 107
Perry, Oliver Hazard, 234
Pfander, Landsman, 65
Philbrick, Carpenter's Mate, 72
Phillips, George, 199
Picayune, 207
Piekett, George E., 245
Pierce, Joseph, 206, 230
Poody, 124
Pook, Samuel M., 41
Pook Turtles, 41, 44
Porter, David, 111
Porter, David Dixon, vii, 52, 56, 212
    background of, 111–113
    Civil War career of, 120–121
    Hatteras-Alabama and, 130
    Mississippi Squadron and, 111, 116
    New Orleans and, 114, 115, 117–119
    post-Civil War career of, 121–122
Porter, Evalina Anderson, 111
Porter, Henry O., 124, 127
Potomac flotilla, 214–223

Powhatan, 113, 114
Price, Marcus W., 134
Princeton, 36
Prize money
    for Confederate sailors, 85
    Porter and, 121
    for Union sailors, 58, 60

Ramming, 40
Randolph, Victor, 225
Recollections of a Naval Life (Kell), 183
Red River Campaign, 121
Reindeer, 153, 155, 157
Reliance, 214–217, 244
Report of the Secretary of the Navy in
    Relation to Armored Vessels, 41
Reynolds, Alfred H., 159
Rhodes, James Ford, 16
Rinaldo, 108
Roan, 251
Roanoke, 50
Roanoke Island, 142, 150
Rodgers, John, 54, 145
Rodman, J. T., 37
Roland, Charles P., 133
Roosevelt, Theodore, 2
Ruskin, John, 13
Russell, William Howard, 236

Sachem, 155, 157
Salvery, Semmes and, 33–34
Sandler, Stanley, 20
Sarah A. Boyce, 247
Schley, Winfield Scott, 74
Schultz, Fred L., ix
Scomp, Henry A., 186–187
Scott, Winfield, 24
Sea King, 11
Searle, Joshua, 189
Semmes, Raphael, 250
    Alabama and, 28–34, 84–85, 90,
        128–130, 166–181

    arrest of, 252
    background of, 23–26
    Bullock and, 1, 7–9, 12
    grog ration and, 90–93
    James River Squadron and, 87–88, 98
    recruitment by, 85–86
    Service Afloat by, 183
    slavery and, 33–34
    on Slidell, 104
    Sumter and, 27–28, 33, 34, 84, 169–170
Semmes, Samuel, 24
Service Afloat and Ashore During the Mexican
    War (Semmes), 25
Service Afloat (Semmes), 183
Seward, William H., 101, 107, 108, 113,
    114
Shark, 2
Shaw, William, 157
Shea, Daniel B., 152, 153
Shell guns, 38
Sherman, William T., 116, 121, 136
Simmes, Raphael, vii
Sinclair, Arthur, 85, 90–91, 183
Sinclair, George T., 8, 172, 178
Singer, Isaac, 17
Slidell, John, 101, 104, 107, 110, 172
Slidell, Rosina, 104
Smith, Andrew J., 117
Smith, Kirby, 83, 238
Smoothbore guns, 37, 47, 49
Soley, James R., 133
Somers, 24
South Atlantic Blockading Squadron, 54,
    65, 70, 74, 141
Spencer, Anne Elizabeth, 24, 26
Spitfire, 112
SS *Bahama,* 7–9
St. *Mary,* 125
Steam propulsion
    adoption of, 35–37, 39–40
    importance of, 50
Still, William, vii, viii

Stribling, John M., 6
Submarines, 49, 50
Sumner, Charles, 107
Supply, 112
Sutlers, 73–74

Tasmanian, 197
Taylor, Anne Mackall, 242
Taylor, John, vii
Taylor, Richard, 242
Taylor, Zachary, 156, 242
Technological advances
    ironclad warships as, 35, 40–47. *See also*
        specific ships
    ordnance developments as, 36–38,
        47–51
    overview of, 35
    steam propulsion as, 35–36, 39–40, 50
    strategy implementation as, 38–40
    undersea warfare as, 49–50
Temperance movement, 72
Terry, Alfred H., 120
Theodora, 101–102
Timby, Theodore R., 18–19
Tise, Larry E., 16
Trent, 103–110
Turtle, 38
Two Years on the Alabama (Sinclair), 183
"290," 7–8. *See also* CSS Alabama

Undersea warfare, advances in, 49–50
Uniforms
    for Confederate sailors, 96–97
    for Union blue jackets, 60–62
Union army, 56
Union blue jackets
    alcohol use among, 71–74
    blacks as, 56–57
    on blockaders, 76–77
    disciplinary problems among, 79
    enlistment terms for, 57
    experience of, 57–58

food for, 7476
foreigners as, 57
grievances of, 76
illness among, 78
importance of, 54
liberty for, 70–72
on monitors, 78
pay of, 58, 60
recruitment of, 53–55
shipboard entertainment for, 68–70
shipboard life for, 63–68
uniforms and clothing of, 60–62
Union navy
    blockade of, 52, 53, 131–139
    personnel of, 53
    preservation of Union by, 52
    recruitment for, 53–55
    vessels used by, 53
USS *Brazileira,* 68–69
USS *Chickasaw,* 77
USS *Colorado,* 57, 58
USS *Conamaugh,* 75
USS *Dictator,* 69
USS *Fernandina,* 56, 62, 71, 75, 78
USS *Florida,* 1, 7, 11, 30, 57, 69, 76
USS *Hartford,* 52, 57, 71, 210, 211
USS *Hatteras,* 29, 32, 172
    CSS *Alabama* and, 126–130
    salvage of, 123
USS *Kearsarge,* viii, 10, 30, 32, 52
    Alabama and, 57, 90, 98, 123, 166–181,
        184
USS *Lackawanna,* 66, 70
USS *Manhatten,* 77–78
USS *Mattabesett,* 65, 67
USS *Merrimack,* 14, 15, 45, 82, 221, 243
USS *Minnesota,* 57, 62
USS *Monitor*
    background of, 13–14
    battle with *Virginia,* 14, 42, 43, 144,
        145, 243–244, 253
    description of, 41

Hampton Roads engagement and,
   14–16, 42, 43
importance of, 16–20, 54
provisions on, 75
Sundays on, 66–67
unseaworthiness of, 46
USS *Mound City,* 69
USS *Nahant,* 60, 68–69, 75
USS *Niagara,* 203
USS *Penobscot,* 69
USS *Portsmouth,* 58, 71–73
USS *San Jacinto,* 102–105
USS *Silver Lake,* 64
USS *Tyler,* 64, 75–76
USS *Valley City,* 69, 75
USS *Vanderbilt,* 68
USS *Wachusett,* 11
Utah, 129

Vance, Zeb, 251
Vandiver, Frank, 134–136
Venereal disease, 72, 78
Vicksburg, 116, 117, 121
Virginia II, 86–87

Wabash, 54
Waddell, James, 11, 12, 85, 86, 250
Wamsutta, 163, 164
Ward, William, 252
Ware, James A., 159, 160, 164
Warrior, 38
Wash, Charles, 55
Water Witch, 161

Watson, Robert, 88–89, 94, 95
Weehawken, 78
Weitzel, Godfrey, 118
Welles, Gideon, 41, 44, 54–56, 103, 106,
   110, 113, 115–116, 120–121, 131,
   141, 143, 153, 214, 249, 250
Wells, Thomas, 184
West Gulf Blockading Squadron, 209
West Point, 217
Whiting, W.H.C., 251
Wiley, Bell I., viii
Wilkes, Charles, 102–106, 108–110, 146
Wilkinson, James, 209
Wilmington, North Carolina, 118, 137,
   138, 145, 245
Wilson, Joseph, 177, 179
Winslow, John, 30–32, 52, 167–168, 173,
   174, 176, 178, 180, 181
Wirt, Elizabeth Gamble, 142
Wirt, William, 142
Wood, John Taylor, viii, 84, 242–253
Wood, Robert Crooke, 242
Worden, John L., 52, 244
Worth, William, 24
Wyman, R. H., 215
Wyoming, 30, 169

Yancey, William L., 101
Yellow fever, 78
Yonge, Clarence R., 5–6, 9, 12
Young, James, 189, 191, 192
Youngblood, Wilson, 212